D0086818

Fable's End

DAVID H. RICHTER

Fable's End

COMPLETENESS
and
CLOSURE
in
RHETORICAL
FICTION

The
University of Chicago
Press
CHICAGO & LONDON

To Sheldon Sacks

David H. Richter is assistant professor of English at Queens College
of the City University of New York.
[1974]

The University of Chicago Press, Chicago 60637
The University of Chicago Press, Ltd., London

© 1974 by The University of Chicago
All rights reserved. Published 1974
Printed in the United States of America

International Standard Book Number: 0–226–71317–2
Library of Congress Catalog Card Number: 74–10344

Preface

The essay that follows is concerned with the architectonic principles of coherence, completeness, and closure in a group of novels whose structure is generated not by plot but by doctrines, themes, attitudes, or theses. These rhetorical fictions (or, as we shall alternatively call them, fables or apologues) make up one of the most significant subgenres within the contemporary novel, where under the hands of such craftsmen as Barth and Heller, Golding and Burgess, Sartre and Camus—a few among a host of novelists who have used the form—some of the most productive experimentation of our day is currently going on. It is not only one of the most important chapters in modern literary history, but also one of the least understood: there have been few serious attempts to come to grips with it. (The only full-length study that comes to mind is Robert Scholes's *The Fabulators*, which is concerned with content more than with form.)

My motive for taking up the problem of completeness and closure in the fictional fable came not, however, from the neglected state of that subgenre but rather from the more general problems of poetic unity and wholeness in prose fiction, and particularly from my reaction to a number of studies concerned with the "open-ended" novel. I will go into the various theories of literary openness in much greater detail in chapter 1; here I shall say only that some of the works most commonly termed open-ended (like *To the Lighthouse* and *Herzog*) seem complete to me, not only in the trivial sense of having a final page with "The End" obligingly inscribed upon it, but in the sense of recounting a completed process of change, either in external circumstances or in internal consciousness, taking place in the protagonists. As readers we would react to any continuation of the narrative as though it were a sequel, and we would find any interpolation of material digressive at best. I planned a study of wholeness and completeness in the novel at large, only to find that I had bitten off more than I could chew. Seeking a more restricted area better suited to my powers, I selected that of the rhetorical novel since (in a sense which I shall define) all of them can be seen as at least *potentially* open-ended. Remnants of my earlier, more universal plan persist in this essay as allusions, digressions, and (especially in the final chapter) hints on how the conclusions arrived at here might be generalized. And although I have not, strictly speaking, adopted a literary-historical method, my conclusions will also make some suggestions toward a formal history of the rhetorical novel.

The problem of literary openness is currently more fashionable than the problem of closure and completeness, but I was gratified to find two brilliant studies which seemed to be in my camp rather than in that of the "enemy": Frank Kermode's *The Sense of an Ending,* and Barbara Herrnstein Smith's *Poetic Closure.* My study can be seen as complementary to both these works, although in quite different ways. In *The Sense of an Ending,* Kermode is concerned, just as I am, with closure in the novel, but he looks at the poetic process from an entirely different perspective. His focus is on the metaphysical and psychological needs of man-as-reader for a form which will console him for his arbitrary placement in a world without beginning and end. My focus, to adopt Kermode's terminology for the moment, will be on how the literary work provides this "consoling" form. The psychology of the audience will not be the principal subject of investigation; it will rather find its place as a factor in the author's rhetorical strategies in the creation of aesthetic forms. *Poetic Closure* is complemented by this study in an obvious way: Mrs. Smith's book deals with the lyric, mine with the fable. But there is a less obvious connection as well. Late in her book, in discussing the problems posed by the "weak closures" characteristic of modern poetry, Mrs. Smith suggests the existence of a new principle, "what might be called 'hidden closure,' where the poet will avoid the expressive qualities of strong closure while securing, in various ways, the reader's sense of the poem's *integrity*" (Smith, 1968, p. 244; italics mine). The notion of two independent but mutually related principles of form—which I shall deal with under the terms "completeness" and "closure"—is only hinted

at in Mrs. Smith's book: in the works she analyzes, closure is by
far the more important principle, while the other (this "sense of
the poem's integrity") is terribly difficult to define for lyric
poetry. In my essay closure—which remains far easier to define
than completeness, even in the novel—is the less significant of
the two, being frequently sacrificed to completeness in the pursuit of the fable's end.

Although many of my debts of honor—my borrowings from
published sources—are acknowledged in the footnotes and the
bibliography, I would like to take this space to record what I owe
to teachers, friends, and institutions. My thanks, first, to the
Regenstein Library of the University of Chicago and to the New-
berry Library for their cooperation in assisting my research. My
former colleagues in the doctoral program at the University of
Chicago, who have influenced my ideas on fiction through their
conversation and their hitherto unpublished writings, are also
my creditors: I should like to single out Robert V. Wess (now at
the University of Texas) for his help in molding my notions of
form in the novel, and Brian Corman (now at the University of
Toronto), whose ideas on Pynchon's *V.* contributed greatly to my
own. Professors Wayne C. Booth, Norman Friedman, and Elder
Olson have all read my manuscript at various stages of revision,
and I am deeply grateful to them for their comments and criticism, which have affected its final form.

To my wife, Janice, I owe a special debt of thanks for going to
Bloomingdale's without me and allowing me the time to write
and revise this essay. And finally, as an inadequate gesture of
recompense for my shameless pillage of his ideas, with the respect
of a disciple and the affection of a friend, I have dedicated this
book to Sheldon Sacks.

1 · Open Form and the Fable

The problem of open form

"And they all lived happily ever after"—so goes the conventional ending to many a fairy tale or romance. It is a powerful ending, for with those words "ever after" any lingering curiosity we might have about the prince and his lady is dispelled; they are in eternal bliss and we need not look far into our imagination to picture their never-ending summer's day.

Fictions are different nowadays—or so we are told—and the final chord no longer is "happily every after"; now it is Edouard's note on the art of the novel in Gide's *The Counterfeiters*: "Might be continued." Our heroes no longer ride off into the sunset; more typical of the ending patterns of twentieth-century novels are those of James's *The Ambassadors*, showing Lambert Strether looking into the uncertain future ahead of him back home at Woollett, and the uncomfortable explanations he must make to Mrs. Newsome; of Joyce's *Portrait of the Artist*, showing Stephen Dedalus just beginning his foray into a new life; and of Hemingway's *The Sun Also Rises*, showing Jake Barnes riding in a Spanish taxi next to the woman he loves but can never possess, his life circumstantially unaltered from the opening page. We now have "open form," defined by Robert Martin Adams as "literary form . . . which includes a major unresolved conflict with the intent of displaying its unresolvedness" (1958, p. 13). This "open form," which is typical of much of twentieth-century fiction, has as its principal characteristic the "open end."

A number of theoretical studies have concerned themselves with the unresolved conclusion as the product of a new view of experience. Ihab Hassan's *Radical Innocence: Studies in the Contemporary American Novel* is among the most celebrated; another

1

more recent study is Alan Friedman's *The Turn of the Novel*, which is concerned primarily with the psycho-cultural factors which produced the new form of fiction. The new novel, according to Friedman, "is open presumably because the new novelist conceives that experience in life itself is open. . . . In general terms, the modern novelist exposes innocence to essentially unlimited experience" (1966, pp. 179–80). By contrast, the earlier novel presents a closed experience, one which, Friedman states, "traditionally tends to conclude in marriage or death" (1966, p. 18).

David Daiches, writing before the phrase "open form" became current, takes a similar if somewhat less simplistic view in his *The Novel and the Modern World*. For Daiches, formally interesting modern fiction "represents an attempted adjustment between literature and a certain state of transition in civilization and culture generally, and . . . this adjustment explains most of the differentiating features of the twentieth century novel" (1939, p. 2). The transition between civilizations, which Daiches felt we were undergoing in the early decades of this century, has had as one of its effects a breakdown of public values and beliefs. Since "it is public truth which provides the artist with his means of communication," with his ability "to communicate emotion and attitude by simply describing incidents," and with "a storehouse of symbols with guaranteed responses" (1939, p. 5), it is clear that the modern novelist, lacking these, must come up with some way of making art out of *private* values—and Daiches suggests that it was new techniques and means of expression which allowed art to continue when its foundation in culture was being cut from under it.

Much of this seems true enough—almost self-evident, once it has been expressed thus cogently—and yet the implications of this view of literature are a bit disturbing to me, for these notions would ignore, I believe, much of the complexity of form in the eighteenth-century novel, and, as I shall argue later, it presents what I consider an overly simple relationship between a novelist's beliefs (conscious or otherwise) and the forms he creates. Daiches writes: "For a love story to end in marriage was a 'happy' ending, since the convention was to accept marriage as the final reward of virtuous love—as a conclusion rather than as a beginning" (1939, p. 4), and he can point to *Tom Jones*, to *Humphry Clinker*, to *Emma* as examples of that public truth expressed in fiction. And yet there are love stories in which the formula does not work. *Pamela*, for instance, is a novel in which our desires center in the marriage of the heroine, and indeed the book has its climax in the engagement and wedding of Pamela to Mr. B. Though one may stop reading here—how many thousands of readers have done so?—it is not here that the novel ends: in the last third or so of the novel Richardson chronicles the adjustment of both Pamela and Mr. B. to the misalliance—and we do not read these pages as a sequel. (Richardson did write a sequel to *Pamela*, but that is another story.) While it is not true that Richardson considered Pamela's marriage to be any less final than Fielding considered Tom and Sophia's, the marriage does not in itself exhaust the created form.

In *Fiction and the Shape of Belief*, Sheldon Sacks suggests why: in the first place both partners to the marriage have formed relationships with other characters in the novel which are not resolved by the marriage, and in the second place the marriage alone is no guarantee of Pamela's happiness, for doubts remain as to whether she and Mr. B. can really make a go of it. Pamela, Sacks points out, changes more after her marriage than before it, as this is necessary for the full resolution of the represented instabilities of Richardson's plot. (1964, pp. 63–64n). Now Daiches could probably have worked *Pamela* into his generalization by slightly altering his wording, but my point is not a mere quibble with Daiches's language: it is rather that, within any system of public beliefs, many aesthetic forms are possible, and acceptable conclusions to novels—ones which leave us with the sense of completeness—depend less upon the particular conventions of society than upon the kinds of instabilities which, once represented in a fiction, must be resolved.

Thus the determinist notion that the "modern" novel is "open-ended" par excellence, while the older forms of the novel are typically closed due to the fact that "modern novelists . . . make special new consistent assumptions about the shaping character of the process of experience" (Friedman, 1966, p. 35), can be seen as at least partially inadequate. *Pamela*, as "traditional" an eighteenth-century novel as one could select—it marks the start of many traditions, at least—could perhaps be technically thought of as a case of "open form" according to the criteria of either Robert Martin Adams or Alan Friedman. In Adams's terms, the "major unresolved conflict" is that between the world-views of the lower-middle-class servant and her arrogant and aristocratic husband; the "unresolvedness" is purposely displayed in the postmarital section, where we are forced to see the marriage of Pamela and Mr. B. as one of dynamic rather than static equilibrium, of strong forces held in check rather than a conflict now lapsed and settled. Similarly, Alan Friedman, who defines "open form" not in terms of the "structure of meanings, intents and emphases" (Adams, 1958, p. 13), but as the expansion of "the flux of conscience, the progress from innocence to experience" (Friedman, 1966, p. 34), might well be convinced that *Pamela* was an "open" novel. Richardson's work ends, after all, not merely with the determination of Pamela's fate, with Mr. B.'s surrender to Pamela's conditions for cohabitation, but with a narrative sequence in which we are shown the attempts at accommodation by both husband and wife to each other's personalities and views. Needless to say, Mr. B. is initially as "innocent" of the experience which his partner's consciousness represents as Pamela is of his; both are altered ethically as well as circumstantially by the alliance, and the alterations—the last we are allowed to see is Pamela's attempt to come to terms with her husband's libertine past—are shown as continuing past the end of the novel, rather than artificially limited by that boundary.[1]

On the other hand, even the most modern novels—modern in terms of their technical innovations—are similar to the old-fashioned variety in that both types usually come to an end in aesthetically satisfying ways. However "unlimited" the flux of experience portrayed, however expansive the ethical framework, novelists have never quite managed to get around Aristotle's dictum that a work of art must be "whole, complete, and of sufficient magnitude" (*Poetics* 6: 1449b, 25). And this is far from surprising: "open form" is hardly a license to demonstrate a vision of chaos in an equally chaotic narrative—the word "form" in "open form" is fully operative, after all. Despite his evident sympathy and admiration for the practitioners of the expanding "stream of conscience," Friedman recognizes that the practical necessities of novel-writing demand some sense of completeness and closure; the writer must, or at least frequently does, "suggest at the end of his novel that these are the final pages of this particular rendering of experience."[2] To this problem, according to Friedman, the "solutions are as various and intricate as novels" (1966, p. 180)—and he quotes approvingly the final words of

John Barth's *The End of the Road*, Flannery O'Connor's *The Violent Bear It Away*, and Joseph Heller's *Catch-22*. He also congratulates Saul Bellow for the "resolute skill" with which he achieves the "balanced irresolution" at the end of *Herzog*, with the hero "poised in the end between two (or three) worlds, the latest still powerless to be born" (1966, p. 182).

The question of just which sorts of "balanced irresolutions" will provide a fully satisfactory ending for novels like *Herzog* lies beyond the scope of Friedman's book, but it is nonetheless an interesting question, and one which goes some way toward solving the problem of completeness in the open-ended novel.

Just what it is that is open-ended about *Herzog* is readily apparent: the hero is enmeshed in a net of shifting, unstable relationships with his ex-wife Madeleine and her lover (and his former friend) Valentine Gersbach; with his girl friend Ramona Donsell; and with a host of friends and kinsmen. By the end of the novel, the patterns have shifted somewhat—not very much— but the relationships are as far from true stability as before. The circumstances of Herzog's life do not define his fate: whether he will make Ramona the third Mrs. Herzog, whether he will establish a satisfactory relationship with his daughter by Madeleine or with his son by his first wife, even whether he will finish his projected book on romanticism: all these threads of what used to be called the fable are left hanging loose at the novel's end. Now we could achieve this effect with any closed novel—a Scott romance, for example—merely by publishing it without the last signature of pages, but no one would suggest that *Herzog*, however open-ended he found it, is open in that trivial sense; it is not an abortion, but a novel which, we feel, is not ended until it has come to full term. And what is over at *Herzog*'s end is a particular spiritual development on the part of the protagonist, along both ethical and intellectual lines—what we might describe as a middle-age identity crisis whose resolution brings about a reshaping of the hero's mental energies, leaving him better able to cope with the circumstances which brought the crisis on.

What we have described as the architectonic principle of *Herzog* was defined by Ronald Crane (in an essay written before *Herzog* itself) as a "plot of character," one in which the synthesizing principle is "a completed process of change in the moral character of the protagonist, precipitated or molded by action, and made manifest both in it and in thought and feeling" (1952,

p. 621). Since there is no "completed change, gradual or sudden, in the situation of the protagonist" as in "plots of action," which make up "most of the familiar, classic plots" (Crane, 1952, p. 620), *Herzog* by comparison with these would seem unresolved, open-ended in one sense, whole and complete in another. Perhaps it is the dissonance between these frames of reference that makes Friedman refer to the ending of *Herzog* as one of "balanced irresolution."[3]

Where I must quarrel with Friedman, and with other apostles of open form, such as Beverly Gross,[4] is in the way their glorification of the openness of open form, while exalting their favorite fictions as supreme expressions of the present-day spirit, at the same time denies them the dignity of art. Open form may well be, as Friedman says, "an ethical vision of the process of experience in life" (1966, p. 187); it may be, as Miss Gross says, a reflection of "our being and the essential openness of the movement of life itself" (1966, p. 376). This is all very well. But if we must also believe, as Miss Gross evidently does, that in such open-ended novels as Joyce's *Portrait of the Artist* and Virginia Woolf's *To the Lighthouse*, "no central issue has been resolved, that the action is not really terminated, that 'the story' is not really over, and indeed that there may never really have been a story at all" (1966, pp. 362–63), then it is uncertain whether, whatever virtues these works may have as mythic embodiments of the contemporary zeitgeist, they are entitled to any artistic status. Certain minimal conditions of art—for Aristotle, that the aesthetic object be whole, complete, and of proper magnitude; for Aquinas, that it possess *integritas* and *consonantia*, wholeness and harmony— would appear, in Miss Gross's view, to have been intentionally violated.

Fortunately, the relationship between the form of a work and its creator's beliefs is not as simple as Friedman and Miss Gross would have us believe: it is fallacious to assume that form is simply an imitation of the artist's ethical or intellectual vision, that to express "the essential openness of the movement of life itself" the artist must refuse to resolve his central issues. The ultimate extension of such a view would be that, for a novelist to express a vision of life as chaos, his novel ought to be as chaotic as possible, with no plot at all, inconsistent characters, incomplete thoughts, and ungrammatical or unfinished sentences —but such a work, if thus written, would not express chaos, for it could express nothing at all. To be expressive, a discourse must minimally be coherent; to be expressive as an aesthetic object, a work must minimally be one whole object, not a fraction of one. In her practical criticism of Joyce and Virginia Woolf, Miss Gross shows that she very well realizes this. When she tells us that we may look upon Stephen Dedalus or Mrs. Ramsay as central consciousnesses but not as characters per se, or that Virginia Woolf substitutes "for the unity of action the traditionally lesser considerations of unity of place and unity of time," she may merely be playing word-games (Gross, 1966, p. 375); her syntheses of the two novels show her to be at least intuitively aware of the distinction between plots of action and plots of character:

> The whole book [Portrait of the Artist] can be viewed as a preparation for something which of course it cannot contain: Stephen's maturation as an artist. . . . Joyce's Portrait is a spiritual biography in a literal sense since what it records is the growth of Stephen's spirit and not the history of Stephen's accomplishments. The book is less a portrait of the artist than of the accretion of the artist's temperament (p. 370).

Miss Gross has described, in terms other than R. S. Crane's, a plot of character which is complete and closed, in which our expectations and desires hinge not upon Stephen's fate, his circumstantial fortunes, but upon the development of his "artist's temperament" from the inchoate beginnings deep in his childhood up to his decision to sacrifice family, religion, and nationality to the fruition of that temperament. Similarly on Virginia Woolf:

> Mrs. Ramsay's passionate battle against the flux of life is ultimately held up as a delusion. We learn by the end that Mrs. Ramsay's real antagonist was not life, but precisely that escape from life that she sought from eternity. And this is ironic because Mrs. Ramsay was the one who, more than any other person in the novel, knew how to live life best—her consciousness could most fully and sympathetically penetrate that of the others. In Part III we see her survivors finally achieving something of this ability (p. 374).

What Miss Gross has defined in her descriptive analysis of To the Lighthouse—perhaps not entirely by design—is a unique form of

Crane's plot of action, one which sets up desires for the fates of the characters, expectations of what the future will bring, and a resolution which helps to maximize the power of the representation. The peculiar thing about *To the Lighthouse*, relative to the more usual sort of plot, is that the fate of the characters is not defined in the usual terms—happy marriages, tragic deaths, fortunes gained or lost—but rather as happiness (or the reverse) gained through the harmony (or discordance) of the interactions of the self with the environment, human and otherwise. Mrs. Ramsay is a character whom we are made to admire (despite her limitations) because of her masterly orchestration of the little things which make up the texture of life for us. Part I represents her uphill battle against chaos and discord which, in the main, she succeeds in winning; in Part II she dies, and the waves, symbol of the disorder she fought, strive to reclaim the little area in which she held out against them. In Part III we see Mrs. Ramsay's "survivors," especially her friend Lily Briscoe, attempting to recapture the quotidian happiness which Mrs. Ramsay had carved out from the invading chaos, with nothing but their memories of her to go by; the novel ends with their success (a success, however, which Mrs. Woolf insists is but a temporary and qualified one). The limitation of their success, its temporary victory in a battle which we are made to see as eternal, makes it not unreasonable, in one frame of reference, to call *To the Lighthouse* an open-ended novel. But on the other hand, from the point of view of plot as Crane has defined it, the ending of Mrs. Woolf's novel —because it gives the answer to the plot-question "How shall Lily Briscoe, Cam, James, and the others manage to live without Mrs. Ramsay?"—provides the sense of completeness and closure.[5]

In any case, whether one calls the principle of organization in works like *Portrait of the Artist* and *To the Lighthouse* "plot of character" or "unity of time," the fact remains that these works are indeed organized artistic wholes whose endings make us feel that the works are over, and whose construction is such that our intuitions tell us that nothing of importance has been left out. Clearly, new principles of novelistic structure are operative here: the unresolved narrative lines of *Portrait of the Artist* or *To the Lighthouse* would hardly do in a work like *Pride and Prejudice*. Yet this irresolute narrative ending is only possible when narrative has been subordinated to something else—in this case the alteration in the states of consciousness (and the ethical character) of the protagonists. The question of the form of the novel has not been avoided or even made less important in the novels of open end; as form becomes a matter of changes in consciousness rather than in fortune, the problem of shape, of completeness, of closure becomes, if anything, more urgent.

Open form and rhetorical fictions

If the question "What is the form of open form?" is an intriguing and fertile one to ask of novels of character like *Portrait of the Artist* and *Herzog*, how much more eagerly might we seek the principles of construction, the sources of the sense of completeness and closure, in novels whose mainspring is neither action nor character, but thought. How do novelists provide a sense of ending for works which have as their formal end not the emotion attendant upon the completed change of fortune or consciousness on the part of the protagonists (although they may include such changes as an element of the narrative, these must remain in some sense subordinate aspects), but the inculcation of some doctrine or sentiment concerning the world external to the fiction? The pursuit of the answers to this question—answers, because each "novel of thought" will require a somewhat different solution to the problem of form—will provide the primary focus for the essay which follows. But before embarking upon that pursuit it is first necessary to explore the genre with which we will be working.

Novels of thought, or rhetorical fictions, were not late-comers to the scene of English fiction: quite the reverse. One of the most influential, *The Pilgrim's Progress*, predated *Pamela* by more than sixty years. But it was not until "recently," according to M. M. Liberman and Edward E. Foster, that the term *apologue* came into use to "describe didactic, moral tales, whether the characters are beasts or not"; the category includes the simplest allegories and fables as well as highly sophisticated fictions. Here is the rest of the Liberman-Foster article on apologues from their *Modern Lexicon of Literary Terms*:

> In this sense, it implies a different kind of technique of construction than, say, the novel. In an apologue like Samuel Johnson's *Rasselas* or Katherine Anne Porter's *Ship of Fools*, characterization and plot are functions of the author's moral or philosophical ideas. This should not be taken to imply that these are poor narratives, but only

that they are constructed on the basis of different principles
and should be evaluated accordingly (p. 7).

A more careful and sophisticated definition of the apologue is
to be found in Sheldon Sacks's article, "Golden Birds and Dying
Generations"; according to Sacks, an apologue is a fiction in
which:

> characters are represented in complex relationships in a
> narrative manner and choice of style designed to alter
> our attitudes toward or opinions of the world we live in.
> The attitudes themselves are formulable critically as
> statements about the external world, though the aesthetic
> response required fully to appreciate the apologue need
> not go beyond an altered "feeling"—a sentiment—about
> the external world. . . . More simply: in an apologue all
> elements of the work are synthesized as a fictional example
> that causes us to feel, to experience as true, some formula-
> ble statement or statements about the universe. The state-
> ment itself can be so simple as "there is no happiness on
> earth" or it may be so complex as to require a book-length
> treatise, a *Myth of Sisyphus*, for its explication (1969,
> pp. 276–77).

The important thing here, if we may isolate one part of a definition as more crucial than the rest, is that the generic distinction
is being made on the basis of the work's final cause, its power to
affect, its "intention" (if we may legitimately speak of a work,
as opposed to an author, having an intention). This should come
as no surprise, for we have been doing this all along, the last time
but a few pages ago when we specified "the emotion attendant
upon the completed change of fortune or in state of consciousness
on the part of the protagonists" as the distinguishing characteristic of a class of novels which are *not* apologues, including such
diverse members as *Tom Jones, Persuasion, Crime and Punishment, Sister Carrie, Portrait of the Artist,* and *Herzog*; we shall
call this class, following Sacks, "represented actions."

The distinction between the class of apologues and that of
represented actions, as it is one of final cause, is an absolute one;
although represented actions have elements of thought, and although apologues have elements of action and character, in each
case these are subordinate to their respective powers. (In apologues, in fact, even the element of "thought" on the part of the
personages of the fiction which is simply expressive of character

will be subordinate to the "thought" which is the ruling principle of the fiction as a whole.) The way in which this distinction is absolute can be seen by analogy with the previous generic distinction we made between plots of action and of character. In Jane Austen's *Persuasion*, the characters' states of consciousness, especially Anne Elliot's, are represented with much greater depth and vividness than in Fielding's *Tom Jones*. Because later writers (like Joyce and Bellow) took advantage of the techniques Jane Austen used in *Persuasion* (along with other techniques developed by other novelists) in writing represented actions with plots of character, and because these techniques for representing states of consciousness were necessary for the creation of works in that genre, *Persuasion* can be seen as a "step towards" the creation of *Portrait of the Artist* and *Herzog*. But, on the other hand, no matter how important we might think *Persuasion* in the development of plots of character, it does not possess such a plot, nor would it even make sense to say that it had "more" of a plot of character than *Tom Jones* did. Both these novels are comedies whose instabilities are resolved and whose protagonists are rewarded by a happy marriage; in both cases the object of the novelist is to maximize the delight attendant upon such an outcome. One of the ways Fielding does this is by first keeping Tom and his Sophia apart by a closely woven net of circumstance—the more closely woven the net, the more affecting will be the subsequent release. But Anne Elliot is not separated from her beloved Captain Wentworth merely by circumstance: their disparity of wealth is no bar to their union, and her superiority of birth is carefully shown not to be worth the having. How then can Jane Austen maximize the joy attendant upon their reunion in love? How, but by showing Anne's suffering in his absence, her misery when she supposes him engaged to another, her hopes and fears when she feels his affections returning to her? And how can Jane Austen do this, but by using all the art at her disposal to represent vividly the changing states of consciousness through which her heroine goes? This representation of consciousness, then, is not an end in itself, but a means subordinate to the end, a method used to increase the power of a plot of action.

It is much the same with the element of thought as it is with that of character. Represented actions may vary a good deal in the quality, quantity, and prominence of thought, but so long as that element, however important, is held subordinate to a power, to the emotion attendant upon a change in fate or in consciousness, the work is different in kind from true apologues or rhetorical fictions. When a represented action possesses a prominent element of thought directed at exposing social injustice or the like, we usually call such a fiction a thesis novel (or *roman à thèse*); *Sister Carrie* may stand as a representative of the type. When, on the other hand, thought is directed to less utilitarian concerns, to metaphysics, to theology, to aesthetics, or even to abstract ethics, we call the fiction a novel of ideas—like *Crime and Punishment* or *Herzog*. In each of these cases the novelist will include a great deal of material explicating ideas, usually ideas which, as we may know from biographical evidence, the author was interested in for their own sake. Yet *within the novels* these ideas do not appear for their own sake but rather in the service of other ends. The serious power of *Sister Carrie*—to take only one example—depends in large measure on our pleasurable relief when Carrie attains her carefully qualified success in the arts, which in turn depends upon her being kept fairly sympathetic throughout the novel. Dreiser's problem, of course, is that the road to her success leads Carrie through a series of actions which are highly dubious ethically. From her initial appearance as a pure if ambitious farm girl, she must first become Drouet's concubine, then leave that benevolent libertine to take up seemingly better prospects with Hurstwood. Whore and gold digger are the conventional names for a woman who behaves in this way; what Dreiser had to do was to keep us from feeling that his heroine deserves them. Here is where his "thesis" material finds its use: to the extent that we can be made to feel that the industrial milieu of the American city turns the worker into a dehumanized helot, to that extent we see Carrie's rejection of the life of the factory girl and her acceptance of Drouet's proposals as a step up, not a fall, the guilt is transferred from Carrie to "the system." Similarly, to the extent that we can be made to agree that love is essentially a matter of chemistry rather than ethical values, we can see Carrie's desertion of Drouet for Hurstwood as a deed as inevitable as any test-tube reaction. Thus Dreiser's sermons on the industrial system and on the chemistry of love are not digressions included for their own sake; they establish norms by which we learn how to judge the characters, and upon these norms our ultimate reaction to the characters' fates depends. As Sacks puts it, "in the represented action, the most intellectual belief, the most extended social criticism, the most penetrating ethical comment, become integral parts of a whole work only as they move us to the appropriate response to the created characters, which, finally, make possible the appropriate experience." In rhetorical fictions, on the other hand, "the most poignant experience, the most subtly created character, the most eloquent prose, become integral parts of a complete work only as they move us to some realization—implicit or formulated— about the world external to the literary creation itself" (1969, p. 277).

Just how does a fiction move us to a "realization . . . about the world external to the literary creation itself"? What relationship is set up between the fictional world and the real one? There are two basic patterns, and perhaps they can best be illustrated with examples from the greatest master of the short apologue:

> The kingdom of heaven is likened unto a man which
> sowed good seed in his field:
> But while men slept, his enemy came and sowed tares
> among the wheat, and went his way.
> But when the blade was sprung up, and brought forth
> fruit, then appeared the tares also.
> So the servants of the householder came and said unto
> him, Sir, didst not thou sow good seed in thy field?
> from whence then hath it tares?
> He said unto them, An enemy hath done this. The
> servants said unto him, Wilt thou then that we go and
> gather them up?
> But he said, Nay; lest while ye gather up the tares, ye
> root up also the wheat with them.
> Let both grow together until the harvest; and in the
> time of harvest I will say to the reapers, Gather ye
> together first the tares, and bind them in bundles to
> burn them: but gather the wheat into my barn
> (Matt. 13: 24–30).

> A certain man went down from Jerusalem to Jericho,
> and fell among thieves, which stripped him of his rai-
> ment, and wounded him, and departed, leaving him half
> dead.
> And by chance there came down a certain priest that
> way; and when he saw him, he passed by on the other side.
> And likewise a Levite, when he was at the place, came
> and looked on him, and passed by on the other side.

> But a certain Samaritan, as he journeyed, came where
> he was; and when he saw him, he had compassion on him,
>   And went to him, and bound up his wounds, pouring in
> oil and wine, and set him on his own beast, and brought
> him to an inn, and took care of him.
>   And on the morrow when he departed, he took out two
> pence, and gave them to the host, and said unto him,
> Take care of him: and whatsoever thou spendest more,
> when I come again, I will repay thee.
>   Which now of these three, thinkest thou, was neighbor
> unto him that fell among the thieves? (Luke 10: 30–36).

The parable of the tares is in the allegorical mode; that is, there is set up a one-to-one correspondence between objects and characters in the fiction and beings, persons, and ideas in the real world external to the fiction. If the parable represents, as its author states, the kingdom of heaven, then the householder—that fatherly man of power—can represent none other than God. The rest of the symbols fall more or less into place accordingly: if the householder is God, then his enemy must be Satan, and the householder's servants must be the loyal angels; the wheat, lovingly gathered in at the end, must be the good men of the world; the tares, which are to be burnt, the wicked; and the harvest itself the Last Judgment. This is the general pattern of allegory; what is perhaps a bit unusual is the mildness of the human interest implicit in the fiction—the allegorical apologues in the book of Revelation have far more exciting vehicles (although this may not necessarily be a virtue in a short parable: the parable of the tares, though not particularly fascinating on the fictional level, excites strong interest on the level of its symbolic meaning, while the more vivid apologues of St. John the Divine are so symbolically dense as to be confusing, at least at a distance of two millenia).

The parable of the good Samaritan, on the other hand, does not possess this one-to-one correspondence between objects in the fiction and ideas in the external world. We may see the Samaritan as the archetype of the Good Man, but the other characters fail to fall so firmly into place: what do the priest and the Levite represent—or the man who had fallen among the thieves, or the innkeeper? Even when the characters seem to suggest ideas, the tight relationships we found in the parable of the tares do not obtain. We might posit that the priest and the Levite represent

clerical hypocrisy or some such thing, but once we have assigned
the idea we find nothing else that works to support it, and practically any other ideological hypothesis would work as well. In
actuality, the parable works not in terms of the interrelationships
among symbolic parts but as a symbolic whole, in representing
the meaning of the abstract statement, "Love thy neighbor as
thyself." But all the elements of the fable work towards the inculcation of that meaning. First the Samaritan's actions: in ad-
ministering first aid, in taking the victim to shelter, in paying for
his care (and, incidentally, writing the innkeeper a blank check
for the expense of the man's convalescence), the Samaritan has
done what we would wish anyone to do for him, what he would
have had done for himself had he been the victim. Then the
characterization: it is perhaps interesting that the uncharitable
priest and Levite, like the Samaritan, are motiveless, and that the
victim is wholly uncharacterized except as victim and perhaps by
implication as a member of the Jewish community to which the
Samaritan significantly does not belong. The Samaritan is motiveless, of course, because to give him any impetus to action except
the love of doing good would be to give him an ulterior motive,
which would not only detract from, but destroy the parable. The
behavior of the priest and the Levite likewise goes unexplained:
to give them any rationale for their lack of charity—it is possible,
for example, that they are on their way to Jerusalem to officiate
at a Temple sacrifice and are loath to handle what may become or
already be a corpse, for that would make them ritually unclean
—would likewise excuse our everyday lack of charity; to give
them evil intentions or even call very strong reprobation on their
sins of omission would be to emphasize their wickedness at the
expense of the Samaritan's goodness: the focus of the parable
would be thrown off. So the priest and the Levite are merely
characterized by their occupations, whose holiness makes us
expect them to do the right thing, and we are the more disappointed when they do not. Similarly, the Samaritan is a member
of an outcast group, and his charity is the more striking because,
unlike the Chosen People, he claims no moral mission in life. In
sum: the parable of the good Samaritan is a fable, a rhetorical
fiction in which each detail of plot, characterization, and language is chosen in order to make us understand something in the
external world—the disciple to whom Jesus recounts the parable
indicates that he does understand, and Jesus replies, "Go thou

and do likewise"—but in which the individual details generally do not have symbolic significance that can be detached from the fiction and equated on a one-for-one basis with ideas in the external world. Fable and allegory are the two main types of apologue, though there may well be other methods of forming a relationship between the fictional and the real world, either existing now or to be discovered in the future.

What is it that makes us feel that the fiction we are reading is an apologue rather than a represented action? This is a good and simple question; we only wish that there were available a single good and simple answer to it. The answers we now know are partial at best, at worst unsatisfactory. For a few rhetorical fictions, the solution is trivial: we are told, or as good as told, that the work that follows is exemplary of the real world rather than a story told for its own sake. The beginning of the parable of the tares, "The kingdom of heaven is likened unto . . ." immediately sets up the story as an extended metaphor. Similarly, Bunyan's opening for *The Pilgrim's Progress*, introducing characters named Christian, Evangelist, Obstinate, and Pliable, and the tale itself as a vision in a dream, establishes its position in the rhetorical mode; there is little Bunyan could do after such an opening that would not be taken on the symbolic level. (On the level of the vehicle, however, the story of Christian, Faithful, and Hopeful is in fact a serious action.) Again, Samuel Johnson, in his opening sentence of *Rasselas*, labels it with a placard reading *apologue*:

> Ye who listen with credulity to the whispers of fancy,
> and pursue with eagerness the phantom of hope; who
> expect that age will perform the promises of youth, and
> that the deficiencies of the present day will be supplied
> by the morrow; attend to the history of Rasselas prince
> of Abyssinia.

There are even some relatively modern apologues which, as it were, hang out a sign proclaiming themselves rhetorical fictions, whose characters are exemplary of ourselves, and whose protagonists' problems are therefore our own. The opening of Camus's *The Plague*, for example, stresses the "ordinariness" of the town of Oran. Its citizens work hard, but only to get rich; they live to do business; they do not, however, neglect "such simpler pleasures as love-making, sea-bathing, going to the pictures." And the narrator realizes that this characterization hardly individuates Oran: "really all our contemporaries are much the same" (1948, p. 4). The only thing that is special about Oran, in fact, is that the modern habit of living in the present is ingrained to a somewhat higher degree; its inhabitants have no inkling that anything else exists. In other words, the narrator of *The Plague* defines his home town as being like everyplace else, but ever so much more so. The stage is thus already set for a fable in which the effects of bubonic plague upon the town may become emblematic of man's confrontation with the absurdity of the universe. Again, the preface to Hermann Hesse's *Steppenwolf* establishes the protagonist, Harry Haller, as the type for modern man; according to the anonymous bourgeois who (more or less reliably) narrates the preface, Haller's manuscript is "a document of the times, for Haller's sickness of soul . . . is not the eccentricity of a single individual, but the sickness of the times themselves, the neurosis of that generation to which Haller belongs" (pp. 26–27). After such a hint, it is easy to take Hesse's cues that Haller's spiritual odyssey is not simply self-referential but describes a mental disorder—its etiology, course, and cure—which is rampant in the Western world today. (One word of caution here: the fact that a town or a character is described as "ordinary" or even as exemplary does not necessarily make the novel in which it appears a rhetorical fiction. After all, *Tom Jones* opens with a character [Mr. Allworthy] whose name might fit into a Bunyanesque allegory and whose description is as suited to a type-character as one could wish, and yet *Tom Jones* is anything but an apologue. So even if an apologue starts with a healthy signal of its generic nature, it must continue to reinforce those signals [*Tom Jones* stops doing so almost immediately] if we are to continue to read it as a rhetorical fiction.)

One of the ways in which these signals are reinforced—and it may, in fact, be substituted for those signals—is a kind of organization which Barbara Herrnstein Smith terms "paratactic structure" (p. 98). In paratactic structure thematic repetition takes the place of narrative sequence (fictional "cause and effect") as the principle of coherence. Typically, the novelist will present a series of incidents whose chronological sequence is more or less arbitrary and which set up no narrative lines. Though the minor characters who appear in the incidents *may* recur, they more usually do not. What holds the various episodes together is simply a common theme, or thesis, or view of the world, and the reader, who by the end of this sequence is willing to grasp at any sort of coherence he can find (how avidly we try to make logical sense of what we read!), is forced willy-nilly into the rhetorical mode. Only after the pattern is very firmly established can the novelist then piece together the narrative sequence, or what there is of it. We shall see more clearly just how the reader is cajoled into reading a work as a fable by means of paratactic structure when we get to the chapters on *V.* and *Catch-22.*

Frequently the methods are combined, and exemplary characters are placed into a sequence of events paratactically ordered: in *Candide,* the eponymous hero is described as an Everyman, then placed in a series of situations in which his optimistic philosophy is ludicrously inappropriate; in *Catch-22,* Yossarian is portrayed as an Everysoldier in a world whose only coherence lies in its grim absurdity; in *V.,* we have both an Everyman (Stencil) and an Everyslob (Profane) placed in interweaving narrative lines which ultimately merge, but not before we have discovered that the significant link between them is thematic. But not all rhetorical fictions employ either method; some, like William Golding's *Lord of the Flies,* present a reasonably coherent line of action peopled by characters who may be universal but who seem no more to be types than the characters in most represented actions. And yet *Lord of the Flies* is so obviously an apologue that nary a critic has expressed doubts that its story is symbolic in character. One might point to the ending—as indeed we will later—as being of the sort that is usually considered inartistic in represented actions but which seems to work well as it stands. But the fact that we find Golding's deus ex machina denouement effective merely confirms that we were indeed reading *Lord of the Flies* as an apologue; it does not explain how we came to be doing so. The celebrated symbolic intrusion, the talking pig's head, comes into the story far too late to be a signal, for I would guess that we begin to read *Lord of the Flies* as a fable from the first chapter or thereabouts. Perhaps it is Piggy's oft-reiterated question, "What would the grown-ups think?" that makes us see the boys on the island as a symbol for what is wrong at the heart of humanity. Or perhaps—and here I begin to speak mystically—it is the very pattern of action and character that makes the reader intuit the novel's form as rhetorical, simply because it is the hypothesis which best fits the total syncresis of details. And if this is true, then it may be that we do not intuit a fable's form as that of an apologue because we have observed signals that would lead us to such a conclusion, but that we interpret details or patterns of events as "signals" after the fact and only because we have already formed our intuitive sense of the genre. Perhaps there are a small finite number of possible "shapes" into which a fiction may be formed, few enough so that we can guess at a novel's form by creating and discarding hypotheses until we find the one that fits. Whether the knowledge of these possible shapes is entirely learned or—as some think—partly innate is a moot question; in either case the establishment of genres which are more than arbitrary or conventional, which are relevant to the psychological process of reading fictions would become one of the most significant critical tools that could be developed.

We have strayed somewhat from the problem of open form while discussing the characteristics of rhetorical fictions which make that problem interesting. Apologues, both the allegory type and the fable type, are informed by attitudes towards the real world, rather than by the relationship between our attitudes towards represented characters and our expectations or desires concerning their fates. But these attitudes, themes, doctrines, theses cannot as such exhaust a form, for there are an infinite number of situations, characters, and actions which could be used to exemplify a given theme, and in this sense all apologues, from the classically formed *Rasselas* down to one of Alan Friedman's favorites, *Catch-22*, could be thought of as *potentially* open in form. What then is it that determines the completeness of these fictions, and what makes us feel that they are over when they end? As we shall see, the principles of completeness for fables are distinctly different from those of represented actions.

The problem of completeness and that of closure cut broadly across chronological lines: they are as relevant to *Catch-22* as to *Rasselas*, to *The Stranger* as to *Candide*. Because of this, I may seem to be submerging the differences—great and obvious differences—between the eighteenth-century novel and that of today. And indeed it is important to demonstrate the ways in which modern fiction, with all its thematic and technical innovations, with its many "opennesses," conforms in certain basic ways to the principles of form which are common to all earlier fiction. At the same time, it would be doing a disservice to the extraordinarily inventive authors of our era to suggest that nothing was really new about their work. This is of course not the case. In my earlier discussion of the fallacy that form directly imitates thought, I rejected the notion that modern novels are open-ended simply because we now see experience as essentially unbounded. But we cannot deny that new knowledge makes new forms possible—or even necessary—in a more indirect way. To take just one example: traditional fables (let *Rasselas* be the type) make little appeal to the emotions of the reader; we are required to invest little psychological capital, and the novel, while amusing and edifying, could only by a great stretch of the imagination be called powerfully moving. But some recent apologues, like *Catch-22*, have been organized around theses which, it seems, can be best embodied in a work which makes strong demands upon the reader's sense of the ridiculous and the horrid: it is funnier than most comedies in some places, while in others it produces an emotional catharsis reminiscent of fully effective tragedy. Somehow Heller has managed to create a work which makes strong emotional demands, but in which the emotion is always kept subordinate to our understanding of his thesis about the world outside the novel. This is certainly an achievement that could not have been attained but for developments in the psychological novel during the nineteenth and early twentieth centuries; it is the creation of new forms of fable, with new forms of completeness and closure.

Our focus in this inquiry, then, will be twofold, for our concern will be, on the one hand, with the ways in which rhetorical fictions, potentially open in form, conserve their well-formedness through techniques giving us the sense of completeness and closure, and, on the other hand, with the kinds of formal innovations which are responsible for the development of that genre from Johnson's day to our own.

It is my hope that this study will provide some insight into what, in Frank Kermode's phrase, gives us "the sense of an ending." In his recent book published under that title, Kermode reminds us that "in our perpetual crisis we have, at the proper seasons, under the pressure perhaps of our own end, dizzying perspectives upon the past and the future, in a freedom which is the freedom of a discordant reality. Such a vision of chaos or absurdity may be more than we can easily bear." And it is our novelists who, while creating in their fictions a paradigm of life, give us the consolation which, Kermode feels, comes with the sense of ending. "We have our vital interest in the structures of time, in the

concords books arrange between beginning, middle and end; and
. . . we lose something by pretending we have not. . . . Out of . . .
experience of chaos grows another form—a form in time—that
satisfies by being a repetition and by being new" (1967, pp.
178–80).

2 · *Aspects of the Eighteenth-Century Rhetorical Novel: Johnson's* Rasselas *and Voltaire's* Candide

Despite considerable controversy over the sources and analogues of Johnson's text, two centuries have produced substantial agreement about the quality of *Rasselas*. Contemporary readers, like Hester Mulso Chapone, a friend of Richardson's, might dub the novel an "ill-contrived, unfinished, unnatural and uninstructive tale."[1] No one would dare call *Rasselas* uninstructive today; its message is its distinguishing feature. In his literary history of the eighteenth century, George Sherburn sets *Rasselas* down as an "oriental apologue," and rates it over the *Rambler* essays as Johnson's "best piece of moral writing" (Baugh et al., 1948, p. 994). Frederick W. Hilles agrees that the moral of Johnson's story, rather than its plot, is what most interests the contemporary reader:

> We do not read *Rasselas* for the story. We read it for a view of life that is presented majestically in long sweeping phrases. We read it, to adopt Johnson's terminology, for the colours of varied diction, for the music of modulated periods. What Johnson achieves in this "artificial" manner is the grandeur of generality (1965, pp. 114–15).

For some critics, the message of *Rasselas* is more than merely a distinguishing feature: it is the principle of its structure. Sheldon Sacks uses *Rasselas* as the primary example in his brief investigation of the apologue genre (1964, p. 28), and over a decade earlier Gwin J. Kolb had suggested that the message of *Rasselas* was the element which could best explain its construction:

> The most cursory reading is enough to convince anyone that . . . *Rasselas* is no ordinary "eastern" tale. For either the work shows Johnson to have been an incredibly inept writer of the

Arabian Nights type of story or else one must conclude that
the tale as tale is not the principle which best explains what
the book contains. . . . Clearly the problem of happiness rather
than the element of "story" emerges . . . as the determinant
by reference to which questions about the book's structure
may be most adequately answered (1952, pp. 699–700).

Like Sacks and Sherburn and, as he himself says, "many com-
mentators," Kolb considers *Rasselas* an apologue: "The narrative
about the prince may be considered as a device for presenting certain notions concerning happiness and the moral and emotional
attitudes to be drawn thence by the reader." (1952, p. 700).
Rasselas, in other words, represents a peculiar inversion, relative to most fictions, of the roles of the plot and the norms. In
actions of whatever kind, from the *Iliad* to *Herzog*, the extractable
normative statements function as a means of understanding and
evaluating the story and its characters. In *Rasselas*, as in all rhetorical fictions, it is the other way about: the values the novelist
wishes to inculcate become the plot's raison d'etre. And this
creates special problems for our investigation of the nature of
completeness and closure in a novel of this sort. Because the work
is a novel rather than a treatise, it presents us with an experience
that is contrived so as to alter (or reinforce) our beliefs in a manner
consistent with the thesis it embodies. In what terms could we
reasonably talk of the completeness and closure of such a work?
If its structure is provided by a normative statement about the
world outside the novel itself, when could we say that the created
fiction had most "fully" or "completely" embodied its thesis? As
we hinted in chapter 1, a series of exempla, no matter how extensive, could never exhaust a thesis—however they might exhaust
any reader: there would always be new characters, new situations
that might be created and added to the series. This is the sense in
which all apologues could be thought of as possessing "open
form": they all "might be continued" in the manner just mentioned. At the same time it is intuitively obvious that successful
apologues conclude before their readers have been bored to death
through multiplicity of examples—that rhetorical fictions give the
theses they embody not only life but shape as well. By examining
Rasselas and *Candide*—two traditional eighteenth-century apologues—we may acquire some general insights into what gives
rhetorical fictions the sense of finality they possess, insights which

will prove useful in our later investigations into the development
of the fable in our day.

Formal closure

The thesis in *Rasselas*, the series of statements around which the
novel is organized, has been succinctly expressed by Gwin J.
Kolb:

> Human limitations make happiness in this world ephemeral,
> accidental, the product of hope rather than reality, and almost
> as nothing compared to the miseries in life; consequently,
> searches for permanent enjoyment, although inevitable to
> man as man, are bound to end in failure. The wise man,
> therefore, will accept submissively the essential grimness of
> life, seek no more lasting felicity than is given by a quiet
> conscience, and live with an eye on eternity, in which he
> may perhaps find, through the mercy of God, the complete
> happiness unattainable on earth (1952, p. 700).

This summary is surely accurate in the main, although one who
has read Kolb's lines but not the novel itself might expect the book
to be far more pietistic in tone than it is. Paul Alkon justly draws
attention to the difference in emphasis between *Rasselas* and Johnson's twelfth sermon, whose main subject, the vanity of man's
search for happiness in this life, is identical. The sermon, Alkon
points out, underscores the Almighty's providential guidance and
help for the mortals whose pride in their own resources he hum-
bles; *Rasselas*, however, gives us no such assured consolation
(1967, pp. 195–98). *If* the soul is immortal, *if* there is a just God,
and *if* he rewards his virtuous and faithful servitors, *then* eternal
bliss awaits the good and the wise who were unable to find permanent happiness here on earth; in *Rasselas*, Johnson never lets us
ignore the ifs. The balancing truth to Johnson's main demonstration of the nonexistence of perfect earthly happiness is not so
much the conventional Christian belief in heavenly paradise as it
is the sense that this life is not entirely a vale of tears, that our
sorrows are as impermanent as our joys, that the flux of life brings
delight as well as dole, much as we may lament the predominance
of the latter. We might paraphrase this in the words of Imlac, who
surely speaks for Johnson when he tells Prince Rasselas that
"human life is everywhere a state in which much is to be endured
and little to be enjoyed" (p. 27). We note that Imlac says "little,"
not "nothing," and that this is typical of the balancing which goes

on in this work; the very gusto of the narrative helps to balance the melancholy inherent in its moral.

So much for the thesis of *Rasselas*, the set of ideas which the fiction embodies, and which might well have been (and, with variations were, for Johnson) fit subject-matter for an essay, a sermon, or a didactic poem. *Rasselas* is, of course, none of these things; it is a fable whose fictional framework presents us with an experience designed to alter (or reinforce) our beliefs in a way consistent with the statements we have just outlined. And if we are permitted to reason backward from this essence to the literary superstructure to which it gives shape (in the manner of Kenneth Burke in his celebrated essay on *Coriolanus*)[2], we shall see just how cunningly Johnson's fictional framework is constructed to achieve its end. What he must present to our view is a vision of universal human discontent, especially, as Kolb points out, in those persons who "might be expected to be happy" (1952, p. 702). Our hero, Prince Rasselas, is just such a person, an inhabitant of the "happy valley," an earthly paradise whose bounteous resources would seem to provide every means to human bliss, but whose cultural stagnation makes it more prison than paradise. A quarter century in this intended utopia has produced in Rasselas a profound melancholy and frustrated restlessness, which are further provoked by one of the prince's former tutors who, observing Rasselas's distemper, informs him that, were he to have experienced the world outside, he would better appreciate the security of the "happy valley." This idea excites Rasselas to a desire to see all the employments of life, looking for the mode of existence which will provide the perfect happiness he is unable to find where one would most expect it. His character is admirably suited to the quest in the outside world: he is intelligent, so that he can sensibly investigate the world on his own; he is young— twenty-six—too young to have adopted the cynicism of age towards such a search. He is a prince of royal blood, sufficiently wealthy to bear the expense of a quest of some length through the world and to provide him with the requirements of ease no matter how humble the calling he should choose. He is stubborn and tenacious, unwilling to believe that happiness is simply not available. Furthermore, his life has been spent in a sort of cloister, and hence it comes as a fresh surprise to Rasselas—a surprise through which Johnson makes his thesis more vivid and compelling—that our quotidian states and occupations provide but ephemeral joys. Since to send Rasselas alone on his survey would not only diminish the possibilities inherent in the fiction, but also leave the reader in a position to suspect that women or older men have possibilities open to them which Rasselas has not, Johnson provides the prince with suitable companions: the older Imlac, who can serve as Johnson's voice during the pilgrimage; and two girls, one bond and one free—Rasselas's sister Nekayah, and Pekuah, her servant and companion. This "prophecy after the event" gives us the terms upon which *Rasselas* rests: we have an intelligent, noble, wealthy young man, whose boyhood was spent far removed from our world, together with his tutor, his sister, and her companion, on a quest for a way of life which will provide perfect happiness.

Given this framework, the problem of closure is easily solved. Any quest—including that of Rasselas and his friends—has three possible conclusions: either the desired object is found, or the quest is abandoned unfulfilled, or we must be made to feel that the search will go on forever. The ethical statement which shapes *Rasselas* dictates the second possibility (although, as we shall see later, the first and third are also slyly incorporated into the conclusion), so that after their long search the party of four returns to the cloistering "happy valley" from which they had set out many years before.[3] This is the minimal condition, if you like, for formal closure.

The end opens

This framework determines the boundaries within which *Rasselas* takes place. But while a frame, like the initiation and the subsequent abandonment of a quest, can provide a rationale for the closure of a work, it cannot explain our sense of its completeness. The latter can come only from our understanding of the appropriateness of the closure device itself, and the appropriateness of its placement. In the case of *Rasselas*, the fable is closed because the hero abandons his search for perfect happiness, but it is complete because we have been made to feel that Rasselas was right to abandon that search—that he was not rash or premature in doing so, that in fact he had investigated and correctly judged all of the significant possibilities. But if experience is at least potentially infinite, how could Rasselas explore it all with his finite means of investigation?

The method Johnson actually uses in *Rasselas* is to divide experience into categories which are both mutually exclusive and ostensibly exhaustive; the prince (or one of his party) can then sample specimens from each category and thus seem to do justice to the whole of experience. We may take as an example of how this is done one such set of categories: the class structure. Since one may belong to either the aristocracy or the bourgeoisie or the proletariat, Rasselas and Nekayah arrange a neat division of the job of investigation: Rasselas will go to the court of the Bassa and see whether happiness is to be found amongst the nation's rulers, while Nekayah visits the homes of the middle classes. (The lowest class of citizens is eliminated ex hypothesi: their "penury and distress" prevent their being the seat of happiness [p. 51].)

Accordingly, Rasselas takes a position at court and is initially impressed with the life led there: "the man must be pleased with his own condition," he thinks, "whom all approached with reverence and heard with obedience, and who had the power to extend his edicts to a whole kingdom" (p. 51). But familiarity with the Bassa and his court breeds not contempt but wisdom: Rasselas finds that "almost every man who stood high in employment hated all the rest and was hated by them, and that their lives were a continual succession of plots and detections, stratagems and escapes, faction and treachery" (p. 51). When the plot against the Bassa brings him in chains to the imperial capital, Rasselas reflects that security belongs only to the sultan in Constantinople —and later learns that even he is not safe, for one may be displaced by revolution from below as swiftly and arbitrarily as by loss of favor of those above.

Meanwhile, Nekayah is having equally bad luck: the bourgeoisie are in the first place rather ignoble companions for the gently-born princess; accordingly, "she found their thoughts narrow, their wishes low, and their merriment often artificial." And even thus they are not happy: the pressures of competing in ostentation with their neighbors "embitter" what poor pleasures remain. Their loves and griefs are trivial, they themselves merely "inoffensive animals" (p. 52).

Having found that the high are insecure and envious, that the middle are narrow and quarrelsome, and that the low are impoverished, Rasselas and Nekayah know, in a sense, that happiness is nowhere to be found, for the categories as set up are exhaustive. But Johnson does not rest with these observations;

his heroes break experience down into other categories in order to exhaust in other ways the sources of perfect happiness. Previous to the critique of the class structure, Rasselas had investigated the various philosophies of life: the hedonists lead ignoble, shameful lives, while the stoics are found to be incapable of practicing the virtues they preach; the ascetic hermit has tired of his solitary existence and longs for the fleshpots of Alexandria, while the philosopher who preaches the "life led according to nature" cannot explain in the least particular what course of action a man should take. Thus many of the major ethical philosophies Johnson knew of are tried and found wanting. Again, Rasselas and Nekayah discourse on whether man is happier married or single, only to find that neither state is without its problems: Nekayah is forced to conclude that "marriage has many pains, but celibacy has no pleasures" (p. 56). And this depressing view is further extended by Pekuah, who can report, after her abduction by the Arab chieftain, that polygamy offers no better alternative, neither for the men nor for the women (p. 85). Again, the four pilgrims explore the pastoral, rural existence, looking for its classic virtues; as usual, they are disappointed, for the workers are merely rude and ignorant, while the wealthy proprietor, like the courtiers, is insecure because of his dependence upon the politics of the capital (pp. 43–45).

At this point, we are faced with the same structural problem that confronted us at the outset. Had Johnson chosen *one* set of categories exhausting the possibilities of experience, and then put Rasselas and his friends through their paces, judging each situation and finding it unproductive of perfect happiness (while at the same time not wholly productive of complete misery, in accord with the other half of *Rasselas*'s organizing doctrine), it would have been obvious where Rasselas would be justified in abandoning his search. But Johnson is not content with this: he has Rasselas exhaust not one but at least four such sets of categories, and, once he has done so, it is not nearly so clear where Rasselas ought to stop.[4] For if there is not one but many ways of categorizing reality, then experience again becomes infinite, and the quest for happiness potentially infinite in its duration. Having exhausted four sets of categories, why should not Rasselas exhaust four more? Or, to put the question in its original form, how does Johnson satisfy us that the quest, when abandoned, was truly over?

Closing the open end

I believe that the key incident in the solution of this problem is that of the old astronomer. Part of its importance, of course, stems from the fact that it eliminates from consideration a way of life in which both Rasselas and Nekayah are interested. But its major import comes, I think, from the fact that it elicits a lecture from Imlac on "the dangerous prevalence of imagination." The old astronomer is a man who has long devoted himself to investigating the heavens—the planets, the stars, and their influence on mankind. In the course of his long investigations he has come to believe that it is his observations that cause the heavenly phenomena to appear: in short, he has gone mad, and madness is, as Imlac tells us, "the heaviest of human afflictions" (p. 92). Imlac draws a picture of the course of this mental illness, and immediately the three others, seeing the similarity between their own imaginative daydreaming and the mad astronomer's, resolve to put themselves under better control. But although Johnson never explicitly tells us so, it is clear that there is one further parallel to be drawn: with the quest for perfect happiness itself. At best the quest is a chimera, a pointless search for something that does not exist. At worst it is as mad as the old astronomer's idea; like the astronomer, whose fixation takes the form of striving to keep the physical universe in good order, Rasselas is seeking for something that God has already provided. Rasselas, of course, is looking in the wrong place, in this world rather than in the next. And it is to the next world that the four pilgrims are directed in a conversation with the old sage, who finds little comfort (except his quiet conscience) in old age, much comfort in his faith in a world to come. After this conversation, and the one Imlac holds with his three young friends in the catacombs, the search is abandoned; Nekayah speaks for them all, I believe, when she declares: "To me . . . the choice of life is become less important; I hope hereafter to think only on the choice of eternity" (p. 109).

With the incident of the old astronomer, the course of the novel shifts. Johnson ceases to record the progressive and systematic elimination of modes of life; in effect he dismisses the continuation of the quest along the same lines with the warning: "This way madness lies." At the same time he enlarges the terms of the investigation to include the possibility of an eternal life after this brief existence, an eternity of perfect happiness.

Earlier we mentioned three ways in which a quest novel could be completed: success, failure, and eternal search. We have just established the way in which Johnson develops the first two possibilities, both of which give a very strong sense of closure: within the original sublunary terms of the action, the search for a life of perfect secure happiness has been a failure; within the terms expanded so as to include the afterlife, Johnson holds out at least the bare possibility of success. But there is also more than a hint of the third type of ending. In "the Conclusion, in Which Nothing Is Concluded," Johnson shows that after all their experience showing its vanity—including the cautionary tale of the old astronomer—Rasselas, Nekayah, and Pekuah are still dreaming, still attempting to imagine a perfect life: Nekayah wishes to found a women's college, Pekuah dreams of being made prioress of the convent of St. Anthony, while Rasselas imagines a kingdom—only a little one, of course—over which he would rule. "Of these wishes that they had formed they well knew that none could be obtained," Johnson suavely interposes, indicating that, in some small sense, the three young people have learned from their experiences (p. 110). They have become wiser, more realistic. And yet they are human, and therefore must dream of progress and perfection until they die. If this is so, then Johnson has used not just the first two but all three methods of concluding his quest apologue, for the last chapter gives us the sense that, though the circular journey is shortly to end in the "happy valley," the search will go on as long as men hold vain hopes. It should be emphasized that the "eternal search" ending is decidedly weaker as a closure than either of the other two, and it must be mentioned, in the same connection, that by leaving his foursome dreaming in Egypt instead of taking them back full circle to their point of origin, Johnson has forgone an obvious narrative closure device. But in the process he has increased our sense of the novel's completeness, and in a way which hammers home the moral: the vanity of men's dreams of perfect bliss.

Completeness as experience

Another structural element which contributes to our sense of *Rasselas*'s completeness in no small way is the categorically arranged set of sources of happiness which, we saw earlier, was *not* an important source of good closure. Looking back upon the novel, it would be possible to arrange the categories in such a scheme that it would be hard to find broad areas which Johnson had not touched. From the center outward, as it were, the sources of happiness tested could be thus arranged: "internal" sources, especially mental schemes like those of the hedonist, the stoic, the man who leads "a life according to nature," and the like; "external" sources. The external could be further divided into those derived from the *family*, including the debate on marriage, the question of when to have children, Pekuah's insights into polygamy, and the like; those derived from one's position in *groups larger than the family*—especially the researches into the preferability of living out of society rather than in it (the hermit), of living in rural society rather than urban (the shepherds and the landowner), and finally of living in the various classes within the more highly structured urban society; those sources of happiness derived from observation and participation in things *larger than human society*—the universe as a whole (here the only important incident is that of the old astronomer, though it is, as we have seen, a crucial one); sources of happiness *greater* even *than the physical universe*, that is, God. Here the centrifugal series has to stop, not only because it has run out of room, but because the investigators are obliged to confess that human methods of research cannot achieve certainty about the Godhead. The ostensible exhaustiveness of the pattern is undeniable, and thus provides a strong sense of the completeness of *Rasselas*, yet the schema is not responsible for the novel's closure —we have just seen how Johnson provided that. There are several reasons why the schema does not provide closure: for one thing, it is too complex to be easily carried in the mind at once, and so it would be hard to know precisely when it was "over." For another, it is not developed in the order given here. Third and last, the divisions in the schema are nowhere explicitly stated within Johnson's novel: it is a framework which we can use to display the author's seeming exhaustiveness, but we must not forget that it is our framework and only implicitly Johnson's.

We have been outlining the elements within the structure of *Rasselas* that contribute to the ordering of the narrative, which in turn is necessary to our sense of the novel as a completed whole. To leave *Rasselas* at this point would be to leave much undone, for while we have explained the way in which a structured argument is represented so as to seem to be narratively exhausted, we have not touched upon the way Johnson sets up his imitation of a logical demonstration, nor upon the ways in which he makes us feel that most of the important issues in the general problem of happiness have been dealt with. *Rasselas*, whatever its argumentative structure, is an imitation, in some sense, of human action; it is a novel, not a sermon, and the vitality of the experience of reading the book is not unrelated to our sense of it as a concrete poetic whole. It is this aspect, I feel, to which W. K. Wimsatt refers when, in his essay "In Praise of *Rasselas*," he complains that critics' efforts (like Kolb's or Hilles's—or mine) to chop the work into its functional parts are irrelevant to the intense enjoyment which two centuries of readers have found in the fable. Part of this enjoyment is indeed to be sought where Wimsatt himself looks, in the "local colours, the geography, the flora, the fauna, the architecture, the costumes" of faraway places, which give *Rasselas* its exotic flavor (p. 123). At the same time, it is certainly true that, given the romantic locale, Johnson's scenario makes precious little use of the materials. The element of the marvelous, so common in Oriental fables, is wholly lacking, and even the customs of the country are virtually identical with those of Johnson's Europe, barring a stray janissary or *harim*. We should indeed cultivate what Wimsatt calls "a warmer affection for the story (plot and character)" (p. 124), but I am not sure that this is to be gained from close attention to the Oriental mise-en-scène which, as Louis E. Goodyear has pointed out (in Wahba, 1959, pp. 21–29), tends to reflect Johnson's haste in writing more than his redoubtable Oriental scholarship. Close attention to the particular incidents out of which Johnson builds his grand morality play, and the way in which the materials of narrative are absorbed into general propositions, may provide something of what Wimsatt is looking for without doing violence to the generic nature of the work.

For an instance of how we might go about doing that, let us take a glance at chapter 18, which is devoted to Rasselas's disillusionment with the stoic philosopher. The function of this chapter within the larger argument is obvious: it is a part of the examination of philosophy as equipment for living, or, as Kolb terms it, the investigation of "those who follow particular schemes designed to produce happiness" (p. 702). The first section of the chapter adumbrates the great expectations that Rasselas is given of the man: he holds forth in "a spacious building," into which a "stream of people" has come to listen to his wisdom.

The "sage" is "raised above the rest," literally referring to his position relative to his audience but figuring forth his lofty discourse. He has all the qualities of the great orator: "his look was venerable, his action graceful, his pronunciation clear, and his diction elegant" (p. 40). And his lecture is filled with the highest wisdom. Johnson refrains from giving the slightest hint during his précis of the discourse—as he does later in chapter 22, the episode of the "life led according to nature"—that the doctrine has its weaknesses; quite the contrary, the substance of the speech is made as impressively sage as possible:

> He shewed . . . that human nature is degraded and debased, when the lower faculties predominate over the higher; that when fancy, the parent of passion, usurps the dominion of the mind, nothing ensues but the natural effect of unlawful government, perturbation and confusion; that she betrays the fortresses of the intellect to rebels and excites her children to sedition against reason their lawful sovereign (p. 41).

Perhaps this is even a bit too impressive: the homiletic style here is even more orotund, more figurative, than Johnson's own essays in the grand style in his *Rambler* papers; it may be that the stylistic shift to the very verge of parody prepares us for what is to follow.

What follows, of course, is the deflation of the bubble, and it begins at once. At the close of the lecture, Rasselas waylays the philosopher at the door and requests "the liberty of visiting so great a master of true wisdom. The lecturer hesitated a moment, when Rasselas put a purse of gold into his hand, which he received with a mixture of joy and wonder." This emotional response to the gold, so unlike the lecturer's heroes, "immovable by pain or pleasure," prepares us to accept Imlac's skeptical doubts about him as dictated by experience rather than by cynicism or even envy (p. 41).

It should be pointed out here, I think, that Imlac's warning to Rasselas—"Be not too hasty . . . to trust or to admire the teachers of morality: they discourse like angels, but they live like men"— is expressed in the most general terms (p. 42). Imlac casts no particular aspersions upon stoicism as such, nor does Johnson explicitly identify the orator with any particular school of thought; Imlac's remarks are addressed against "teachers of morality," all and sundry. This is no mere accident of language: Imlac's words dispose not only of the particular moral philosophy of the stoic, but of all moral thought which enjoins man to be more than he by nature can be. In one deft touch Johnson frees himself from the necessity for separate chapters dealing with epicureanism and other systems of spiritual calesthentics; by being inclusively general here, he saves himself the trouble of being exhaustively particular later. We respond, I believe, to more than the grandeur of generality here; our sense of the completeness of Rasselas's investigations of the philosophers depends on our "inductive leap" from the failure of a single stoic teacher to the failure of all moral philosophy to preserve us from the miseries of life.

The final deflation of the stoic's pretensions follows like the conclusion of a syllogism. When, a few days after the impressive lecture, Rasselas fulfills his intention to visit the master, he is "denied admission." The prince must produce "a piece of gold" for the stoic's corrupt doorkeeper before he can make his way to the philosopher's presence, where Rasselas finds that the man himself, like his servants, cannot live by his teachings. In the same polished phrasing by which he had once won Rasselas over, the philosopher reveals his unphilosophical but very human troubles: "what I suffer cannot be remedied, what I have lost cannot be supplied. My daughter, my only daughter, from whose tenderness I expected all the comforts of my age, died last night of a fever. My views, my purposes, my hopes are at an end: I am now a lonely being disunited from society" (p. 42). In a scene which Wimsatt feels "verges on the uncomfortable" (p. 128), Rasselas repeats the philosopher's advice to him, and comes close to doing what Johnson tells us Rasselas's "humanity" could never allow him to do: insulting "misery with reproof" (p. 42).

One of the most interesting facets of the scene is the way Johnson eschews an easy victory over "the teachers of morality." It could have been made just as plausible for the stoic's distress to have been over something comparatively trivial: a stubbed toe, a broken limb, the illness of a relative, or even the death of some valued pupil. To have chosen something slighter than the unexpected death of an only child would indeed have emphasized more strongly the difference between the philosopher's preachings and his practice. The element of satire in *Rasselas* would have been greatly increased by such an alteration,[5] and Rasselas's unwelcome moralizing to the grieving stoic would be less "uncomfortable" were the source of his grief less touching. Intuitively, though, we can see that such a revision would be wrong: the joke would be too cheap. And the cheapness of the joke would operate against the universality of the moral, for showing a stoic ludicrously departing from his principles as the result of stubbing his toe or biting his tongue[6] would prove his inadequacy in adhering to his philosophy rather than the inadequacy inherent in the philosophy itself. But what drives the stoic in *Rasselas* to display the grief he had condemned is a species of misery to which none of us could feel superior; it is therefore stoicism, not this particular stoic, that is at fault.

The death of the philosopher's daughter also fits into a sort of catalogue of the ills to which mankind is subject, which Johnson has been more or less systematically compiling since the travelers escaped from the "happy valley." In the previous chapter, Rasselas's unwelcome advice to the eudaemonists reminds them of the *diseases* which are the product of youthful follies; the next chapter speaks of the stupid *malevolence* of the shepherds whose ignorance prevents them from relishing their classically fortunate state. Later still, the country squire tells the pilgrims of the *insecurity* of his present prosperity due to the envy of the Bassa in the capital; the hermit's misanthropy is the product of his *frustrated ambition*—he had been many times passed over for promotion. In the last section of the narrative, Johnon focuses upon miseries that may be in store for any man: the *decrepitude* and *loneliness* of old age and the *mental decay* attendant upon senility. None of these evils much resembles a stubbed toe. Johnson feels that the problem with the "teachers of morality" is not that they are obviously charlatans but that life is almost incredibly harder to live, and live well, than their airy systems of thought admit. Johnson's sentiments would be echoed, in language replete with scathing wit, by his contemporary Voltaire. But the similarities in content between *Rasselas* and *Candide* do not prevent the two masterpieces from being extraordinarily different in structure. Let us first take a glance at *Candide*, its rhetorical purpose and the structure Voltaire created to carry out that purpose, and then return to compare and contrast the formal elements of both fables.

The best of all possible worlds

"The resemblance, in some respects, betwixt the tenor of the moral [of *Rasselas*] and that of *Candide*, is striking" (Scott, 1827,

vol. 3, p. 296). Sir Walter Scott was not the most systematic critic
of his time, but his judgments were well worth recording: here, I
think, his intuitions were good, for the resemblance between
Rasselas and *Candide*, both published early in 1759, are indeed
striking. Both novels contain a vain quest for happiness (Candide
calls his vision of perfection "Cunégonde"), both contain a rejected utopia, both end with their heroes giving up dreams of the
ideal and settling for a return to the quotidian. Scott might have
been thinking of such similarities of content when he dumped
Rasselas and *Candide* into the same bucket; he might, in addition,
have thought there were generic similarities in form, that *Candide*,
like *Rasselas*, could "scarce be termed a narrative. . . . It is rather
a set of moral dialogues" or in our terms a rhetorical fiction (pp.
295–96).

Candide's odyssey is a familiar one: after falling in love with
Cunégonde, he is kicked out of doors by her father, a proud
German baron. He is inducted into the Bulgarian (for which we
may read Prussian) army, deserts, and as punishment is made to
suffer four thousand lashes before being pardoned. After witnessing a battle in which tens of thousands of soldiers are killed
and whole towns butchered, he makes his way to Lisbon in time
for the earthquake of 1755. During another flogging—this one
administered by the Inquisition—he is spotted by Cunégonde and
the lovers are temporarily reunited. They flee to Buenos Aires and
are separated once more, this time by the same Inquisition that
had brought them together. Candide, with his servant Cacambo,
wanders through the South American jungle, is nearly eaten by
cannibals, but manages to amass, in El Dorado, an immense fortune with which to search for the elusive Cunégonde. Candide
takes ship to Venice, sending Cacambo to seize Cunégonde and
meet him there. En route, he is cheated by various rogues of most
of his treasure. Cacambo finally turns up—having himself been
robbed, cheated, beaten, and sold into slavery—and tells Candide
that his Cunégonde has become a washerwoman in Constantinople. She has become ugly and cross, but that is no matter: Candide
buys a farm near the Turkish capital, marries Cunégonde, and
settles down with her and their various traveling companions to a
moderately pleasant agricultural life.

These rapid changes of fortune, these incredible sufferings are
by no means peculiar to Candide: all the other major characters
in the novel—Pangloss, Cunégonde, Cacambo, Martin, the Old

Woman, the Baron, Paquette, and Friar Giroflée—suffer as much or more. And yet, though all of them complain endlessly of their sad lot, none of them despairs. The Old Woman makes the most apt generalization on these episodes of the novel:

> A hundred times I wanted to kill myself, but I still loved life. This ridiculous foible is perhaps one of our most disastrous inclinations. For is there anything more stupid than to want to bear continually a burden that we always want to throw to the ground? To regard our being with horror and to cling to our being? In fine, to caress the serpent that devours us until it has eaten up our heart?
>
> I have seen, in the countries that fate has driven me through and in the inns where I have served, a prodigious number of persons who loathed their existence, but I have seen only twelve who voluntarily put an end to their misery (1961, p. 34).

Here the Old Woman speaks for Voltaire, I believe, in her testimony to the resiliency of human nature in the face of natural disaster and human wickedness. This is the first of the themes around which *Candide* is organized.

The second theme is related to the first: it is the philosophical "optimism" after which *Candide* is subtitled. Norman L. Torrey traces this aspect of *Candide* in part to Frederick II and D'Alembert, who "tried to persuade" Voltaire "that men were stupid and ignorant and that nothing could be done about it"—a point of view which would render all efforts at reform futile (1938, p. 48). This ameliorism was systematized in the writings of Shaftesbury, Pope, Leibnitz, Wolff, and (to an extent) Rousseau: the theoretical version of "optimism" maintained that human stupidity and ignorance was part of the grand scheme of things. Faced with the problem of reconciling a perfect deity with his imperfect creations, the "optimists" responded by denying the imperfection of God's world. The problem of evil in nature and in man was solved by defining it out of existence; the "seeming" evil of natural disasters and human vice would, in accordance with God's perfect plan, be the cause of some putative future good. The world thus was, is, and would always remain perfect. As Pope puts it in the *Essay on Man*:

> All Nature is but Art, unknown to thee;
> All Chance, Direction, which thou canst not see;
> All Discord, Harmony not understood;

All partial Evil, universal Good:
And, in spite of Pride, in erring Reason's spite,
One truth is clear, WHATEVER IS, IS RIGHT.

Questioning the order of things, much less attempting to reform the evils one sees, thus becomes a form of sacrilege. Voltaire's proponent of this philosophy within *Candide* is Doctor Pangloss, who believes in "optimism" in its most literal sense: "It is demonstrated . . . that things cannot be otherwise, for, everything being made for an end, everything is necessarily for the best end. . . . Consequently, those who have asserted that all is well have said a foolish thing; they should have said that all is for the best" (1961, p. 4).

Voltaire, persistent social reformer and humanitarian, would have found such a philosophy abhorrent, had it not been on its face so ludicrously perverse; he therefore places Pangloss ("all-tongue" in Greek) and his pupil Candide in the best of all possible circumstances to test this theory: in the midst of disaster and brutality. When Candide wishes to save Jacques, a saintly Anabaptist, Pangloss "stops him, proving to him that the Lisbon roads had been formed expressly for this Anabaptist to be drowned in. While he was proving this a priori, the ship splits open" (1961, p. 14). At dinner with some of the survivors of the Lisbon earthquake, "Pangloss consoled them by assuring them that things could not be otherwise . . . 'For,' he said, 'all this is for the very best. For if there is a volcano in Lisbon, it could not be anywhere else. For it is impossible that things should not be where they are. For all is well' " (1961, p. 16). Were not Voltaire's exposition of the Panglossian philosophy so ludicrous that it is impossible to do anything but laugh, it would be difficult to imagine a more callous response to human suffering. It is true that no possible utterance could "console" victims of disaster, but the optimists' philosophy does the reverse: by claiming actual future good as inherent in each "seeming" evil, the optimists deny the human value in man's heroic resilience after suffering and in his often comic love for his scarcely supportable existence.

Completeness as experience, again

The moral truth which *Candide* embodies might therefore be expressed in this way or some variation of it: the evils that men must face in life, some natural but most of them man-made, are so great, so varied, and above all so senseless that it is absurd to believe in a perfect plan of any sort; in fact, all that keeps man from despair and suicide is his irrational hope for improvement and his equally irrational zest for living.

Accordingly, what Voltaire's fiction makes us experience is a sort of catalogue of the varieties of human misery, similar to the one we found in *Rasselas* but much more detailed, in which each description of suffering is usually shown in ironic juxtaposition to the optimistic philosophy, which is stupidly unable to predict, or powerless to cope with, evil. This philosophy may be in the mouth of Pangloss, the archoptimist, or of Candide his faithful pupil (faithful, that is, until life sufficiently educates him), or even in the sarcastic phrases of the narrator. Before we go into the catalogue of atrocities, perhaps we should have a look at the way Voltaire exposes optimism.

We have already cited Pangloss's optimistic observations on the drowning of Jacques and the Lisbon earthquake—events in which the teacher had no personal stake—but he is even capable of reasoning in this manner about his own troubles. He traces the genealogy of his case of syphilis, caught from pretty Paquette, all the way back to Columbus and explains:

> It was an indispensable thing in the best of worlds, a necessary ingredient; for if Columbus had not caught, in an island in America, the disease which poisons the source of generation, and which is obviously opposed to the great purpose of nature, we should not have either chocolate or cochineal (1961, p. 12).

This is, of course, an utterance similar in the perversity of its logic to Pangloss's previous argument that "noses were made to wear spectacles, and so we have spectacles" (1961, p. 4). It even goes a bit too far, perhaps: the line "obviously opposed to the great purpose of nature" is overly explicit in limning the inherent contradiction in Pangloss's philosophy. Voltaire's use of Pangloss may be most effective when he is allowed to bring forth his absurd generalizations—"private misfortunes make up the general good; so that the more private misfortunes there are, the more all is well" (1961, p. 13).

Candide too is used for this purpose, especially before his enlightenment takes hold. At the outset of his travels he is confronted by two recruiting officers; "Ah, sir," one tells him,

"sit down to table; not only will we pay your expenses, but we will never allow a man like you to lack money; men are made only to help one another."
"You are right," said Candide. "That is what Monsieur Pangloss always told me, and I clearly see that all is for the best" (1961, p. 6).

Subsequently he is manacled, then birched into the *kadaverge-horsam* of the Prussian army. Again, after Candide's escape to Holland, he begs his bread, as he must do, from an orator "who had just talked about charity for one solid hour unaided":

"What brings you here? Are you here for the good cause?"
"There is no effect without a cause," replied Candide modestly, "Everything is linked by necessity and arranged for the best. It was necessary for me to be expelled from the presence of Mademoiselle Cunégonde and to run the gantlet and now to beg my bread until I can earn it; all this could not happen differently."
"My friend," said the orator to him, "do you believe that the Pope is antichrist?"
"I had never heard that before," replied Candide; "but whether he is or not, I have no bread."
"You do not deserve to eat any," said the other. "Hence, scoundrel; hence, wretch; never come near me again in your life" (1961, p. 10).

In both these episodes Voltaire's wit is double-edged: on the one hand we laugh at the philosophy Candide has learned from Pangloss, and at his consequent incapacity for dealing with real life; on the other hand Voltaire gets in sly satirical jabs at the ruses of army recruiters and the hypocrisy of lecturers on morality. In *Rasselas*, as here in *Candide*, a teacher of ethics is knocked off his perch, but while in *Rasselas* the stoic lecturer demonstrated his inability to practice his doctrines only in response to a serious crisis in his life, in *Candide* the mere request for bread is enough to deprive the preacher of that charity about which he had been speaking at such length. Voltaire's picture of human nature is several shades blacker than Johnson's; it is saved from complete pessimism only by his mocking tone.

It is this tone itself which, in the absence of Pangloss and Candide, conveys the caustic juxtaposition of "sufficient reason," "cause and effect," the "best of all possible worlds," and the rest of the Leibnitzian claptrap with the cruel realities of life:

Nothing could be so beautiful, so smart, so brilliant, so well
drilled as the two armies. Trumpets, fifes, oboes, drums,
cannons formed a harmony such as was never heard even
in hell. First the cannons felled about six thousand men on
each side; then the musketry removed from *the best of
worlds* some nine or ten thousand scoundrels who infected
its surface. The bayonet also was *the sufficient reason* for
the death of some thousands of men. The whole might
well amount to some thirty thousand souls (1961, p. 9; italics
supplied).

The ironies here are related to those in a brilliant passage somewhat later in the novel on the aftermath of the earthquake in
Lisbon:

After the earthquake, which had destroyed three-quarters
of Lisbon, the country's wise men had found no more
efficacious means of preventing total ruin than to give the
people a fine auto-da-fé; it was decided by the University
of Coimbra that the spectacle of a few persons burned
by a slow fire in a great ceremony is an infallible secret for
keeping the earth from quaking (1961, p. 17).

This is, according to George R. Havens, one of Voltaire's typical
rhetorical devices; he speaks "of the most atrocious abuses and
absurdities with an affected indifference as though they were the
most natural and commonplace things in the world" (1934, p.
lvi). The actual point Voltaire is making, of course, is that man's
nature is so debased that these atrocities indeed are "natural."
    So common are atrocities and disasters in *Candide* that they are
not merely scattered like plums in a pudding but gathered into
clusters in a series of incidents which (like the previously cited
juxtapositions of optimistic philosophy with evil) are variations
on a theme: a series of incidents which repetitively (though not
repetitiously) underscore a single aspect of Voltaire's thesis. We
might call these variations the Hard Luck stories; there are nearly
a dozen of them within the brief narrative. Except for Candide
himself, each of the major characters recounts at least one; Cunégonde, the Baron, and Pangloss each have two. The Hard Luck
stories run parallel, as it were, to Candide's odyssey; their function is to fill out the catalogue of evil of which Candide's own
adventures can be only part. What Voltaire wishes to do, as we
have stated above, is to paint a picture of the immensity, variety,
omnipresence, and senselessness of evil in the world. He does this

through Candide's experiences, it is true, but nevertheless Candide is only one individual. Through the Hard Luck stories Voltaire implies that regardless of sex, age, or station in life, man's existence is scarcely to be endured—and yet it *is* endured. What is most amazing about the Hard Luck stories is that while they convey a dissertation on the quantity and intensity of human misery in life, they do so without sacrificing our analytic apprehension of this—and its exposure of the absurdity of optimism —to our sympathetic feelings for the victims of life's cruelty. Since Voltaire's success here is what is principally responsible for *Candide*'s effectiveness as a rhetorical fiction, let us take a look at one of these Hard Luck stories in some detail—the Old Woman's is the lengthiest, the most memorable and the most self-contained—to see how the author accomplishes this feat.

A summary of the misfortunes undergone by the Old Woman would provide material for several lengthy melodramas: born to the "Princess of Palestrina," the daughter of the nonexistent Pope Urban X, she is taken by pirates, raped and deflowered, and sold into slavery; she watches her mother torn in pieces before her eyes, is sold again, catches the plague (but does not die of it) and is again resold; during a siege she is mutilated by having one of her buttocks cut off and eaten; again resold, she is made gardener to a Russian boyar, who lashes her every day; finally, on the boyar's death, she escapes and works as a servant from inn to inn across Europe. The moral she appends to her story is a line we have already cited: "A hundred times I wanted to kill myself, but I still loved life."

Wayne Booth implies in *The Rhetoric of Fiction* that, since the effect of a tale depends more on how it is told than on what events are recounted, there is no event, no matter how horrible, to which proper narration cannot give humorous effect (1961, pp. 110–16). Perhaps nowhere in literature is this better proven than in these chapters of *Candide*. One of the narrative techniques by which this is accomplished has already been alluded to: affected indifference. The Old Woman, after describing atrocities in a matter-of-fact way, without subjective detail, comments on the frequency of such occurrences. For example:

> I was a virgin. I was not so for long: that flower that had
> been reserved for the handsome Prince of Massa-Carrara
> was ravished from me by the pirate captain. He was an
> abominable Negro who yet thought he was doing me much

honor. . . . But let's get on; these things are so common
that they are not worth speaking about. . . .

. . . They put their fingers in a place in all of us where
we women ordinarily admit only the nozzle of a syringe.
This ceremony seemed quite strange to me; that is how one
judges of everything when one has never been out of one's
country. I soon learned that . . . it is a custom established
from time immemorial among the civilized nations that
roam the seas. . . . It is a rule of international law that has
never been broken.

. . . my fellow captives, those who had captured them,
soldiers, sailors, blacks, tans, whites, mulattoes, and finally
my captain—all were killed, and I remained lying on a heap
of dead. Similar schemes were taking place, as everyone
knows, over an area of more than three hundred square
leagues (1961, pp. 29–30).

After her buttock has been cut off, the Old Woman is cured by a
French surgeon, who assures her that "the same sort of thing had
happened in many sieges, and that it was a law of war" (1961,
p. 33).

Another technique is that of anticlimax, the irrelevant detail
tossed in at the end of a flowery—or horrific—passage, which
overturns the seemingly intended rhetorical effect. (It is this
technique which we commonly associate with the satire of Swift.)
One example occurs in the Old Woman's account of her wedding
preparations:

I was betrothed to a sovereign prince of Massa-Carrara.
What a Prince! . . . The nuptials were prepared. The pomp,
the magnificence were unheard of; there were continual
festivities, tournaments, comic operas, and all Italy composed for me sonnets not one of which was passable (1961,
p. 28).

The scene of universal carnage, which has just been quoted, ends
with a similar anticlimax: "Similar scenes were taking place, as
everyone knows, over an area of more than three hundred square
leagues, without anyone failing to say the five prayers a day
ordained by Mohammad" (1961, p. 30). And after describing the
skill with which the French surgeon cured her maimed backside,
the Old Woman reminisces: "and I shall remember all my life

that when my wounds were fully closed, he made propositions to me" (1961, p. 33).

It is not, of course, only by narrative techniques that Voltaire makes the Old Woman's potentially pathetic tale into a witty, humorous narrative; the particular atrocities we see perpetrated have no small part in the effect. It is no accident that the Old Woman devotes as much time to the pirates' rummaging for diamonds in the private parts of the women as to the massacre; or that the massacre itself is described in almost slapstick terms; or, finally, that it is not a limb that the Old Woman loses to the cannibalistic beseiged party at Azov, but half her arse—there is nothing particularly funny about someone with one arm or one leg, but despite whatever humanitarian feelings one may have, the idea of a half-arsed old lady is far down the path to the ludicrous.

One result of this technique—the characters' tribulations described so as to seem funny rather than pathetic—is to make the inhabitants of Voltaire's world into Punch and Judy figures: beat them down and they pop right up again. (Cunégonde, the Baron, and Pangloss are even "killed," only to return when the narrative is ready to pick them up once more.) This "mechanization of character, plot, and setting," as Ira O. Wade puts it, has, he says, led many a critic of *Candide* to "believe that therein lies its weakness" (1959, p. 305). It is rather the major source of its strength. In an apologue it is always necessary to subordinate our emotional reactions attendant upon the events described to our understanding of the controlling thesis. And since Voltaire's purpose was not to horrify us with the miseries caused by natural and man-made evil but to make us understand its variety and senseless omnipresence, and hence the folly of believing that "all is well," he quite correctly tinged the passages chronicling at large the evils of life with stronger than usual doses of irony and humor; he thus feeds our analytic intelligence while starving the emotional sensibility that might otherwise have prevented our fullest possible understanding of his ideas. And the ironic humor with which the characters narrate their tales of woe underscores Voltaire's thesis that no matter how horrible existence may be men still go on living, loving their detestable lives.

The fullest possible refutation of the optimistic philosophy, of course, demands the fullest possible demonstration of the variety of evils the world has to show; the completeness of *Candide* depends then, in some sense, on the completeness of Voltaire's catalogue. And it is indeed as complete as it was possible to imagine in the eighteenth century, before atomic bombs, nerve gas, and genocide. There are natural disasters: earthquakes, tempests, and shipwrecks. There is incurable disease visited upon man wholesale in the great pox and the plague. And in great abundance and variety there are the evils, avoidable but for human nature, which man visits upon his fellow man: brutal crimes like rape, murder, and mutilation; the butchery both of war itself and of military tribunals; the merciless cruelty of religious bigotry; theft by force and fraud, by judges and moneylenders, gamblers and whores; the horrors of servitude, as chattel slave or as domestic servant. Nor is any profession exempt: doctors, lawyers, merchants, and priests are as corrupt as the lower orders are bestial. A few good men exist—like Jacques the Anabaptist—but their fate is unlikely to be proportioned to their deserts. If Voltaire managed to leave anything out, either from Candide's own adventures or from those he hears from his friends, it is certainly not very obvious; it was left to the twentieth century to invent new forms of evil.

Narrative sequence and closure

It would be going too far to attribute much in the way of what we usually think of as novelistic structure to *Candide*; the placement of such incidents as the Hard Luck stories is determined, I think, rather by considerations of rhythm and balance than by the subtle and complex ideological relationships between episodes that we found in *Rasselas*. For example, Cunégonde's story is followed by that of an older version of Cunégonde—the Old Woman; Friar Giroflée's tale sets off Paquette's, which it follows; the Baron's and Pangloss's second tales are told successively, as the former's miseries are the result of his homosexual licentiousness and the latter's of his heterosexual lust. Nevertheless, this "mighty maze" is "not without a plan"—not wholly, at least. There is a kind of sequential core to *Candide* consisting of the hero's adventures and his slowly altering attitudes toward the evils he encounters: Candide's education, if you will. William F. Bottiglia sees Candide's opinions changing in a "progression from relative complacency through pessimistic drift to meliorism" and considers this shift to be one of the "vital structural patterns of *Candide*" (1959, p. 167).

Candide's early utterances are thoroughly worthy of his optimistic tutor, Doctor Pangloss. We have already cited some of his Leibnitzian observations, and Candide is even more optimistic in happiness than he is in adversity. After Jacques takes him in, he falls to his knees in gratitude and sighs: "Doctor Pangloss was certainly right to tell me that all is for the best in this world, for I am infinitely more touched by your extreme generosity than by the harshness" of the preacher and his wife (1961, p. 10). Later, as Candide is about to sail for the New World with Cunégonde and the Old Woman, he quiets his lady-love's fears with more optimism: "All will be well . . . the sea of this new world is already better than the seas of our Europe; it is calmer, the winds are more constant. It is certainly the new world that is the best of possible universes" (1961, p. 27). One may detect, even here, a note of realism; Candide hopes that America will be what Europe was not.[7]

This note grows stronger as the novel progresses: with Pangloss gone and Candide on his own (or with the prudent and sensible Cacambo), Candide's references to optimism become steadily more ambiguous. On the boat to Buenos Aires, for example, Candide, having heard the Old Woman's tale of her miseries, begins to find optimism less self-evident:

> "It is a great pity," said Candide, "that the wise Pangloss was hanged contrary to custom in an auto-da-fé; he would tell us wonderful things about the physical evil and the moral evil that cover earth and sea, and I would feel strong enough to offer him, respectfully, a few objections" (1961, p. 35).

In his joy on again meeting up with the Baron, whom he encounters as Father Colonel of the Jesuits in Paraguay, Candide seems to take up the Panglossian strain, although the manner of expression is not the same as his former imbecile optimism:

> "What! Can that be you, Reverend Father? You, the brother of the fair Cunégonde! You, who were killed by the Bulgarians! You, the son of My Lord the Baron! You a Jesuit in Paraguay! I must admit that the world is a strange thing. O Pangloss! Pangloss! How happy you would be if you had not been hanged!" (1961, p. 40).

His mere exposure to the evils of life do not seem to be enough, however, to convince Candide that all is not well; it is only after

Candide sees the true utopia of Eldorado that he is finally moved to reject his tutor's philosophy. The "bad meal" shared by Candide and Cacambo in the "poor village" in Eldorado is sufficient to provoke the travelers to this evaluation:

"What kind of country is this, then . . . unknown to the rest of the world, and where all nature is of a sort so different from ours? Probably this is the country where all is well; for there absolutely must be one of that sort. And no matter what Doctor Pangloss said about it, I often noticed that all was pretty bad in Westphalia. . . ."

. . . "This is very different from Westphalia and the castle of My Lord the Baron; if our friend Pangloss had seen Eldorado, he would no longer have said that the castle of Thunder-ten-tronckh was the best thing on earth" (1961, pp. 48–51).

As a picture of Voltaire's ideal society, Eldorado is only thinly sketched in, so that builders of extravagant theories about the author's social and political ideas can usually read what they like into it. Bottiglia, who sees *Candide* basically as a highly affirmative work extolling the virtues of labor specifically and the *vita activa* generally, emphasizes the fact that Eldorado seems to be a dynamic place, with schoolmasters, innkeepers, physicists, engineers each cultivating his own garden; these things are certainly there, and yet the ethical significance of Eldorado cannot consist only of this. One might claim, on equally good evidence, that Eldorado was simply a picture of Voltaire's France, minus some institutions obnoxious to the author, like lawyers and a militant clergy, and with far greater wealth. Another might see in Eldorado Plato's republic led by a philosopher-king, as ironically seen by Voltaire. The fact is that Eldorado is significant not so much for what it is in itself as for the contrast it provides Candide—and us readers—to the civilizations Voltaire knew.

For it is as though after seeing Eldorado—society as it might be—Candide cannot any longer believe that "all is well" in the world in which he is henceforth to live. At the pathetic sight of a Negro slave mutilated by his master, Candide can no longer hold onto his optimistic doctrines:

"O Pangloss!" exclaimed Candide, "you had not guessed this abomination; this does it. At last I shall have to renounce your optimism."

"What is optimism?" said Cacambo.
"Alas," said Candide, "it is the mania of maintaining
that all is well when we are miserable!" (1961, p. 56).

And as he is bilked of his wealth in Surinam, first by a piratical
sea-captain, then by a rapacious and corrupt magistrate, Candide
falls prey to a pessimism as black as his former optimism was
sunny:

> True, he had endured misfortunes a thousand times more
> painful; but the coldbloodedness of the judge, and of the
> captain by whom he had been robbed, inflamed his bile
> and plunged him into a black melancholy. The wickedness
> of men appeared to his mind in all its ugliness; he fed only
> on sad ideas. . . .
> "That Pangloss," said he, "would be much embarrassed
> to try to prove his system. I wish he was here. Certainly
> if all is well it is in Eldorado and not in the rest of the
> world" (1961, p. 58).

And it is at this crucial point that Candide comes under the influence of Martin, the character whose cynical views come closest
to those of Voltaire. Martin's philosophy, of course, is precisely
the opposite of Pangloss's: he believes that all is for the worst;
a professed Manichean, he holds that God "has abandoned" the
world "to some maleficent being":

> "I have hardly seen a town that did not desire the ruin of
> the neighboring town, never a family that did not want to
> exterminate some other family. Everywhere the weak
> loathe the powerful before whom they crawl, and the
> powerful treat them like flocks whose wool and flesh are
> for sale. A million regimented assassins, ranging from one
> end of Europe to the other, practice murder and brigandage
> with discipline to earn their bread, because there is no more
> honest occupation; and in the towns that seem to enjoy
> peace and where the arts flourish, men are devoured with
> more envy, cares, and anxieties than the scourges suffered
> by a town besieged. Secret griefs are even more cruel than
> public miseries. . . ."
> "Yet there is some good," said Candide.
> "That may be," said Martin, "but I do not know it"
> (1961, pp. 60–61).

This is the period of "pessimistic drift" in Bottiglia's triad; in
this section of the novel Candide serves as a kind of *advocatus*

domini—a devil's advocate in reverse—arguing against Martin's diabolical reasonings, weakly and rather sadly attempting to establish the possibility of good in a world he now knows well to be evil:

> "Do you think," said Candide, "that men have always massacred each other as they do today, always been liars, cheats, faith-breakers, ingrates, brigands, weaklings, rovers, cowards, enviers, gluttons, drunkards, misers, self-seekers, carnivores, calumniators, debauchees, fanatics, hypocrites, and fools?"
> "Do you think," said Martin, "that sparrow hawks have always eaten pigeons when they found any?"
> "Yes, no doubt," said Candide.
> "Well," said Martin, "if sparrow hawks have always had the same character, why do you expect men to have changed theirs?"
> "Oh!" said Candide, "there's a big difference, for free will . . ." (1961, p. 64).

Candide's argument, though it would seem that he is trying to establish the possibility of a golden age from which men have fallen, or of a possible future state of virtue to which they may aspire, has already explicitly conceded Martin's point. The same is true of a somewhat later conversation in which Candide and Martin participate; the poor, cynical scholar at the house of the Marquise de Parolignac is asked by Candide whether he thinks "that all is for the best in the physical world and in the moral, and that nothing could have been otherwise?" Quite the contrary, the scholar replies, "it's an eternal war." Candide tries valiantly to hold up the absent Pangloss's end of the eternal argument, claiming that "a sage, who has since had the misfortune to be hanged, taught me that all this is wonderful: these [evils] are shadows in a beautiful picture." And when Martin cynically reminds Candide that his "shadows" are in reality "horrible stains," Candide does not contest the description; his only reply is that men "can't help" making those stains—which seems virtually an admission of the inevitability of evil (1961, p. 71).

In all fairness, one must point out that Candide's shift from the cheerful optimist to the near-convert to Martin's Manicheanism is not quite as pat as the above quotations would make it appear. Candide's moods play no small part in his opinions, and when he is cheered by the prospect of finding his beloved Cunégonde once more, he can sound as optimistic as the lad who referred his beating at the hands of the Bulgarians to the Great Chain of Being:

> Candide had one great advantage over Martin: he still hoped to see Mademoiselle Cunégonde again, and Martin had nothing to hope for; furthermore, he had gold and diamonds; and though he had lost a hundred big red sheep laden with the greatest treasures on earth, though he still had the knavery of the Dutch captain on his mind, nevertheless, when he thought about what he had left in his pockets, and when he talked about Cunégonde, especially toward the end of a meal, he still leaned toward the system of Pangloss (1961, p. 60).

Or when Martin and Candide land at Venice, where they are to meet Cacambo and Cunégonde:

> "God be praised," said Candide, embracing Martin, "here is where I shall see the fair Cunégonde again. I count on Cacambo as on myself. All goes well, all goes well, all goes as well as it possibly could" (1961, p. 76).

But while these exceptions to the general trend of Candide's philosophizing do exist, one must never forget that these are exceptions. In the first of the above quotations Voltaire carefully qualifies Candide's optimism: which of us would not be sanguine when jingling his money and speaking of his mistress after a good dinner, over brandy and cigars? And as for the second quotation, it is the cynical Martin who has the last word: Cunégonde is not in Venice when Candide arrives, and the erstwhile optimist falls "into a black melancholy":

> ". . . Cunégonde is beyond doubt dead, there is nothing left for me to do but die. Ah! it would have been better to remain in the paradise of Eldorado than to return to this accursed Europe. How right you are, my dear Martin! All is illusion and calamity. . . ."
> Martin was not consoling. Candide's melancholy increased, and Martin never stopped proving to him that there was little virtue and little happiness on earth, except perhaps in Eldorado where no one could go (1961, p. 77).

The general direction of Candide's volatile beliefs is toward Martin's hard-boiled attitude about life, and, at the very end of the novel, when Candide is reunited with Pangloss, his former tutor in metaphysico-theologico-cosmo-nigology, he cannot help twitting him a little: " 'Well, my dear Pangloss . . . when you were hanged, dissected, racked with blows, and rowing in the galleys, did you still think that all was for the very best?' " (1961, p. 95).

This is basically all there is to the "sequential core" of *Candide* —the twist in the final chapter will be discussed a little later—and it is hard to establish much more than this in the way of formal structure in the novel; the episodes seem less to take their places within a sequential argument (as in *Rasselas*) than to lead lives of their own. The Old Woman's story, which we analyzed in relation to the controlling thesis of *Candide*, and in the way in which its rhetoric serves the analytic apprehension of that thesis, is in itself a memorable bit of humorous narrative; extracted from the novel, it would lose, to be sure, the moral and philosophical significance which the rest of *Candide* gives it, but it would certainly retain—like the extant fragments of the *Satyricon*—its biting wit. Its vitality would remain. And the Old Woman's story is merely the longest and perhaps the most brilliantly inventive of the episodes of which *Candide* is composed: many of the others are almost as delightful and equally autonomous.

It is worth mentioning here that no one would pick up the more intricately structured *Rasselas* just to read a page or two: a good many of the aphorisms come out neatly in one piece, but the episodes are generally tightly lashed together. The local effects of wit or pathos are slighter—where they are not wholly lacking —and it would be difficult to suggest a sequence that one would want to extract for isolated enjoyment. It is àlmost as though there were a difference in the "focal length" of *Rasselas* and *Candide*: the former is like a brilliantly composed painting whose outlines, on nearer inspection, resolve into a series of tiny dots; the latter is like a mosaic, each of whose tiles is in itself a witty engraving. With certain qualifications, the two forms are inconsistent, for to the extent that a part is to function in subordination to some larger formal structure, its isolable local effects must be toned down.

Candide is, then, an additive rather than an architectonic structure, in which each episode embodies one or more clauses of the statement which the novel embodies as a whole. It "might be continued" in the sense that Voltaire makes his points repetitively on occasion, and that the episodic narrative sequence could always be rearranged to include a few more Hard Luck stories, or a few more exempla of man's chicanery, brutality, and greed. If he did not do so, it was because Voltaire thought his argument as it stood seemed complete, and we have earlier discussed the completeness of the author's catalogue of the evils of life as a condition for the completeness of his fable.

Closure is, of course, another matter. We could incorporate more episodes into *Candide*—if we felt the need for more—without disturbing the unity of the work, but had Voltaire subjected his Westphalians to further tribulations at Constantinople, we would begin to think we were reading a sequel. Even further elaboration of their agricultural life—sketching in how Candide goes about cultivating his garden—would have had the force of an addendum.

One main factor in the closure of *Candide* is obviously our hero's marriage to the girl of his dreams, Cunégonde. She is, of course, no longer the girl of Candide's dreams: for her to have remained beautiful and complaisant would have been inconsistent with Voltaire's thesis, and the "happily ever after" conclusion would have clashed with the ironic tone of the novel. Just as Candide's trials have sapped his youthful optimism, Cunégonde's have made her ugly and ill-tempered, but Candide is an "honorable man" and marries her anyhow, terminating his years-long quest as finally as did the group in *Rasselas*. A second factor, related to the first, is the settling of the rest of the narrative lines, the formation of permanent situations for the other characters in the novel who appear in more than a single episode. The Baron is shipped off to the galleys whence he came; the rest—Pangloss, Martin, Cacambo, the Old Woman, Paquette, and Friar Giroflée—become part of Candide's ménage. Thus all the story lines of the episodic work are tied off.

More important, and much more puzzling in a way, is the ideological twist by which Voltaire rounds off the philosophical speculation of which his novel has mainly consisted. The elements in this twist are two, the first of which is Pangloss's rebuke by the wise dervish:

> "Master, we have come to ask you to tell us why such a strange animal as man was ever created."
> "What are you meddling in?" said the dervish. "Is that your business?"

"But, Reverend Father," said Candide, "there is a horrible amount of evil on earth."
"What does it matter," said the dervish, "whether there is evil or good? When His Highness sends a ship to Egypt, is he bothered about whether the mice in the ship are comfortable or not?"
"Then what should we do?" said Pangloss.
"Hold your tongue," said the dervish (1961, pp. 99–100).

Evil, in other words, is a matter of perspective. God is as little concerned with the problems of man as a prince would be with the discomfort of vermin. So there is no point in arguing about the subject of evil as though it were, in the long run, important whether one did so or not.

The episode of the dervish is not so finely developed or so elaborate as that of the old astronomer in *Rasselas*, but the two incidents serve similar functions: both close off debate. Rasselas's experience of the astronomer leads him to break off his prolonged search for a perfect life, while the dervish's enigmatic responses convince Candide of the futility of metaphysical speculation. This concludes the duologue between the deistic optimist Pangloss and the Manichean cynic Martin on the origin and nature of evil, and although Pangloss tries to start it up once more in the novel's penultimate line, his former pupil reminds him that the argument is over.

The second element in the ideological closure of *Candide* is the episode of the old patriarchal farmer who gives our hero the solution to the ultimate evil in life—boredom. Although men's miseries in this world are typically represented as the result of natural disaster or their fellows' wickedness, the episode of Martin's and Candide's visit to Count Pococurante shows the travelers that the mere absence of external torments does not in itself produce happiness. The Count of "few cares" is wealthy and intelligent, superior to all his possessions, but the effect of this upon him is only lethargy, ennui, and disgust. And it is into this state that Candide's household falls once its more exciting trials are past. As the Old Woman puts it,

"I would like to know which is worse—to be raped a hundred times by Negro pirates, have a buttock cut off, run the gantlet among the Bulgarians, be flogged and hanged in an auto-da-fé, be dissected, row in the galleys, in short to

undergo all the miseries we have all been through—or to
stay here doing nothing?" (1961, pp. 98–99).

And Martin agrees that "man was born to live in the convulsions
of anxiety or the lethargy of boredom." Candide "did not agree"
—looking, doubtless, for a way through the horns of this dilemma, a way that is pointed out by the old Turkish farmer, who
explains the happiness of his moderate station in life in terms of
the value of labor: " 'Work keeps away three great evils: boredom, vice, and need.' " (1961, p. 100). And the farmer's pure
Mocha coffee and delicious candied fruits—the products of his
labor—make his views worth listening to. It is Martin who draws
together the lessons of both dervish and farmer: " 'Let us work
without reasoning . . . it is the only way to make life endurable' "
(1961, p. 101). One must cultivate one's garden.

This conclusion, according to Norman L. Torrey, is rather con-
troversial:

> Some have interpreted it as an expression of pessimism, a
> counsel of inaction and of withdrawal from all efforts to
> better the lot of mankind. The conclusion is so obviously
> in contrast with Voltaire's own way of life that others have
> sought an allegorical interpretation and have seen in the
> words an exhortation to enter the fight for humanity (1938,
> pp. 49–50).

William F. Bottiglia, in "Candide's Garden," takes the latter view.
Men cultivate their gardens when they "work concretely, each at
his appointed task, and with a minimum of windy theorizing,
toward the diminution of social evil and the spread of social virtue." Candide's ménage thus becomes a "model society" whose
members "can . . . legitimately envision an ideal State which,
though beyond complete realization, may at least be . . . approached through cooperative work, through practical action"
(1968, p. 90). To achieve this formulation of "cultivate your
garden" requires a good deal of fancy footwork: for one thing,
one must somehow make Martin out as much the "villain" of the
piece as Pangloss, which Bottiglia does by taking literally Voltaire's obviously ironic reference to Martin's "detestable principles" and conveniently forgetting about its context. For another,
Bottiglia ignores completely Martin's unanswered arguments for
the universal depravity of human nature. Fortunately, it is not so
difficult to reconcile the pessimistic interpretation of "cultivate

your garden" with Voltaire's known opinions: Voltaire, as Torrey rightly points out, was by no means a consistently enthusiastic reformer, and in late 1758, when he was writing *Candide*, he was hitting the bottom of his curve—he was worn out and depressed (Torrey, 1938, pp. 50–51). Furthermore, it is in a sense possible to reconcile the two interpretations: why may not Voltaire be recommending not altruistic social reform but private self-improvement, developing the little one has in order to create around oneself a tiny Eldorado?

But while Bottiglia is not alone in attempting insistently to reconcile "cultivate your garden" with the main tenor of Voltaire's thought, his persistence may be seen to derive from a fundamental misconception of the nature of fables in general and *Candide* in particular. If one identifies the denouement of a work with its purpose, confounding the two distinct meanings of the word *end*, one will naturally see the thesis of a rhetorical fiction in its final statements. This would very likely be the case, of course, with a long, progressive, logical argument: the last statement would be that which was to be proven. And it would also be the case in rhetorical fictions which were imitations of such an argument: one can treat Plato's *Gorgias* in this way (though not, surely, all the Platonic dialogues), as a fiction whose last moments contain the final steps in a deductive proof. But if *Candide* is a fable of a different sort, in which each incident does not represent a step in the proof of the thesis, but is rather a fictional exemplum of the entire thesis (emphasizing one or another of its aspects); if the parts in *Candide* are not subordinate and progressive, but coordinate and repetitive—as we have tried to show—then there is no reason why we should expect the denouement to have any unique ideological importance. In other words, the significance of "cultivate your garden" is to be found not in its putative relationship to Voltaire's philosophy as expressed in his other works or to his mode of life, but in its function as an ending for the particular rhetorical fiction, *Candide*, with its particular thesis.

There is thus a sense in which it is irrelevant to argue over whether the intended meaning of "cultivate your garden" should be taken to be social reform, or disengagement, or self-improvement, as though one of these were the main point of the novel. For regardless of which sense we give it, it represents the final step in Candide's education which, throughout the novel and not merely at its end, has consisted in his learning about the evil inherent in human life and the consequent contradiction between his own experiences and the philosophy inculcated by his former master, Pangloss.

We should remember, in the first place, that although Candide twice enunciates the phrase "we must cultivate our garden," he never presents it as a thesis for argument: both times Candide sets it forth in reply to a windy theoretical argument of Pangloss's, and each time it is a conversation-stopper. Unlike Martin's discourse, which in a sense meets Pangloss on his own ground by countering one theory explaining the phenomena of the universe with another, Candide's final position rejects not only Pangloss's views but also his penchant for argumentative discourse. "We must cultivate our garden": perhaps we do not go about cultivating others' gardens, but at least we do not assure men, as Pangloss had, that all gardens are by the very nature of things well cultivated—we have realized that man is no longer in Eden and that one's garden must be actively worked at if anything at all is to grow. Implicit in Candide's statement is the denial of a benevolent providence or an immanent rewarding and punishing deity, together with the acceptance of the extremely limited form of self-made happiness that is possible for man on earth.

And so it is perhaps not irrelevant, in the second place, that the two Panglossian arguments which elicit Candide's reply bring us back to the world of Candide's odyssey, with its rapid changes of fortune and exaggerated suffering. The first argument is a catalogue of the host of great men who have miserably perished, rulers who were deposed and murdered; the second is a summary of Candide's own experiences, with the appended conclusion that his suffering, by the chain of causes and effects in this best of possible worlds, was necessary for the present happiness the group shares. Candide's reply would seem to accept the facts of life, but to reject Pangloss's reasoning about them. He knows that kings, like all men, are subject to the vagaries of fortune, just as he knows what he has himself undergone before reaching his tiny corner of contentment; but he also knows that this is not the best of possible worlds, and that any happiness they have will not be ordained but achieved.

One can most graphically see the appropriateness of "cultivate your garden" as an ending for *Candide* by imagining how much the fable would lose in force were some other ending—say, that of *Rasselas*— grafted on in its place. What would happen if instead of cultivating its garden Candide's ménage decided to go off to some sort of combination of Westphalia and Eldorado, of home and utopia, which the "happy valley" represents in *Rasselas*? Probably nothing could do more to dissipate our sense of Candide's education in the immense variety of evil in the universe, in the senselessness and randomness of misery, and consequently in the folly of the optimistic philosophy, than such a conclusion. For Candide to leave Constantinople in search of a better life would imply that things are not the same everywhere, and that one may change one's lot simply by leaving the place where one has suffered. But throughout the novel Candide has found the same brutality and misery in all the countries of Europe and the New World as well. (One might claim that there is a geographical exhaustiveness about *Candide* in addition to the philosophical kind, so careful is Voltaire to show us vice and misery in every major area of the earth's surface!) Searching for the ideal has convinced Candide only of the universality of evil: in cultivating his garden Candide renounces the search and accepts the world as it is, and the work which constitutes his small happiness.

Similarly, the ending of *Candide* would be ruinous to *Rasselas*, for the entire thesis of the latter novel is that no choice of life will guarantee perfect happiness: to show Rasselas and his companions making a contented life for themselves through cooperative labor would be in complete contradiction to the thesis. What modicum of hope *Rasselas* leaves us with depends upon our sense that the miseries of life are as temporary as its joys, and that there is the possibility of eternal bliss for the reasonably virtuous; the return to Abyssinia is a testimony to the failure of Rasselas's quest for earthly happiness. Thus the slight difference between the theses of *Rasselas* and *Candide*—both are concerned with demonstrating the variety and omnipresence of evil in the universe, but *Candide* does so not for its own sake but in order to scuttle, through ridicule, the philosophical theory of optimism— dictates not only the very different tones of the two novels but also their incommensurate endings.

Completeness and closure

But at the same time, the differences between *Rasselas* and *Candide* with regard to their senses of completeness and closure depend less on the particular thesis which governs each novel— these have indeed been rightly felt to be very similar—but on the

particular way in which each statement is embodied within the
fiction. In *Rasselas,* the quest for the hero's "choice of a life" is
used to provide the framework for an illusory fictional induction.
The search for happiness is divided up according to the various
sources of contentment and bliss, and each source—philosophy,
family relations, class status—is further subdivided for investigation by empirical examination. It must be stressed here that only
the illusion of inductive argument is provided us; as a serious
philosophical proof, *Rasselas* could hardly stand much scrutiny.
The sources of happiness, in the first place, are not examined
exhaustively; within a single such source—philosophy, for example—it is clear that there are many unexplored pathways: the
epicureanism of Marcus Aurelius, for instance, or even Panglossian optimism. Worse still, the alternative sources of happiness
are eliminated without the kind or amount of evidence that we
would require in the real world: the failure of his philosophy to
provide solace for a single stoic is taken as proof of the inadequacy of "teachers of morality." To take *Rasselas* seriously as a
set of logical propositions would require a reversal of the fictional
argument: the moral of *Rasselas,* the nonexistence of perfect, secure, earthly happiness, would have to be taken as the major
premise, not the conclusion, of a series of syllogisms; *Rasselas*
would have to be a set of deductive arguments rather than a complex induction. In a sense, this is the case. The *logical* form of
Rasselas is a set of deductive syllogisms; only its *fictional* form is
inductive. The former makes possible and satisfying Johnson's
opening statement, which is logically a premise rather than a
conclusion: "Ye who listen with credulity to the whispers of
fancy, and pursue with eagerness the phantoms of hope . . . attend to the history of Rasselas prince of Abyssinia" (p. 1). The
imitation of an induction, on the other hand, is what gives
Rasselas its shape as a fiction. One might go so far as to argue that
had Johnson been able actually to prove the nonexistence of
earthly happiness, he might have done so in a philosophical
treatise; the difficulty of proving a negative prevented this, and
so he produced the illusion of such a proof in his novel. The form
of *Rasselas* is such that each mentioned source of happiness is
examined and rejected until the search is broadened to include the
possibility of eternal happiness after death, an object which is
shown to be as probable as it is untestable by the searchers'
methods. The rhetorical completeness of the imitation of an in-

duction is the source of the completeness of the novel; the closure of *Rasselas* depends on the consequent abandonment of the hero's quest. The strength of the closure depends thus upon that of the completeness.

Whereas in *Rasselas* each incident embodies a logically discrete aspect of the ethical statement which shapes the work, in *Candide* each incident is a fictional example of the entire thesis (although the variations may emphasize one or the other of its clauses). Thus the episode of the Lisbon earthquake, while it mainly serves to show the ridiculous inadequacy of optimism in dealing with the problem of natural disaster, also demonstrates the resilience of human nature: in the midst of the catastrophe sailors look about them for loose women whose favors may be purchased, and the survivors pick themselves up, dust themselves off, and forage for their dinners. The episodes in *Candide* are thus independent coordinated parts of the whole, while those in *Rasselas* are subordinate parts dependent upon a logical framework.

For example, had Johnson anachronistically wished to include an incident showing that earthly happiness could not be achieved through the use of LSD, he would have had either to include other incidents demonstrating the inutility of other drugs (alcohol, opium, marihuana), or to make us feel that LSD was the most important possibility in this category, and that if happiness could not be gotten through its use, then no other drug could conceivably do the job either. In *Candide*, on the other hand, Voltaire could have added another exemplum of natural or human evil almost anywhere in the novel without disturbing its integrity, so long as it was sufficiently different from the others he had used to make an adequate contribution, and so long as its tone and moral significance jibed with the thesis.

Actually, there are a few incidents in *Rasselas* appearing early in the novel before the "choice of a life" sequences which work like those in *Candide*. The dissertation on flying, for example, symbolically represents not a fragment but the entire thesis of the novel. The abject failure of the artist's much vaunted pair of wings is an objective correlative for the vanity of all earthly ambitions; similarly, just as the lack of perfect happiness does not imply that life is nothing but misery, so the artist's "wings, which were of no use in the air, sustained him in the water" in which the brief, ignominious flight concluded (p. 15). Man cannot fly, but he does not necessarily drown as the result of trying. It is in episodes such as this one that the thesis of *Rasselas,* announced in the opening lines, is "developed" before it is "proved."

The independence of the incidents in *Candide*—except, of course, in terms of their mutual relation to the thesis which each embodies—makes our sense of the completeness of the work depend upon our sense that Voltaire's survey of the sources and quality of evil in the universe has been thorough—that he has neither blinked at evil nor exaggerated it. The sense of ending that Voltaire provides in the denouement of *Candide* is partly the result of saving until the end the balancing evil of ennui—equal in the Old Woman's eyes to all the natural and man-made disasters they have experienced; the rest is the result of the strong closure devices we have discussed above.

Where Johnson and Voltaire are alike in their methods, of course, is that neither of them makes strong demands either on the reader's intellect or on his emotions: both authors are content to think for us rather than let us reason to conclusions for ourselves, and both carefully tone down the emotional impact of the fiction lest, feeling too deeply, we should forget to think. Yet there is no absolute reason why rhetorical fictions should be cold treatises; in fact, so long as our emotional reactions to events in a fable are carefully kept subordinate to our apprehension of the thesis, it is clear that the more involved we become the greater the intellectual impact of the thesis will be. The danger is that things will come unstuck. But narrative techniques had not evolved in 1759 to the point where surmounting this danger was an easy task. New techniques for representing deep states of consciousness in fictional personages were developed in the nineteenth century, a development which made possible the modern apologue, which could combine the emotional force of represented actions with the thematic structure of the fable. The rest of this essay will be concerned with the new possibilities which have opened up for writers of rhetorical fictions in our time. The first one we shall take up is, in a way, a transitional case: *Lord of the Flies.*

Allegory Versus Fable
Golding's Lord of the Flies

Like a good many modern rhetorical novels, *Lord of the Flies* generally adheres to the conventions of psychological realism; where it is unlike most modern apologues is that it has been consistently interpreted as such. Most of the voluminous literature on *Lord of the Flies* has concerned itself with elucidating the nuances of William Golding's thesis within the novel and relating the fictional superstructure to this thesis. This unusual unanimity may have less to do with the transparency of Golding's creation than with his personal candor; unlike many modern novelists who refuse to help out the critics with the job of interpretation, Golding is not at all adverse to stating quite precisely what his novels are intended to mean. Of *Lord of the Flies* Golding has written:

> The theme is an attempt to trace the defects of society back to the defects of human nature. The moral is that the shape of society must depend on the ethical nature of the individual and not on any political system however apparently logical or respectable. The whole book is symbolic in nature except the rescue in the end where human life appears, dignified and capable, but in reality enmeshed in the same evil as the symbolic life of the children on the island. The officer having interrupted a manhunt, prepares to take the children off the island in a cruiser which will presently be hunting its enemy in the same implacable way (p. 189).

Such was the force of Golding's explanation that no one has dared to deal with *Lord of the Flies* as a simple adventure story of boys on a desert island; the novel has, in the twenty years since its publication in 1954, become a standard introductory text through which high school sophomores are initiated into the mysteries of chasing after hidden meanings and trapping elusive symbols. What we shall be concerned with, for the next few pages, is the way in which Golding's thesis (as he himself expresses it in the quotation above) has been expressed as an experience, embodied within a fiction—and especially with the artistic function of the conventionally despised deus ex machina denouement, both as a closure device and as an element in shaping our sense of the novel's completeness.

Structure as symbolic action

The structure of Golding's rhetorical novel corresponds roughly to that of his thesis: "The shape of society must depend upon the ethical nature of the individual and not on any political system however apparently logical or respectable." Accordingly, the novel describes the formation, decay, and re-formation of a society of boys marooned on a Pacific coral island during some future atomic war.

The children (there are several dozen of them, ranging in age from six to fourteen) begin by setting up an elective government with Ralph, the biggest and oldest, as chief executive. Ralph's qualification for office, aside from his size and age, consists of his having been the one to call the society into existence, gathering the boys together by blowing a blast through a trumpet-shaped conch shell he has found. Ralph lacks, as he himself well knows, the intelligence and foresight to run the society, and he therefore gathers to himself a one-man brain trust: Piggy, a fat, asthmatic Cockney who is both literally and figuratively far-sighted. The government is dedicated to maintaining the spiritual and reestablishing the physical link with England: the boys hold daily "democratic" assemblies, using Ralph's conch as the symbol of the freedom and order of organized debate; they build shelters —as though they still had the English fogs to contend with; they plan to keep up a smoke signal during the daylight hours (using Piggy's strong convex lenses to set the fire) in order to alert any passing ship to their presence. Here we have the "apparently logical or respectable" system of government referred to in Golding's thesis, and there would seem to be no reason why it should not work: the island is a paradise, with plenty of fruit, fresh water, firewood for the signal, and pigs to be trapped and slain for meat—enough for all indefinitely; there are no predators, no carnivores but the boys themselves; no women for whom the older, pubescent boys might compete; no danger from the weather or from outside the island where—we may guess—the war is still raging.

But the government is at odds with "the ethical nature of the individual," and as time goes on it begins to decay, first slowly and almost invisibly, then more obviously, and finally with an explosive rupture. Halfway through this process, Ralph tells the group what he sees happening: " 'We have lots of assemblies. Everybody enjoys speaking and being together. We decide things. But they don't get done' " (p. 73). Water is no longer gathered and brought to a shady spot in coconut shells; the huts are no longer built with the joint effort of the whole community; the rocks downstream from the bathing pool are no longer the only spot used as a lavatory; the fire is no longer attended to with any care. Ralph is right to complain about his friends' neglect of their responsibilities, but he does not see why things are falling apart, though the reason is not far to seek. The longer the children are on the island the less real the possibility of returning to civilization becomes for them. As their hopes fade, so does their ambition to retain the amenities of civilized life on the island. Unsupported by the presence or imminent arrival of grownups, the children's behavior changes; the ostensible motivations of civilized men are replaced by deeper and more primitive ones, and their manners change accordingly.

As their hopes fade, their fears grow more insistent. Starting with a "littlun" called Phil, who claims at assembly that he has seen "something big and horrid" moving among the trees at night, panic spreads like an epidemic among the society, dissolving the order that had been maintained up to that time. Ralph and Piggy cannot deal with this outbreak of primitive terror with the organization and method of civilized society, but there is in their company one boy who can not only cope with the panic but can use it for his own ends: Jack Merridew. Jack had been the prefect of a group of choirboys when he and they were deposited on the island in the crash; as such he is a sort of natural leader—he has at least the virtues of command and address—and at the very beginning challenges Ralph's acclamation as chieftain. He is bought off by being made leader of his choirboys again, a team which is now to function as hunting party and as guardians of the signal fire.

Up until the outbreak of terror caused by the "Beast," Jack

had chafed under his role in subordinate authority: he had had
to suffer sharp words from Ralph criticizing his slipshod care of
the fire and his relegation of that all-important duty to a secondary place while he and his hunters developed their skills. Confronted now with the mythical Beast, however, Jack comes into
his own; democracy and fair play have become irrelevant to the
survival of the society, which now comes more and more to depend upon Jack's skill and strict control.

From a battle fought ten miles above the island, a dead airman
floats down until he is caught in his parachute on some trees.
Seen by Sam and Eric, a pair of twins who are special friends of
Ralph's, the airman becomes the objective focus of the children's
fears, which by now have reached immense proportions. Jack
here assumes the de facto leadership of the group, calling up the
hunt on which he takes Ralph and the other bigger boys. All day
they hunt around the island until all but Jack, his lieutenant,
Roger, and Ralph have given up the chase; at last, after nightfall,
they find what Sam and Eric had claimed to have seen: first a
"bulge on the mountain," then "something like a great ape," and
finally the airman's "ruin of a face" (pp. 112–14).

The existence of the Beast established, Jack moves to take full,
acknowledged control of the society which must perforce depend
upon his skills. At the last assembly, Jack moves Ralph's with-
drawal as chief, only to be rejected on Ralph's home ground: he
leaves the society to go off up the mountain on his own. By dawn
the next morning, however, after the terrors that nightfall brings
to the children, almost everyone has joined Jack's tribe of hunters; only Piggy, Ralph, and a few others remain on the beach by
the huts. A new society is established, substituting Jack's paternal
dictatorial leadership for Ralph's democratic assemblies, an
aggressive hunting economy for a passive gathering one, and rule
of terror for rule of law. Jack's most impressive innovation is his
introduction of a mystery cult of the Beast, with the pig as a
ritual sacrifice to propitiate the Beast's putative wrath.[1] The
invention of ritual, the use of war-paint as a mask, the dense
camaraderie of the hunt—these are the elements which hold
Jack's society together. The children, frightened of the unknown,
need each other's supportive closeness by day and the catharsis
of mimetic rites by night to keep back their blind terror.

But these innovations have their social cost as well: when
Simon interrupts a dance celebrating the pig hunt in order to tell

the group that the Beast whom they feared is only a dead man on the hill, the dancers, mistaking him for the Beast, set upon and kill him with their bare hands, a scene reminiscent of the slaying of Pentheus in *The Bacchae*. And it is after this horrific ritual murder that Jack's control of the society becomes rigid—almost totalitarian; Jack's commands are law and become gradually more arbitrarily cruel:

> "He's going to beat Wilfred."
> "What for?"
> Robert shook his head doubtfully.
> "I don't know. He didn't say. He got angry and made us tie Wilfred up. He's been"—he giggled excitedly—"He's been tied up for hours, waiting—"
> "But didn't the chief say why?"
> "I never heard him" (p. 147).

Sentinels are posted at the entrance to Jack's fortress: poor Simon, murdered by mistake, is authoritatively termed "the beast disguised" and a close watch is kept for a possible return. Having consolidated his political triumph, Jack returns to the problem of Ralph, Piggy, Sam, and Eric, and the other few holdouts from his tribe; he seeks a final solution.

The last chapters of the novel return from Jack's point of view to Ralph's, so that we see the final effects of Jack's new mode of society—one based on the savage "ethical nature of the individual," his desires and fears, rather than on "apparently logical or respectable" forms of conduct—so that we see this society from the vantage point of its victims rather than its leaders. Ralph, Piggy, and the rest are isolated now, their only possessions the conch symbolizing the vanished rule of law and Piggy's damaged but effective glasses—their source of fire. The latter object is stolen by Jack in a sudden raid on Ralph's camp—the conch is clearly of no value to Jack's tribe—and when Piggy (now blinded) is remonstrating with Jack to do the fair thing and give the spectacles back, Roger—Jack's lieutenant and "enforcer"—rolls a huge rock down onto him from a height, smashing his skull and the conch he had been holding. With this demonstration of government by terror, everyone but Ralph is absorbed into Jack's tribe, and the last chapter is devoted to Ralph's attempts to hide as the entire group hunts him down as they hunted the pigs—Roger has even sharpened a stick at both ends, a stake on which Ralph's trunkless head would set, gathering flies around it. Ralph frantically seeks a hiding place, hoping to avoid both the line of savage hunters and a forest fire which someone has accidentally started, and which would prove as deadly as the inexorable tribesmen. As the fire engulfs the island, as Ralph is "started"—like a hare—and run down to earth, as he is about to be caught and killed, Golding springs his deus ex machina. "A naval officer stood on the sand, looking down at Ralph in wary astonishment. . . . The kid needed a bath, a haircut, a nosewipe, and plenty of ointment" (p. 185). The rescue, called inadvertently by the forest fire, has arrived: a British warship, ready to carry them aboard to civilization. The "fun and games" on the island are over.

Apologues and allegories

When I mentioned earlier the critical unanimity that *Lord of the Flies* has elicited, I was referring only to the reviewers' tendency to take the novel as didactic in its intent and to take seriously Golding's remarks about its thesis. There has also been some attempt to explain the way in which the fiction "contains" the thesis. Within these limits there are of course many possibilities —the literature on *Lord of the Flies*, for a novel around twenty years old, is quite extensive. Nevertheless, there is one persistent strain in the criticism, one method (if I may call it so) of reading *Lord of the Flies* which a fair number of critics have insisted upon: this is the allegorical. The tendency has been to abstract from the traits of the characters their "essential nature," and to treat them then as though they were identical with these abstracted traits; to deal with the novel, finally, as though its conflicts were identical with the conflicts of "forces" which the characters represent. The effect of the allegorical readings of *Lord of the Flies*— and this is the reason why we shall review them at such length —is on the one hand to distort and oversimplify the experience Golding wishes to make us understand, and on the other to create artificial "levels" of meaning, in which the interaction of forces on the island forms an intellectually closed system, which in turn robs the ending of the novel of its artistic integrity, reducing it to the status of "gimmick." Philip Drew, one of the "allegorists," claims that "the individual characters . . . have symbolic value":

> Ralph is decent, though not very intelligent, and has
> qualities of leadership. . . . Jack . . . is arrogant, brave,
> boastful, unscrupulous, and finally murderous. . . . Piggy
> typifies thoughtfulness and intelligence, the advanced side
> of man's mind which has made for human survival and
> material development. . . . Simon, whom Piggy cannot
> understand, speaks always as the idealist. . . . The twins,
> Sam and Eric, who speak antiphonally and act in concert,
> are types of the ordinary men of good will who do the
> decent thing as long as possible but eventually succumb
> to the opposition. . . . Roger is vicious, Robert and Maurice
> are of Jack's stamp . . . (1956, p. 79).

Drew cannot decide, however, whether "the island represents a society and the boys the various types and classes in that society, or an individual and the boys the various instincts and promptings in the mind or soul of a man" (1956, p. 79). Most other critics have chosen one or the other mode of "fixing" their allegorical attributions, or else have spoken of "levels" of meaning so as to be able to define characters on the one hand in political and on the other in psychological terms.

C. B. Cox, for one, sees the plot of *Lord of the Flies* as "both dramatically credible and capable of allegorical interpretation. . . . On one level the story shows how intelligence (Piggy) and common sense (Ralph) will always be overthrown in society by sadism (Roger) and the lure of totalitarianism (Jack). On another, the growth of savagery in the boys demonstrates the power of original sin" (1960, p. 112). Kenneth Watson both extends and makes more explicit the political forces with which Golding has invested his characters for, as he says, "there is, evidently, not only a moral and intellectual fable, but a social and political one." Ralph is thus the junior archetype of the liberal politician, while Jack is an "authoritarian demagogue." Piggy is a representative of the "rational non-violent person" while Roger is a sort of SS man: "the eager executioner of the cruelties decreed by the Leader." Even very minor characters fit into this typology: the little boy with the birthmark—the "littlun" who is not seen again after one of the group's early attempts at fire-setting gets out of control—is "the Unknown Citizen who . . . exists till obliterated by forces, part human, part natural, which he can neither control nor understand" (1964, pp. 4–6). Even in popular—as opposed to scholarly—journals, which "took up" *Lord of the Flies* in the early sixties, the time of its greatest vogue, we find similar attempts at allegorical typology:

> The chief mover in bringing about a coherent form of self-government is Piggy, who throughout the book stands for reasonableness and decency. . . . [Ralph] is a type of representative man, only of the better sort. . . . Just as Piggy and Ralph stand for reasonableness and social order, Jack stands for irrationality and anarchy. . . . Rounding out the group of central characters is Simon, the young mystic (Kearns, 1963, p. 137).

One unique typology which should certainly be mentioned with these moral, social, and political ones is that contained in Claire Rosenfield's "Men of a Smaller Growth," a Freudian study of *Lord of the Flies*:

> These two [Ralph and Jack] are very obviously intended to recall God and the Devil. . . . But, as Freud reminds us, "metaphysics" becomes "metapsychology"; gods and devils are "nothing other than psychological processes projected into the outer world." If Ralph is a projection of man's good impulses from which we derive the authority figures . . . then Jack becomes an externalization of the evil instinctual forces of the unconscious. . . . On a third level, Ralph is every man . . . and his body becomes the battleground where reason and instinct struggle, each to assert itself (1961, p. 93).

Piggy, according to this analysis, is a "father figure," who is killed by his rebellious sons, as in *Totem and Taboo*; and just as the sons in Freud eat the father whom they have killed, so Piggy's name emphasizes his psychological use as food (Rosenfield, 1961, pp. 98–99).

There are, of course, other allegorical interpretations of *Lord of the Flies*, notably those by Ralph Freeman and by John M. Egan,[2] but I think that by this time the main lines of the typological interpretation are clear. Now the odd thing about these interpretations is not that all of them are wrong but that all of them are in some sense right; that is, each of these interpretations has been helpful in elucidating the relationships between plot, character, and thought in *Lord of the Flies*. But the very fact that this is so casts fundamental doubt on the method of interpretation itself.

Perhaps I can illustrate this point by an example taken from earlier literature. In the second book of *The Faerie Queen*, the hero, Sir Guyon, is an allegorical figure representing some virtue. Now let us assume that six literary critics go to work on the poem, each concluding that Guyon stands for a different virtue, say, Cheerfulness, Thriftiness, Bravery, Cleanliness, Reverence, and Temperance. It is obvious that, unless Spenser has written a very ambiguous allegory, only one of them can be right; only one (in this case the last) will be able to explain the function of such diverse episodes as that of the "cave of Mammon" or the "Bower of Bliss" as expositions of the symbolized virtue. The other five critics will be simply unable to explain much of the poem unless they read badly or dishonestly. For in allegories characters may represent traits or ideas of general nature—"temperance" is a pretty general sort of virtue—but they always represent some *particular* trait or idea, no matter how manifold its application. Now the critics we have cited above have differed quite a bit in ascribing significance to the characters: Jack is described by Watson as an "authoritarian demagogue," by Kearns as representing "irrationality and anarchy," and by Cox as "totalitarianism." It is hard to fit the second ascription in with the first and third (which are similar, although the distinction embodies a significant difference), and yet it would be impossible to say that Kearns is wrong: Jack is certainly irrational, and chafes under authority though he longs to exercise it. Again, Ralph represents decency for Drew, common sense for Cox, liberal politics for Watson, social order for Kearns, and the superego for Miss Rosenfield. All these explain the novel to some extent, all are adequately descriptive of traits in Ralph, yet to suggest that these five ideas were identical would clearly be absurd. Furthermore, Jack and Ralph have many other traits equally important in the structure of the novel which these interpretations simply ignore. Ralph, for example, is childish and ungrateful in his treatment of Piggy—especially in revealing his unflattering sobriquet to the whole group, as he does at his first opportunity—and he is spiteful and tactless in his handling of Jack, who resents his leadership from the first. These are qualities difficult to reconcile with his usual decency, common sense, liberalism, and the rest, but they do not seem false to his nature. The fact is that Ralph is a fully developed, "round" character, and not a walking concept at all, and so any allegorical treatment of the novel must omit mention of his inconvenient inconsistencies. True "walking concepts" like Spenser's Guyon cause the critic no such trouble.

Though all allegories are apologues, in other words, all apologues are not allegories, and treating them as such is certain to oversimplify and likely to distort them. Indeed, if we fail to distinguish between rhetorical fictions that are allegories and those that make use of characters and events more like those in represented actions, we may distort one of the most important chapters in the development of the modern novel. We have already attempted earlier in this essay to distinguish between the two apologetic methods;[3] and Margaret Walters, although she was later to accept C. B. Cox's allegorical structuring of the novel, posed the following distinction between true allegory and what both she and I term "fable":

> In its element of design at least, fable is obviously akin to
> allegory, with its precise correspondences between different
> levels of meaning. In the latter, however, the cross-reference
> between literal narrative and a body of abstractions is
> usually specific, sustained at length, and rather arbitrary.
> And while, as various critics have rightly pointed out,
> most fables use some allegorical correspondences, . . . the
> more important fact to notice is the way the fabulist always
> tries to make his dramatic situation serve as an *analogy*
> of the world at large. A fable really offers its individual
> story as an analogue, a metaphor, of an order to be found
> in a wider reality (1961, p. 19).

I have already implied that one of the distortions caused by typological interpretations of nonallegorical texts is oversimplification of a complex character to correspond better with the type assigned. Another distortion—one which wreaks havoc on *Lord of the Flies*—is neglect of the way in which characters develop or alter. If one says, with C. B. Cox, that "intelligence (Piggy) and common sense (Ralph) will always be overthrown in society by sadism (Roger) and the lure of totalitarianism (Jack)," one is forced to see the novel as the conflict between forces (or ideas) which are themselves static. But this view disregards the way in which even the "flattest" of these characters alters during his stay on the island. Let us take the simplest case, that of Roger: he is briefly introduced as "a slight, furtive boy whom no one knew, who kept to himself with an inner intensity of avoidance and secrecy" (p. 16). This is foreshadowing of what is to come;

at the same time, Roger is described as little more than the sort of sullen fellow we have all known as children. The next major scene in which he figures is more significant:

> Roger stooped, picked up a stone, aimed, and threw it at Henry—threw it to miss. The stone, that token of preposterous time, bounced five yards to Henry's right and fell in the water. Roger gathered a handful of stones and began to throw them. Yet there was a space around Henry, perhaps six yards in diameter, into which he dared not throw. Here, invisible yet strong, was the taboo of the old life. Round the squatting child was the protection of parents and school and policemen and the law. Roger's arm was conditioned by a civilization that knew nothing of him and was in ruins (pp. 56–57).

Golding's commentary on the scene underlines its meaning: there is Roger's nature, which involves throwing stones at boys smaller and weaker than he—and then there is the invisible arm of social convention which bars him from doing so: his actual behavior—throwing the rocks, but so as to miss rather than hit Henry—is a sort of vector sum of these forces. And as the last line implies, the conventions are growing weaker and nature is coming to the fore. Somewhat later in the narrative, Roger is the one who is "fighting to get close" when Jack mimes the pig-killing, using Robert as his "victim"; still later, it is Roger who buggers the sow with his spear in the grisly, fully dramatized scene of orgiastic (I almost wrote orgastic) butchery. The final scenes in the novel, of course, are the ones which really justify Cox's definition of Roger as "sadism": the glee with which he rolls a rock onto Piggy, killing him, or sharpens a stick on which Ralph's head is to be impaled shows a savagery which goes beyond the mean of human nature, even in Golding's pessimistic view, though it is certainly not outside the human possibility. The point of my reciting this sequence, however, is this: Golding's thesis has not only to do with the conflict of people like Ralph and Piggy with people like Jack and Roger. It is at least equally concerned with the change of Roger the sullen choirboy into Roger the fiend; with the way in which the veneer of civilization strips off when that civilization is left far away; with the way, in short, in which human nature in that island comes to be revealed for what it really is—the cause of all "defects of society." And this occurs not only in Roger and Jack but in Piggy and Ralph as well. It is

fascinating—and disheartening—to see how many critics wholly
neglect the fact that Ralph and Piggy are full participants in the
ritual murder of Simon, and the fact that Ralph—our personifica-
tion of "decency," "liberal politics," and the rest—has by the last
chapter, in which he is hunted down, become as cruel and as
savage as any of the rest of the boys. (He is still a sympathetic
character, but that is because he is the isolated underdog in that
fight, and because we see it through his eyes, not because of any
ethical distinction he embodies.)

And to neglect these things is to deny what the Lord of the
Flies had to say to Simon:

> "There isn't anyone to help you. Only me. And I'm the
> Beast. . . . Fancy thinking the Beast was something you
> could hunt and kill!" said the head. For a moment or two
> the forest and all the other dimly appreciated places echoed
> with the parody of laughter. "You knew, didn't you? I'm
> part of you? Close, close, close! I'm the reason why it's
> no go? Why things are what they are?" (pp. 132–33).

Not all critics approve of the explicitness of this scene. To place
the central thesis within a uniquely surrealistic sequence seems a
case of arrogance on Golding's part ("But when in capitals ex-
prest/ The dullest reader smoaks the jest"). Margaret Walters
feels that Simon is "used, needlessly, as a mouthpiece for something that emerges quite adequately from the story," and that the
scene with the Lord of the Flies "is dramatically unconvincing and
obscure, and at the same time over-explicit" (1961, pp. 22–23).
Miss Walters neglects to inform us how a scene can be at once
obscure and overexplicit, and the notion that the scene is dramatically unconvincing is belied by the gut reactions of all those
(including myself) who found it the most powerful single scene
in the novel. Its power derives less from the unreal atmosphere
and the horrific detail than from the *frisson* of recognition that
(as John Peter has put it) "Man is a fallen creature. . . . Beelzebub,
Lord of the Flies, is Roger and Jack and you and I, ready to declare himself as soon as we permit him to" (1957, p. 583). As for
its dramatic function, it is a foreshadowing, a prediction in fact,
of the murder of Simon: "We shall do you. See? Jack and Roger
and Maurice and Robert and Bill and Piggy and Ralph. Do you.
See?" (p. 133).

I confess to being a bit mystified by Miss Walters's reactions to the scene: it seems odd that she, who has praised Golding elsewhere for having provided explicit, reliable narrative commentary on his scenes (including the rock-throwing episode), should lash him for putting such commentary into the mouth of a symbolic figure in a nightmarish sequence. Her reaction, however, is not unique—John Peter says much the same thing—and one might try to explain it by suggesting that sensitive readers (like Samuel Johnson in the case of the catastrophe of *King Lear*) turn away from *overly* powerful scenes as one's eyes turn away from too much light—and then rationalize their blenching by terming such scenes inartistic. Certainly the "Lord of the Flies" sequence is not pleasant to read; it is too penetrating for that, not least because its truths are expressed by the horrid decomposing pig's head in such off-hand, donnish, slangy terms. They are home truths, and we cannot but blink at the homely way they are put.

Deus ex machina *and the sense of completeness*

Other sequences besides the "Lord of the Flies" scene have been the targets of various critics, one of which is the deus ex machina denouement, in which a naval officer appears literally out of nowhere to rescue the seemingly doomed Ralph. One early critic, Philip Drew, finds the significance of the sequence obscure:

> A minor difficulty confronting the reader is to know what to make of the ending. In the simple context of the story it comes suddenly and arbitrarily at a time when Ralph is doomed. Since it springs from nothing in the book but comes like the waking out of a nightmare it is hard to attach any symbolic significance to it or to the final irony by which the boys hunting Ralph in fact kindle the fire that leads to the rescue. This paradox and the final episode cannot be given a consistent allegorical status, but they may be accepted without strain as part of the narrative. The eye is, as it were, taken away from the microscope at the close, the boys become twelve-year-olds again, and the book ends in the naturalistic mode (1956, p. 80).

Somewhat later, James Gindin termed the ending a "gimmick":

> Just when the savage forces led by Jack are tracking down Ralph and burning the whole island to find him, a British naval officer arrives to rescue the boys. Ironically, the smoke of barbaric fury, not the smoke of conscious effort, has led to rescue. Throughout the novel, frequent references to

possible rescue and to the sanity of the adult world seemed
the delusions of the rational innocent. Ralph and Piggy
often appealed to adult sanity in their futile attempt to
control their world, but, suddenly and inconsistently at the
end of the novel, adult sanity really exists. The horror of the
boys' experience on the island was, after all, really a
childish game, though a particularly vicious one. The British
officer turns into a public school master: "I should have
thought that a pack of British boys—you're all British
aren't you?—would have been able to put up a better show
than that." The officer's density is apparent, but the range
of the whole metaphor has been severely limited. Certainly
the whole issue, the whole statement about man, is not
contradicted by the ending, for, as Golding directly points
out, Ralph has learned from the experience. . . . But the
rescue is ultimately a "gimmick," a trick, a means of cutting
down or softening the implications built up within the
structure of the boys' society on the island (1962, p. 198).

I have quoted Drew and Gindin at length because they raise
the two most significant questions about Golding's conclusion:
first: is the rescue arbitrary and inconsistent? (and should this,
if true, matter aesthetically?). And second, does the denouement,
as Gindin claims later, tend to simplify and palliate, rather than
to enrich and intensify the experience of *Lord of the Flies*?

The answer to the first question is a qualified no. The rescue
is indeed improbably opportune—a traditional "nick of time"
coincidence that the gunboat should arrive at the precise moment
Ralph is at bay: a moment later and he would have been beyond
help. At the same time, there is a sense in which the melodramatic
aspects of the coincidence are irrelevant to a novel such as this
one. We may be irritated by last-minute escapes in Dickens or
by tragic coincidences in Hardy because the authors try to suggest
that their scheme of probability includes, not mere chance, but
"divine providence" or "malevolent fate." But there is no hint
that Golding would have us read any special providence into
Ralph's rescue, and we tend to accept the workings of chance
here as we do in, say, *Pride and Prejudice* or *Catch-22*.

The rescue is not, of course, wholly arbitrary: it is, after all,
just the sort of rescue for which the late Piggy had planned, and
for which, ironically, he had died. The children, we know, are
powerless to leave the island (all but Simon and Piggy, whose
corpses are washed out to sea), but at the same time Golding never

pretends that the island is inaccessible. Ships certainly do pass from time to time—Ralph and Piggy even catch sight of one, though they are unable, because of Jack's irresponsibility about keeping the fire alight, to hail it—and it is obvious that a smoking island would be more visible from a ship than the ship would be from the beach of an island. There is even an air battle near the island—the one which drops the dead airman—so the place may even have some sort of strategic importance. In any case, Golding's ending fits into the pattern we have seen building up; it is, after all, a ship and not a seaplane or a time machine which arrives to pick up the castaways.

The question of the inconsistency of the ending has in one sense already been answered by Golding himself: "The officer having interrupted a manhunt, prepares to take the children off the island in a cruiser which will presently be hunting its enemy in the same implacable way. And who will rescue the adult and his cruiser?" (p. 189). We shall go into this statement in greater detail shortly. But if what Gindin means to say is that the ending brings about an abrupt shift from the "symbolic" to the "naturalistic" mode of narration, Golding's commentaries seem to lend him support, especially where he says that "the whole book is symbolic in nature except the rescue in the end." I can see an abrupt shift in point of view, even in frame of reference, but I am afraid I cannot take the rescuing officer and his gunboat as any more or less symbolic in nature than the boys themselves and their society. In fact, I find rather confusing the notion that "naturalistic" sailors could rescue "symbolic" children: by the last pages of the novel, it would be difficult for the reader to take any newly introduced character or event as simply self-referential.

And Golding's detail helps us work out the significance of the rescue. The officer, with "white-topped cap. . . . white drill, epaulettes, a revolver, a row of gilt buttons," is a kindly fellow—so it seems from his conversation—but he does not take "his hand away from the butt of his revolver" until he sees that the little boys pose no threat to him (Golding, 1959, p. 185); but the sailors had come expecting trouble—witness the petty officer in the stern of the cutter holding a submachine gun ready for action. The rescuers who stop the island war are themselves men of war, as Golding says, "dignified and capable, but in reality enmeshed in the same evil" we have seen in all the children: the viciousness and savagery of human nature. War is one manifestation of this "evil," and crime, of course, would be another; all the sad variety of human life in which man's inhumanity to man, the "darkness of man's heart," is revealed bears witness to the truth about the adult world for which the "friendly" sailors stand as symbols. There is no shift to the naturalistic mode, although, as Drew put it, "the eye is . . . taken away from the microscope." By the introduction of actual adults, Golding's symbolic narrative is broadened to include the grownup world about which the children had metaphorically been speaking all along. The mode of their introduction underlines the truth of Golding's thesis respecting them. The "microscope" becomes a wide-angle lens. This is the answer, then, to our second question: far from tending "to simplify and palliate" the experience, the denouement broadens and extends beyond its own immediate significance the morality play which has been enacted on the island. "The darkness of man's heart" is not evinced merely by the slackening of the bonds of civilization; it is not to be found only on coral islands: it is, in fact, always with us, the ultimate source of all human pain and misery.

In terms of the form of the novel, what Golding has done is to choose a possible ending for the book which best satisfies and completes the rhetorical structure, though it is not necessarily the most probable closure for *Lord of the Flies*. What Gindin and Drew seem to be objecting to, at least in part, is that the rescue is on the face of it much less probable than alternative closures Golding could have used; Ralph's death would have been the most probable outcome of all, given the narrative sequence (though since Ralph has not been the sole center of consciousness, this would not have been as strong a closure as it might have otherwise been). Another possibility Golding might well have thought of and rejected would be for Ralph to have killed Jack in a fight and then settled down to lead his tribe in the same autocratic manner Jack had adopted; this would have been far less probable, but it would have ironically underlined the thesis that life in society reflects the savage nature of the individual.[4] The ending Golding actually chose is in some sense the least probable of the lot, because it comes from outside the closed society of boys, even though it has been prepared for at some length; admittedly it is unexpected. Everyone would concede that it is a firm closure—the ship is even an English cruiser, so that the boys are in a sense already "home"—but its main virtue for Golding was, as I have stated earlier, the way in which the denouement extends the significance of his thesis by pointing out the evils in the grownup world which derive from the original evil in men's souls.

And there is some sense in which Gindin's annoyance with the ending of Lord of the Flies, like Miss Walters's and Peter's criticism of Simon's interview with the pig's head, are artifacts of critical terminologies, pointing rather to defects in our exegetical vocabularies than to deficiencies in Golding's work. All three, in their different ways, seem to be worried about a possible conflict between the "symbolic" and the "naturalistic" modes of narration, or the inherent loss of cohesion caused by obtruding "fantastic" elements into a "realistic" work. What I should like to make explicit here is something I slyly suggested a few pages ago: that the question of whether this or that event in Lord of the Flies is "naturalistic" or "symbolic" is ultimately irrelevant. If by "symbolic" we mean that the characters in their relationships with each other and the chain of events affecting these characters' fates are not simply self-referential, but rather that the experience which these characters and events embody is designed to alter our opinions concerning people and objects in the outside world, then Lord of the Flies is "symbolic" from beginning to end. If by "naturalistic" we mean that the characters behave the way real people would do, in a manner consistent with their age and station in life, with all the complexities and inconsistencies which real people are known to evince; and that the incidents are such as may happen in life, as opposed to "supernatural" events; and that the characters' dialogue and represented thoughts are probable, given the ethical nature and existential situation of each: then Lord of the Flies is "naturalistic" from beginning to end. The fact is that Lord of the Flies is both "symbolic" and "naturalistic." But neither of these terms is really an adequate description of the novel or of the logic which underlies its system of probability: Golding's fiction is actually an apologue the apprehension of whose thesis depends upon the use of techniques developed for and associated with represented actions, including the techniques of representing character and changing states of consciousness. Unlike Johnson and Voltaire, who stylize character and event in order to achieve an "alienation" effect, Golding uses all available resources to move us, to make us vicariously experience what the boys on the island go through, in order to turn that experience into a terrible knowledge.

We can see this best in "Cry of the Hunters," the final chapter of *Lord of the Flies*, which is told almost exclusively from the point of view of Ralph as he is hunted down by Jack and the rest of his tribe. There is no distancing commentary here of the sort Golding used earlier in the book, as in the incident we cited in which Roger throws rocks at little Henry. Our apprehension of Ralph is direct—almost a form of stream-of-consciousness narrative:

> They had smoked him out and set the island on fire.
> Hide was better than a tree because you had a chance of breaking the line if you were discovered.
> Hide, then.
> He wondered if a pig would agree, and grimaced at nothing. Find the deepest thicket, the darkest hole on the island, and creep in. Now, as he ran, he peered about him. . . . The cries were far now, and faint (p. 182).

No matter how this sequence had been narrated, it would be difficult to avoid some degree of imaginative sympathy with Ralph: this is, after all, not a game but a hunt to the death, with the "stick sharpened at both ends" to complete the picture of horror. But by conveying Ralph's every action, every perception, every thought in the disjunctive style of rational terror, where the language seemingly imitates the quick over-the-shoulder glances and rapid, fearful steps of the man pursued, Golding succeeds in imparting an intense empathy with the object of the hunt that is nearly unbearable. The last sequence is feverish:

> He forgot his wounds, his hunger and thirst, and became fear; hopeless fear on flying feet, rushing through the forest toward the open beach. Spots jumped before his eyes and turned into red circles that expanded quickly till they passed out of sight. Below him someone's legs were getting tired and the desperate ululation advanced like a jagged fringe of menace and was almost overhead.
> He stumbled over a root and the cry that pursued him rose even higher. He saw a shelter burst into flames and the fire flapped at his right shoulder and there was the glitter of water. Then he was down, rolling over and over in the warm sand, crouching with arm up to ward off, trying to cry for mercy (pp. 184–85).

This is the point at which the Seventh Cavalry arrives—or in this case the naval officer from the cruiser with cutter and crew. The mood of crude melodrama ended by the deus ex machina (if my memory of B movies is any guide) would seem to demand some sort of expression of relief, some suitable version of "Saved! At last! And in the nick of time!" together with the appropriately modest rejoinder from the officer. And if this kind of "Perils of Pauline" conclusion had been what Golding had been aiming at, his critics would have been right to roast him for an "arbitrary" and cheap denouement. But as the narrative proves, this was no part of Golding's intention. Immediately after the objective description, through Ralph's eyes, of the "white-topped cap . . . white drill, epaulettes," and the rest of the naval officer's regalia, the point of view shifts to that of the officer "looking down at Ralph in wary astonishment" (p. 185). The brilliant and faithful film treatment of *Lord of the Flies*, directed by Peter Brook, achieved precisely the right effect here, I think: the camera, which had been closely following Ralph through his flight in the jungle, suddenly lights on a pair of highly polished shoes, then, from ground level, slowly pans upward, revealing crisp and immaculate white duck trousers, a decorated coat, and finally the officer's astonished and horrified face. Brook understood the novel better than most of Golding's literary critics, I think; he apprehended, at least, that Golding did not bring the naval officer to the island merely to effect an eleventh-hour rescue, but because he needed an appropriate vehicle through which to view the savage and brutal society which the children had constructed:

> "We saw your smoke. What have you been doing?
> Having a war or something?"
> Ralph nodded. . . .
> "Nobody killed, I hope? Any dead bodies?"
> "Only two. And they've gone."
> The officer leaned down and looked closely at Ralph.
> "Two? Killed?"
> Ralph nodded again. Behind him, the whole island was shuddering with flame. The officer knew, as a rule, when people were telling the truth. He whistled softly (pp. 185–86).

The adult, an officer in the British Navy, the embodiment of discipline and good order, is led to the island to observe the result of a society based upon "the ethical nature of the individual" and he sums it up in typically understated English fashion: "I should have thought that a pack of British boys—you're all British, aren't you?—would have been able to put up a better show than that—I mean—" (1959, p. 186). As an officer on a ship of war, moreover, he represents, as we have already pointed out, the evil at the heart of our seemingly civilized world.

J. D. O'Hara is distressed at this double use of the officer. Our author, O'Hara claims,

> tries to eat his cake and have it too. He shows us Jack's society as an image of ours, yet he criticizes and condemns it by our standards. He tells us that civilization reflects man's dominant qualities and that those qualities are evil; yet in the novel the influence of society is always a good one. . . . Golding's choice of children, rather than adults, for his utopian experiment suggests that he considers them better and more likely to succeed in establishing an ideal society. . . . Yet time and again he shows that he really thinks children worse than adults. . . . The fable has become willy-nilly a defense of society rather than an attack on it (1966, pp. 419–20).

But there is little cause for alarm; Golding does not contradict himself: he criticizes and condemns not society but human nature, which is at odds, basically, with the structured restraints of which civilization, taken at its best, consists. What the officer's presence suggests is not, of course, that civilized society is as bad as Jack's tribe, but that, men being what they are, human nature is always below the surface restraints, able to break forth at any time, with the added momentum that the organization of social institutions can provide. The officer can thus both comment on the results of untempered original sin and represent its product.

The point of view in the final sequence does not, however, rest with the officer; Golding returns to the depths of Ralph's consciousness, not, even this time, for the representation of the relief of melodramatic tension, but for the moving evocation of what the boy had learned from the sum of his experience:

> For a moment he had a fleeting picture of the strange glamour that had once invested the beaches. But the island was scorched up like dead wood—Simon was dead—and Jack had. . . . The tears began to flow and sobs shook him. He gave himself up to them now for the first time on the island; great, shuddering spasms of grief that seemed to

wrench his whole body. His voice rose under the black
smoke before the burning wreckage of the island; and infected by that emotion, the other little boys began to
shake and sob too. And in the middle of them, with filthy
body, matted hair, and unwiped nose, Ralph wept for the
end of innocence, the darkness of man's heart, and the fall
through the air of the true, wise friend called Piggy (pp.
186–87).

The last line returns to the officer who, "moved and a little em-
barrassed" by the messy truth, looks toward the trim cruiser
whose neatness and discipline, on the one hand, and grim purpose, on the other, embody the fierce tension within the term
"civilized man."

The designations "symbolic" and "naturalistic" simply do not
do justice to Golding's achievement in *Lord of the Flies*; it is even
wrong, I think, to speak of his novel as a synthesis of the two,
if by synthesis we would mean a cunning combination of an-
tithetical elements. What Golding has done is to utilize all the
increasingly subtle narrative techniques for the revelation of
deep states of consciousness developed during the nineteenth
century by Jane Austen, George Eliot, and Henry James within
the English tradition—and by Stendhal, Flaubert, and Proust on
the Continent—but to utilize them for a didactic rather than a
purely representational purpose. That is, we are shown the intricate and shifting patterns of awareness in characters like Simon
and Ralph not simply to fully realize the tragic (or melodramatic)
impact of their fate but through the emotional realization of the
characters' potential to maximize our sense of the moral and
intellectual *significance* of their fate. The relationship between
fictional form and ideological content thus becomes incredibly
more complex in *Lord of the Flies* than in earlier apologues like
The Pilgrim's Progress, Rasselas, and *Candide*: here the characters are not walking concepts whose fictional relationships on one
level imitate ideological relationships on another; nor are the
incidents a series of exempla each embodying a determinate aspect of the fictionalized thesis. Instead, *Lord of the Flies* presents
us with a complete experience in narrative form which, taken as a
whole, is designed "to alter our attitudes, to make us feel new
truths about the external world" (Sacks, 1969, p. 290). And the
sense of completeness of works like this depends, as we have
seen, on the choice of a denouement which most completely turns

the emotional experience of the fictions into knowledge of the fictions' significance.

I mentioned, at the end of the last chapter, that *Lord of the Flies* represented a transitional case between the eighteenth-century and the contemporary fable. This refers to the fact that Golding has not fully explored the inherent possibilities of this new form of apologue. For despite the new complex relation between fictional narrative and the structure of ideas, Golding's thesis itself is relatively simple and uncontroversial: Golding himself expressed his novelistic purpose in a few brief sentences, and the idea might be thought of as one of our received opinions.[5] It is in this sense that Golding fails to sound the limits of the new form, for it would seem that one might use the sophisticated representational techniques to embody within a fiction a thoroughly novel moral and intellectual philosophy of such complexity that entire books might be devoted to its exposition. This brings us to Albert Camus's *The Stranger*.

4 · Novel Forms of Thesis
Camus's The Stranger

In his "Explication of *The Stranger*," Jean-Paul Sartre cites
Camus's dictum in *The Myth of Sisyphus*, "The feeling of the absurd is not the same as the *idea* of the absurd. The idea is grounded
in the feeling, that is all. It does not exhaust it." Sartre concludes
from this that "*The Myth of Sisyphus* might be said to aim at
giving us this *idea*, and *The Stranger* at giving us the feeling" (in
Brée, 1962, pp. 108–10). In the sense that *The Stranger* is not a
treatise but a novel, this goes without saying; but at the same
time *The Stranger*, although it uses many of the techniques of
the modern psychological novel, uses them to different purposes.
As a rhetorical fiction, even if what it conveys is properly spoken
of as a feeling rather than an idea, the narrative is designed precisely in order to *convey*. And in any case, the feeling/idea dichotomy is unnecessarily rigid: perhaps it would be best to speak
of the formal end of Camus's novel as the communication of some
form of intuitive knowledge, a philosophy understood immediately through experience rather than mediately through the terms
of logical argument. Either way, it is past dispute that (like Golding's discussion of *Lord of the Flies*) *The Myth of Sisyphus* can
be taken as more-or-less reliable commentary on the ideological
substructure of *The Stranger*.

Thus Camus can use the language of reasoned argument in
The Myth of Sisyphus:

> A world that can be explained even with bad reasons is a
> familiar world. But, on the other hand, in a universe sud-
> denly divested of illusions and lights, man feels an alien,
> a stranger. His exile is without remedy since he is deprived
> of the memory of a lost home or the hope of a promised

land. This divorce between man and his life, the actor and
his setting, is properly the feeling of absurdity (1955, p. 5).

This is, in a sense, a more precise, thoroughly conscious account
of the feeling which *The Stranger* conveys. Meursault, the narrator, is just such an individual making his way through a world
which, for him, is without the sources of value which we usually
think of as giving our lives significance. Since the world is devoid
of meaning, Meursault is indifferent about events and ideas which
we might expect to call up passionate response or intelligent
choice. So that when Meursault's employer offers him the opportunity of transferring to Paris from provincial Algiers, he replies
that he is prepared to go, but that he doesn't really care very much
one way or the other; asked "if a 'change of life,' as he called it,
didn't appeal to me, . . . I answered that one never changed his
way of life; one life was as good as another, and my present one
suited me quite well" (1946, p. 52). He accepts Marie's proposal
of marriage, but adds that whether they marry or not is of no
importance to him; when she insists that marriage is a serious
matter, he politely demurs. What this means within the narrative
is that our first experience of Meursault profoundly shocks our
sensibilities, for his indifference extends to the death of his
mother, a deeply tragic event in the lives of most men. For a
while we read Meursault's narrative holding ourselves aloof
from this immoralist, just as we keep our emotional distance
from, say, Jason's narrative in *The Sound and the Fury*. But it
quickly becomes obvious that Meursault is not a moron with
arrested sensibilities: quite the contrary, we soon find out his
sensitivities, skewed as they are. His view is accurate, lucid, precise, honest: his observations of the petty annoyances during the
trip to Marengo, the vigil, and the funeral procession show that
he is open to experience of some kind. But our sense of moral
shock returns when he seduces Marie on the day after his
mother's burial—like her, we shrink from Meursault as we too
are overpowered by the proximity of the two events—as well as
when, after his dull Sunday, Meursault reflects that his mother
was buried, he'd be returning to work the next day, and nothing
for him had really changed.

But gradually, through the seductive first-person point of view,
we absorb Meursault's perspective on life and begin to see as he
does "a world of incoherence, a world where rational analysis has

little scope, and where moral purposes and responses are con-
spicuously absent" (Cruickshank, 1959, p. 152). And I think that,
by the time we get to such incidents as the employer's offer of
transfer and Marie's proposal of marriage, we already see Meursault's indifference less as mere insensitivity than as the conscious
rejection of all forms of involvement, participation, commitment.
Ambition, love, and morality mean nothing to Meursault, do not
even interest him, because they refer to coherent relationships
between one event and another, between past and present, or
present and future, or the real and the ideal. There is in fact a
sense in which past and future—let alone the ideal—do not even
exist for Meursault, who lives happily without the "structure"
which these concepts lend reality by giving his attention to nothing save the immediate present. Here is a world in which Meursault is truly at home: the pleasures and pains of the moment,
which he feels deeply himself and describes so that we can feel
them with him. The critical discussions of narrative tense in *The
Stranger* explain this aspect of Meursault's character—and our
growing empathy with it as we continue to read. According to
John Cruickshank:

> . . . the story is recorded almost exclusively in the perfect
> tense. This use of what is called in French *le passé composé*
> . . . is unusual in a straightforward literary narration of
> past events. It may be argued, of course, that Camus uses
> this tense simply because it is the most natural form of
> spoken narrative in French but . . . the peculiar quality of
> the perfect tense lies in the fact that although it describes
> a past action it also retains, to a considerable degree, a
> feeling of presentness. . . . The use of the perfect tense in
> *L'Étranger* helps to impart directness, to bridge the gap be-
> tween the novel as author-narrative and as reader-experience.
> It gives to events an actuality . . . (1959, pp. 159–60).

Other elements of Camus's style contribute to our understanding
sympathy with Meursault's view of an absurd, incoherent world:
we are made to see the world through Meursault's eyes which,
Sartre tells us, are "transparent to things but opaque to meanings" (Brée, 1962, p. 117). Stylistically, this is achieved through
Meursault's short, choppy sentences in which ideas are joined (if
at all) by coordinating conjunctions:

> I heard the warden tell me that the hearse was waiting on
> the road outside and the priest began his prayers. Starting

right then, everything went very quickly. The men went
up to the coffin with a cloth. The priest, the altar-boys, the
warden and I left. In front of the door was a woman I didn't
know. "M. Meursault," said the warden. I didn't hear the
woman's name and I understood only that she was a
delegated nurse. She bowed without a smile on her long
bony face. Then we stood aside to let the body go by. We
followed the bearers and left through a hall. Outside the
door, there was the hearse (1958, pp. 80–81; my translation).

Camus did not feel, as Hemingway may have done, that there was
any inherent virtue in such a style—it merely served his purpose;
in an interview with Jeannine Delpech, Camus remarked: "la
technique romanesque américaine me paraît aboutir à une im-
passe. Je l'ai utilisé dans L'Étranger, c'est vrai. Mais c'est con-
venait à mon propos qui était de décrire un homme sans conscience apparente" (Cruickshank, 1956, p. 251).

We have seen a few of the methods by which Camus aims to
make us conscious of the absurdity of the universe; the question
remaining is whether Meursault is conscious of it himself. And
this is important because, as Camus says in The Myth of Sisyphus,
"everything begins with consciousness and nothing is worth anything except through it" (1955, p. 10). A good many critics feel
that Meursault is not conscious of the absurdity; Thomas Hanna,
for one, criticizes Sartre for neglecting the fact that

> In terms of Camus' later position, Meursault is a paradox,
> because from the beginning he shows the absolute indiffer-
> ence of the absurd hero, but at the same time does not
> possess the absurd hero's consciousness of the absurdity of
> life and the revolt against it. . . . Meursault acts like he is in
> an absurd universe but is not conscious . . . of the conse-
> quences which this entails (1958, pp. 39–40).

I think that Hanna is wrong, but he points to a dilemma which
Camus had to face in writing The Stranger: the more obviously
conscious of the metaphysical and existential problem of the absurd Meursault becomes—the more, in other words, he resembles
the witty and compassionate author of The Myth of Sisyphus—
the less Camus will be able to convey directly to us how the world
will appear to a man for whom all its meaning is lost, that feeling
of the absurd. But unless we can somehow be made to understand that Meursault is conscious of all this, Meursault's fate—

his final awakening to freedom—will lose its significance. The solution is that Meursault must be, as Camus said in the Delpech interview, without *apparent* consciousness; only occasionally may he remind us, as in his remarks to his employer and to Marie which are cited above, or in his reflection, while holding Raymond's revolver, that "one might fire, or not fire—and it would come to absolutely the same thing," that he is thoroughly aware of his view of life and of its implications (Camus, 1946, p. 72). What this means is that, as Philip Thody points out, "it requires a very careful reading and interpretation of the text to see through Meursault's apparently complete indifference to life and unawareness of what is happening, and perceive the truly exemplary and conscious character beneath" (Thody, 1961, p. 43).

Paradoxically, Meursault demonstrates most consciousness when he least appears to do so. On the beach, wandering towards the shadow of the rock—and the Arab—Meursault is seemingly at the mercy of the forces of nature, unconscious of everything except the burning blades of sunlight and the hot breath of the sea. He shoots the Arab, as he later tells the court, because of the sun, without any intention of doing so; the text does not even have it that Meursault actively shot—it merely says that "the trigger gave way" (1958, p. 113; my translation). And it was thus, Meursault tells us, that it all began: and yet the chapter does not end here. With the sound of the shot Meursault's mind becomes lucid, shaking off the sweat and the sunlight to which he had passively responded: for a brief moment he realizes his own condition, the irreconcilable disparity between himself and the universe that Camus, in *The Myth of Sisyphus*, calls the absurd. And in an act of existential revolt he consciously fires the four additional shots—those four sharp blows on the door of his unhappiness—a revolt which is defined by Camus as "the certainty of a crushing fate, without the resignation that ought to accompany it" (1955, p. 40). These shots are what the examining magistrate cannot understand, nor can Meursault explain them to him; perhaps on an initial reading the shots are enigmatic—I suspect, in fact, that such was Camus's intention, for it is through the attempt to penetrate Meursault's mystery that this fable gains its essential force. And if this is true, one gains an insight into why Camus wished to write about this man without apparent consciousness: the intriguing opacity of Meursault's narrative would provide a double experience; on the one hand, the life of the absurd hero as seen through his own eyes, and on the other, the experience of the difficulties of reading "Meursault's" text, the incongruities and enigmas that are strewn across our paths. The former provides us with imaginative sympathy; the latter encourages us to think, to reason about the absurd, and finally in a sense to duplicate in our own minds, at least on an intuitive level, the understanding of the absurd contained in different form in *The Myth of Sisyphus*.

The extent to which we actually do this is nowhere more clearly seen than in the chapters concerning Meursault's trial. There we watch the prosecutor build up a damning picture of Meursault's guilt: how he had been unfilial in sending his mother to the Old People's Home in the first place, in never visiting her, in smoking cigarettes and drinking *café au lait* during the vigil, and, most of all, in showing no signs of grief; how he had callously taken up with Marie immediately after his mother's burial; how he had interested himself in the sordid affairs of Raymond the *maquereau*, written the letter which culminated in the Arab girl being beaten, and finally taken a cold-blooded revenge on her brother. It is a damning case, designed to be "convincing," positing a "rational" explanation for every one of Meursault's actions, predicated upon his "criminal nature." And yet, even on a first reading of the novel, we know as well as Meursault could how absurdly unjust such an "explanation" of his behavior is, for we have absorbed and identified ourselves with his rejection of purpose and abstract ethics; we have understood the indifference with which he has always acted, and find the term "criminal" as irrelevant as he does. These scenes are thus a grim sort of comedy, with both prosecutor and defense lawyer trumping up explanations which fail in the most elementary sense to explain Meursault's character and actions, both of them burrowing in the kitchen-garden of rhetoric to make the jury agree with their portraits of the man whom neither will ever understand. Both are equally ridiculous; the prosecutor is simply more competent at this insanely silly game. Our ability to read the courtroom scenes in this way is a token of Camus's success at inculcating the point of view of absurd man.

"For all to be accomplished . . ."

The final chapter, with Meursault's reflection on his coming execution, his argument with the chaplain, and his mysterious illumination, consummates the rest in other than the most obvious sense. If what we have earlier experienced is how absurd man faces life, it is here that he faces the ultimate absurdity: death. This is a problem, it goes without saying, for all of us, but for Camus it is, par excellence, the most truly philosophical problem. For an immortal, life would not be absurd—the term for him would have no meaning—because it is the fact of our death and extinction that makes us sense the incommensurability of the universe with ourselves, the meaninglessness of life, the emptiness of all our ambitions, hopes, and fears. Under these circumstances, how can man confront the certainty of death?

One possibility Meursault explores is that of dreaming in fantasies that it simply will not occur. "The problem of a loophole obsesses me," Meursault tells us; "I am always wondering if there have been cases of condemned prisoners' escaping from the implacable machinery of justice at the last moment, breaking through the police cordon, vanishing in the nick of time before the guillotine falls" (1946, p. 136). He dreams of being in the position not of "the patient" but of one of the spectators at a decapitation "who comes to see the show and can go home and vomit afterward." And the very thought of being free, of living, "flooded my mind with a wild, absurd exaltation" (1946, p. 138). Later, he fantasizes in terms of new laws with new modes of capital punishment, like poisons that kill the condemned man ninety-nine per cent of the time, giving him a slim chance of life —the chance that enables the prisoner to rebel against his own death. As things are, Meursault recognizes, "the condemned man had to hope the apparatus was in good working order . . . it was in his interest that all should go off without a hitch"—otherwise, if the guillotine should by some almost unimaginable mischance fail to do its job, the whole procedure would have to begin all over again. These fantasies of Meursault's, mutatis mutandis, represent the method most of us use in the midst of our lives in contemplating our own coming death: pretending it will not occur. But whatever courage it gives us is false, and in the end it will not do.

Perhaps it would be well at this point to note that my use of the first person plural in the last few sentences was not merely a matter of rhetoric, for in the final scenes after Meursault's death-sentence our hero's problem becomes quite explicitly our own. If Camus has been successful in the courtroom scenes he has foreclosed any identification that might remain between the society on the other side of the bars and ourselves. The "free" men—prosecutor and defense attorney alike—are mere caricatures, and their reasoning is a parody of logic. These scenes are scarcely up to Camus's standard for subtlety, but they are not meant to be subtle: for us to appreciate the utter absurdity of the machinery of justice, ironies stronger than Camus's usual doses were required.

But this "absurd" justice is still capable of condemning Meursault to death, a death not only gruesome—that is the least of the matter—but inevitable. And as we experience with Meursault the approach of this unavoidable end, we are forced, perhaps against our will, into the knowledge that we are condemned to death as inevitably as he is. Meursault's "unique" experience is thus extended into our own lives, transforming what might have been narrated as personal tragedy into an apologue telling us about *our* condition in the world outside that of Camus's novel. Having already been forced to side with Meursault against society, we now see his coming death as representative of our own mortality, so that his rationalizations—the fetches he must use to hold off the horrid confrontation with the inevitable—are much like our own, and his solution—when he finds it—will hold good for us and for all mankind.

After trying in vain to pretend that death will not come, Meursault explores a second possibility, the consolation that life, after all, is not worth living, and therefore it is not such a great matter to die. It makes no difference, he tries to comfort himself, whether one dies a young man or an old, since in any case one is dead and the world goes on without one as it had before. He pictures his feelings years later when, as an old man, he is finally run down by death: "once you're up against it, the precise manner of your death has obviously small importance." But the "galling reminder" of the forty years or so between his present age and man's allotted three-score and ten deprives this line of reasoning of its expected comfort, while the thought of his appeal succeeding, of his having those forty years in front of him, sends him into "a sudden rush of joy," and even brings tears to his eyes (1946, p. 143). As Haskell M. Block has observed, "assailed by his recollections of a life now dead, he finds temporary refuge in the conviction that life is not really worth living, and that how and when one dies is immaterial. The drama of Meursault's final crisis rests in the subversion of this indifference" (1950, p. 356).

The third possibility is presented to Meursault by the priest; it is the consolation of religion, the assurance of a life everlasting following one's earthly death. But Meursault has little trouble rejecting this: he does not believe in God, and he is too honest with himself even to attempt to make himself believe in this sort of lie. Meursault's honesty in these matters is absolute—he is a stranger in the world, loathed by his "respectable" fellow men, because he will not lay claim to feelings he does not actually have. It was, after all, on account of this honesty, his refusal to pretend grief for his mother or remorse for shooting the Arab, for which he is to be executed: even Meursault's lawyer, despite his incompetence, could have gotten a reduced sentence for a more cooperative murderer.

Yet despite his honest rejection of the chaplain's offers, Meursault is not unmoved by this notion of a life after death: he is stung by the difference between the chaplain's pallid notion of an afterlife and the intensities of real human pleasures and pains. Meursault has a better idea of the life beyond the grave: "I fairly shouted at him: 'A life in which I can remember this life on earth. That's all I want out of it'" (1946, p. 150).

For Meursault really does love this earth very much, as the chaplain half-accuses him of doing. The face which Meursault has tried—without success—to see on the walls of his prison cell is not a divine face but a human one, the passionate countenance of his mistress, Marie. And we may recall at this point the brilliantly colored descriptions of Meursault's earthly pleasures, how lying on Marie's lap on a raft in the midst of Algiers harbor, "I had the sky full in my eyes, all blue and gold, and I could feel Marie's stomach rising and falling gently under my head" (1946, p. 23). This is the sort of experience which has touched Meursault's heart, touched it so that he knows that, though he is about to die, he has well understood what it was to have lived.

And this is what Meursault's harangue to the chaplain signifies: to the examining magistrate and the court he had said nothing, but staring into the face of death he finally expresses in one passionate outburst his sense of the ultimate unmeaning of life, the unimportance of all the ideas by which men structure existence in a vain attempt to wall out the "dark wind" of death streaming in from the future. But at the same time men are not simply poor deluded wretches: "every man alive was privileged" for the simple experience of living is in itself the highest of privileges and, indeed, the only value worth retaining (1946, p. 152).

Meursault's exposition of these ideas is brief, almost incoherent; Camus left their full expression for *The Myth of Sisyphus*, where he explains:

> If I convince myself that this life has no other aspect than that of the absurd, if I feel that its whole equilibrium depends on that perpetual opposition between my conscious revolt and the darkness in which it struggles, if I admit that my freedom has no meaning except in relation to its limited fate, then I must say that what counts is not the best living but the most living. . . . A man's rule of conduct and his scale of values have no meaning except through the quantity and variety of experiences he has been in a position to accumulate (1955, p. 45).

What this implies is that Meursault's "sudden rush of joy" at the idea of a successful appeal and an additional forty years of life is not a puerile or unmanly reaction: it is rather the only rational attitude one can have. If life has no meaning, then what counts is not *how* one lives—for there is no absolute scale by which we might measure that—but simply *how much* one lives, the quantity and intensity and variety of one's experiences. And therefore happiness is not the result of what one accomplishes in life—the very notion of accomplishment makes little sense in Camus's scheme—but rather of the moment-to-moment sensation of living.

And it is these sensations which flow through Meursault when, after the chaplain has gone, he awakens with the "stars shining down on my face":

> Sounds of the countryside came faintly in, and the cool night air, veined with smells of earth and salt, fanned my cheeks. The marvelous peace of the sleepbound summer night flooded through me like a tide. Then, just on the edge of daybreak, I heard a steamer's siren. People were starting on a voyage to a world which had ceased to concern me forever (1946, p. 153).

Having contemplated his fate, Meursault has silenced all the false rationales of life which offer their absurd consolation for his death so that

in the universe suddenly restored to its silence, the myriad
wondering little voices of the earth rise up. Unconscious,
secret calls, invitations from all the faces, they are the
necessary reverse and price of victory. There is no sun
without shadow, and it is essential to know the night. . . .
For the rest, he knows himself to be the master of his days.
(1955, p. 91).

Meursault's final illumination is of the freedom and happiness
which the absurd man may find in the face of death. The illusions
of hope and fear, of the existence of absolute values by which he
may be judged, make man a slave to his unknowable future;
once one comprehends "the benign indifference of the universe,"
the absurdity of life, and the finality of death, these illusions lose
their power over us; and once the idols are silent, we can assume
the personal liberty that belongs to man. So Meursault's mother
must have felt, he now understands; facing her coming end without the illusory comfort of religion, she took a "fiancé," a man
as old as herself, disregarding the social conventions that now
ceased to keep her their thrall. In her relationship with Perez,
her "fiancé," Mme Meursault affirmed her liberty and the value
of life's experience: for she thereby showed her readiness to begin
life all over again. Man's tragic triumph over the meaninglessness
of existence is achieved through living life to the very end; Mme
Meursault's last moments were such a triumph; she rose above
pity so that "no one in the world had the right to weep for her"
(1946, pp. 153–54). And her son, too, faces death, revolting
against it by feeling himself ready to begin life anew. Such is
Meursault's freedom, a freedom which makes irrelevant his
prison's walls.

His happiness too consists in this conscious revolt of life
against death.[1] To assert his happiness he must live as he had
been living—in the present and to the final moment. He has been
washed clean of hope . . . but there is one thing left for him to
desire: that his last moment should sum up the totality of his experience; it must therefore be rich in sensation, and it must also
contain somehow his role as a stranger among mankind, participating in their common fate and yet alienated from them by his
consciousness of its absurdity. He therefore wishes that "there
should be a huge crowd of spectators and that they should greet
me with howls of execration" (1946, p. 154). And the lucidity of
Meursault's revelation, born of his final revolt against death and

the absurd; his refusal to accept death meekly—to commit by
collaborating morally a form of suicide—and his consequent in-
sistence on the vital confrontation between himself and his fate:
these represent Meursault's triumph. And he will retain these
tokens of his grim victory, we assume, to the end, when all is
accomplished.

Visions of the end

I do not know how much of this interpretation is available on a
first reading. Wayne C. Booth is certainly correct when he claims
that "it is very difficult to make out the relation of the final
affirmative point to the many negations of the work" (1961, p.
296). And because of this fact it is clear that Camus has taken
a very real risk in constructing his novel as he has, placing his
moments of greatest moral and metaphysical import in the form
of metaphorical, enigmatic utterances made by a narrator who is
occasionally incoherent and frequently seemingly unconscious,
whose way of life is in itself hard to understand. The danger is
that Camus's point of view, tightly embedded in the text, will be
thought not worth the trouble to dig out, or that the reader, too
little rewarded for his initial efforts, will give it up, throw in the
towel, and go back to his detective novel. Perhaps, as Philip
Thody suggests, such easily frustrated readers are not worth
reaching: Camus, he says, "had every right to present his readers
with a book that needs to be looked at more than once if its true
meaning is to be understood. Like Gide, he might well say: 'Hard
luck on the lazy reader. I want readers of a different sort' " (1961,
p. 44). I doubt, however, that the difficulty of *The Stranger* is the
product of any intellectual snobbery on Camus's part. Our understanding of the absurdity of the universe is a product of our immediate involvement in the narrator's consciousness—to approach Meursault from the outside would have been disaster—
and if Camus has buried the affirmative "answers," he had to do
so in order to get us interested in the "questions." Besides, there is
a sense in which it is merely the *interpretation* of *The Stranger*,
not its meaning, that is buried. To have read the novel sympa-
thetically is to have absorbed, however intuitively, its significance:
interpretations of the work make sense—or make nonsense—
according to how well they explain this already attained intuitive
knowledge. Or, as Hayden Carruth implies through his character,
"Aspen," in *After the Stranger*, one need not be able to write a
critique of Camus's novel to have one's life changed by it.

What all this implies is that *The Stranger* is complete when its experience is, within the one hundred fifty-odd pages that make up its length; it is not, in other words, a work like Samuel Beckett's short drama, *Play*, wherein the author requires the actors to read their lines through once, then again, and yet a third time.[2] As diligent readers, we *do* give *The Stranger* the second and third readings which this fine work deserves, and perhaps we are intrigued enough to read as well, as a short cut, the philosophical works of Camus which bear on the intellectual questions the novel raises. But it is wrong, I think, to suggest, as Carl A. Viggiani does, that *The Stranger* "is incomprehensible except in the context of all [Camus's] works" (1956, p. 865). The essential completeness of *The Stranger* is not found in the second or third reading, nor in *The Myth of Sisyphus* and *The Rebel*: this would be to mistake what the repeated readings and outside forays accomplish for us. Having already felt the absurdity of the universe, the importance of revolt, the final happiness and liberty which Meursault achieves, we seek the logic underlying the experience, an explicit expression of our intuitions, a formula which will satisfy us of the intellectual viability of the ideas whose emotional impact we have already felt. We want to be able to add things up.

What *The Stranger* adds up to, what its completeness consists in, is an answer to a question Camus was later to raise philosophically in *The Myth of Sisyphus*, "whether or not life had to have a meaning to be lived" (1955, pp. 39–40). And the answer Camus reaches here is the same as in *The Myth*: "It now becomes clear, on the contrary, that it will be lived all the better if it has no meaning" (1955, p. 40). Put this way, we can now see the denouement of *The Stranger* as a test of this philosophical conclusion in the harshest possible case. We are shown Meursault finding happiness not in the pleasures of sun and surf—though he finds it there as well—but in contemplating his last moments on earth before the guillotine puts an end to his existence: in his act of revolt he concludes "that I'd been happy, and that I was happy still" (1946, p. 154). As a proof that despite (or, indeed, because of) the fact that life is meaningless, it is all the more worth living, Camus could not have gone further: it is the ultimate test. It is also, in a way, the final step in Camus's argument, the redaction of *The Myth of Sisyphus* which *The Stranger* can be seen to represent. And I am not sure that Camus made his conclusion more convincing in the later, more explicitly philosophical work than he did in Meursault's last illuminating reflections. Perhaps Camus

himself sensed the higher lucidity of fiction, and for this reason
chose to end *The Myth of Sisyphus* not on a dialectical but on an
imaginative note:

> ... Sisyphus teaches the higher fidelity that negates the
> gods and raises rocks. He too concludes that all is well.
> This universe henceforth without a master seems to him
> neither sterile nor futile. Each atom of that stone, each
> mineral flake of that night-filled mountain, in itself forms
> a world. The struggle toward the heights is enough to fill a
> man's heart. One must imagine Sisyphus happy (1955, p. 91).

But while the completeness of *The Stranger* is strongly en-
forced by Meursault's final reflections, its closure is correspond-
ingly weak. It is true that Meursault is in prison, waiting for the
end, with no further possibilities of action, and with a philosophy
of life that could not be carried a step further; it is true, furthermore, that in the last few pages we are given a recapitulation,
courtesy of Meursault's memory, of his relationships with all the
other major characters of the narrative: Marie, Raymond, Mas-
son, Céleste, Mme Meursault, her fiancé Perez—even old Sala-
mano. (This recapitulation serves the same closure-function as it
does in the musical sonata form.) But at the same time, Camus
does not take Meursault to the final narrative point as he could by
representing his *actual* thoughts on the way to the guillotine
rather than just his projected ones. And this must have been a
significant aesthetic decision for Camus, for he had already written the scene; in his notebooks is recorded (under the date of December 1938) something which can only have been an ending,
later rejected, for *The Stranger*. It is fascinating enough to quote
in its full length:

> "I worked it out. I tried to control myself. There was my
> appeal. I always assumed the worst. It was rejected. Well,
> then, I would die. Perhaps sooner than others. But how
> often had not the idea of dying made me see life as absurd?
> Since we are going to die anyway, it doesn't matter how and
> when. Therefore I must accept. Then, at that moment, *I had
> the right* to consider the other possibility. I was pardoned.
> I tried to tame the upsurge in my body and blood which
> made my eyes smart with desperate hope. I tried to make
> this cry less intense, so as to make my resignation more
> plausible if my first assumption were correct. But what
> was the use. The dawns came, and with them the uncertain
> hour. . . .

"But here they are. Yet it's still very dark. They've come
earlier. I've been robbed, I tell you I've been robbed. . . .
"Run away. Wreck everything. No, I'll stay. Cigarette?
Why not. Time. But at the same time he's cutting my shirt
collar away. At the same time. I haven't gained any time
at all. I tell you I'm being robbed. . . .
". . . How long this corridor is, but how quickly these
people are walking. . . . As long as there are a lot of them,
as long as they greet me with cries of hatred. As long as
there are a lot of them, and I am not alone. . . .
". . . I'm cold. How cold it is. Why have they left me in
my shirtsleeves? It's true that it doesn't matter any more.
No more illnesses for me. I've lost the joy of spitting out
my lungs, of being eaten away by a cancer under the gaze
of someone I love.
". . . And this starless sky, these black windows, and
this man in the front row, and the foot of this man who. . . ."

END

(1963, pp. 66–67)

One reason why Camus may have rejected this ending is the inconsistency between the present tense in which the last moments
must necessarily be spoken and the *passé composé* of the rest of
the novel. But surely this is a weak objection: one is not much
jarred by the shift between the first and second paragraphs of the
above quotation, and besides, the present perfect tense already
conveys the feeling of presentness. Furthermore, there is no consistent vantage point in time from which Meursault is telling his
story: it reads like a diary in which the word "today" always
refers to the narrative present rather than to some future moment
from which all that is said is being recalled. It is far more likely,
I think, that Camus rejected this scene—while incorporating into
the finished novel its philosophically significant content—in order
to avoid the pathos attendant upon the grisly preparations for a
a decapitation, the "last mile," and the narrator's thoughts cut off
in midstream by the blade of the guillotine. The apologue is, after
all, complete without all of this, and the overly intense vision of
horror would perhaps blind us to the meaning of Meursault's
tragic triumph. It would furthermore be a mistake to narrate such
a scene, if for no other reason than that we would slip, in spite of
ourselves, out of the grasp of Meursault's vision, become spectators at the decapitation who "can go home and vomit," rather
than empathic participants in Meursault's ultimate confrontation
with the absurd universe.

For us, Camus's audience, to become "empathic participants" in the sufferings and triumphs of fictional characters should be nothing new, not if we are habitual readers of novels. One could practically chart the course of the development of fictional techniques in the nineteenth and earlier twentieth centuries in terms of a group effort toward the vivid portrayal of increasingly deep and subtle shifting states of consciousness. And indeed, one could match the profound internal view of Meursault here in earlier work by Flaubert, or Conrad, or Joyce. What is distinctively new in *The Stranger* is not the techniques themselves but the use to which they have been put: the exposition of a surprisingly complex set of ethical and metaphysical ideas.

When we look back to *Rasselas* and *Candide*, we can see that in *The Stranger* Camus has forged a new relationship between work and audience which necessitates a new form of completeness. In *Rasselas* the thesis which the novel as a whole represents as an experience is announced (more or less) in the opening sentence: as we read of how Rasselas's quest for supreme earthly happiness is initiated, carried through, and finally abandoned, we do so in full ironic consciousness of its ultimate futility. And so, from our olympian position of foreknowledge, we are amused, informed, perhaps impressed—but we cannot be deeply moved: except in the most rarefied intellectual sense, Rasselas's quest never truly becomes our own. Similarly, in *Candide*, we are made to understand the ludicrousness of philosophical optimism before we have read more than two or three pages; although Voltaire does not fully develop his rationale for the rejection of optimism until much later, the witty, urbane, confiding tone of the narrative places the reader on the same plateau as Voltaire, as a detached observer of the human comedy and its manifold ironies. And in both these novels the final scenes represent not the most radical expression of the theses which govern the fables but rather the most telling revelation of the extent to which the principal characters have learned from their experiences and have adopted into their own set of beliefs the theses which had been explicitly or implicitly announced from the very beginning.

These patterns do not hold for *The Stranger*. Far from looking down from some sublime intellectual and moral height at the struggles of the hero, we are forced into accepting with at least notional consent the point of view of Meursault, even to the extent that we perceive as meaningless or absurd, events whose significance we understand perfectly well in our daily lives. And, as Wayne Booth says of *The Fall*, Camus's last completed novel (for it is equally true of *The Stranger*): "in so far as we read this book properly, we are . . . taken in by it, tricked by the narrator into playing a role in the action" (1961, p. 294). Without willing it, and perhaps without even being conscious of it, we become accomplices in Meursault's view of the universe: the seductive first-person point of view cozens us into the understanding of life that Camus intended to convey. *Candide* could be called a novel of education in some conventional sense, but to speak of *The Stranger* as a novel of education, we should have to specify that it is not so much that Meursault learns from his experience as that we ourselves do.[3] The consequence of this may be seen in the form of denouement in *The Stranger*. Meursault's perception of his happiness and his freedom in the most extreme existential situation functions, as in *Rasselas* and *Candide*, as the revelation of the hero's acceptance of authorial norms. But since until Meursault's final illumination we cannot ourselves fully comprehend the beliefs Camus means to inculcate, the conclusion becomes for us the final step in *our* understanding of Camus's ideas as well.

We should appreciate the risk Camus takes in presenting his philosophy in such a way: no one capable of reading could miss Johnson's thesis, while Voltaire's, although fraught with irony, is made no less explicit in the long run; the effect of Camus's apologue, on the contrary, depends upon the author's skill in manipulating us into an empathic participation in Meursault's consciousness—sympathy, by itself, would ` not have been enough. If we rejoice at Meursault's illumination without understanding, at least intuitively, the grim metaphysical premises behind it, then Camus has failed. And to make things more difficult still, our understanding of the tenets of Camus's philosophy must be achieved without the controlling devices of explicit authorial commentary, which Golding used freely in exposition of a far less complex set of essentially received opinions. Camus's ideas were not only highly original but, as we have seen, he was forced to present them without even the mediation of a character (like Marlow in *Lord Jim*) who can act as *raisonneur*—can speak for Camus in his own terms whether or not he fully represents the author's point of view.

Despite the risks, Camus succeeded[4] in creating a new form of rhetorical novel, one which harnessed the psychological techniques developed over the preceding century and a half to a didactic purpose. And in so doing he paved the way for a group of mid-twentieth century novelists who have constructed their fables in similar ways, either entirely void of narrative commentary from outside the characters, or else using narrators who function well in ordering the represented sequence of events but who are by no means allowed to tell all the author knows. Some of these novelists have created—as Camus and Meursault did—fantastic parodies of the universe we live in, mock worlds that speak more eloquently about our age's moral dilemmas than the authors could do in their own voices. We shall next be examining two of these works, Thomas Pynchon's *V.* and Joseph Heller's *Catch-22*, in an effort to fathom the formal structure of a genre that has had its renaissance in our time.

5 · *The Failure of Completeness*
Pynchon's V.

For the last two chapters we have been discussing the way in which authors in the twentieth century, like Golding and Camus, adapted techniques which had been developed for use in represented actions to create a new form of rhetorical fiction. So complex are the problems of the form, though, that it is not surprising to find an author of immense talent, a master of all the various techniques for interesting us in his characters' fates while still subordinating this interest to our perception of a thesis about the external world, using these techniques with a brilliance which excites our admiration but nevertheless failing to produce a work that moves us as a coherent whole. Such an author is Thomas Pynchon; such a work is his first novel, *V.*

Pynchon's failure—a magnificent and instructive one, to be sure—comes not in spite of his bravura technique but because of it, so that, ironically enough, his novel is memorable precisely for its faults. *Finnegans Wake* springs to mind immediately as a parallel: a novel whose local effects are so striking and new that they constitute the work's raison d'être, and yet because of the innumerable Finneganswakisms the book cannot be read, can only be studied. Though one could scarcely claim that *V.* is as immensely significant an experiment as *Finnegans Wake*, Pynchon, like Joyce, insists that the reader participate in the solution of intricate verbal puzzles simply to get at the meaning of his novel, and in the case of *V.*, at least, the novel as a whole fails to justify, much less make a virtue of, its paralyzing complexity.

Many of the critics who reviewed *V.* on its first appearance recognized this fact, even as they praised Pynchon himself as a novelist for whom the term "promising" would be condescending understatement. Whitney Balliett, in the *New Yorker*, compared Pynchon's novel with the Music Minus One recordings, in which the disc provides the orchestral accompaniment to the purchaser's solo performance: Pynchon, Balliett said, is willing to provide all the plot, characters, images, symbols, so long as the reader provides his own interpretation (1963, p. 113). Christopher Ricks struck a similar note in the *New Statesman* when he compared *V.* to that elusive and allusive novel by William Gaddis, *The Recognitions*, about which little clubs have formed for elucidation and criticism: Ricks suggests that the same fate will attend *V.* because of its open invitation to critical parlor-games:[1] "it is long, quirky and allusive, a pile of faggoted notions, styles, and subjects, including a pocket *White Goddess*, an anthology of atrocities, and a curdling set of boozy, horny grotesques." Ricks goes on to say that the one package symbol that might have been able to hold the novel together, the quest for V., simply does not accomplish its end: it leads instead "to disquisitions on Venezuela, Venus, Vheissu, Veronica, Valletta, etc., none of which is without interest and none of which has such centripetal force as would demonstrate a real centre" (1963, p. 492).

It is, of course, possible to posit that these qualities in *V.* are not faults but virtues. John W. Hunt sets up an ingenious theory that Pynchon's characters reluctantly forge meanings which his narrator consistently undercuts, creating a "tension"; according to Hunt, "justification of this tension lies in the vision the novel is trying to suppress" (Scott, 1968, p. 99). For Hunt, in other words, the novel is created not so much to establish a thesis—which Hunt calls a "vision"—as to suppress it. An antiapologue par excellence, if Hunt's theory is valid. We shall examine Hunt's notions more fully later in this chapter; meanwhile, let us only point out that Hunt, like the weekly reviewers, is not convinced of the success of *V.* He compares it unfavorably with Joseph Heller's *Catch-22*, suggesting that Heller—unlike Pynchon—has given his novel "a shape which counters the chaos." Pynchon, he explains, has not yet experienced "the deepening of perception to which he may be led by his technical innovations," a desirable change because the "technical stratagems" used in *V.* "appear . . . labored," measured even against Pynchon's second novel (Scott, 1968, p. 111).

The fact that even Pynchon's most enthusiastic admirers—myself included—look upon *V.* as a work seriously flawed, not fully achieved, poses special problems for the critic. He cannot, in all honesty, simply discuss the author's vision and the way in which he bent the available narrative techniques so that all the novel's elements work together to communicate that vision, as one could do with a more successful book. The vision may be clouded because the techniques (however brilliantly carried out in themselves) do not, in fact, serve to communicate it at all but rather tend to obscure it. What one must do, in a case like this, is to form a hypothesis as to what Pynchon was attempting to do in *V.*, to explain the basis for this theory in terms of those elements of the novel which lend it support, and then try to explain where it all went wrong. Obviously any number of hypotheses could be raised to this end; the criterion for selecting one over another, however, should be clear.[2] The hypothesis we choose should be one which would explain as virtues those elements of the novel with which we feel intuitively more or less comfortable, those elements which move us, which seem to "work"; it should explain as faults those sins of commission or omission against which we instinctively rebel as we read. It should, in other words, be a coherent explanation for the intuitive experience of reading the novel.

A pattern in pieces

What Pynchon was attempting to do in *V.* is nothing less than an explanation of the course of Western civilization in the twentieth century and a prophecy of its fate. The complex thesis developed in *V.* holds that, sometime in the latter half of the nineteenth century, Western civilization contracted a disease—just how Pynchon does not say, although he allows us to make some interesting inferences—from which it has been suffering ever since; that this disease is manifested in spiritual decadence of many forms, all connected with the replacement of vital human elements of culture by the Inanimate; that the disease is chronic, progressive, and mortal; and that some form of apocalypse, with either a bang or a whimper, is around the next corner.

Like Heller in *Catch-22*, Pynchon abolishes the sort of interest typical of represented actions and makes us structure his novel as an apologue, through the development of a paratactic form;[3] like Heller, furthermore, he purposely distorts temporal sequence and both naturalistic and literary probability to achieve an intended sense of "formlessness." Pynchon even has an extra trick up his sleeve: instead of concentrating, as Heller does, on the history of a single individual, he develops his thesis through two separate narrative lines each of which is given equal importance. The first of these is taken up, for the most part, by the wanderings of Benny Profane (*bene profane*: thoroughly secular), "a schlemihl and human yo-yo," whose picaresque adventures in Norfolk, Virginia, New York City, and Malta in 1955–56 make up what there is of the narrative present (Pynchon, 1963, p. 9). The second is the story of the lady V. for whom the novel is titled, presented in five "historical" chapters and an epilogue, which take us from 1898 to 1942. These chapters, however, are not arranged in chronological order, so that the reader is left with the responsibility of piecing together her history. For the most part, the story of the lady V. tells of the disease's inception and its progressive character, while the Profane chapters tell of the stage which it has reached by 1956, and indicate something of the future; actually the connections are not quite as simple as that, though it is useful to deal with the novel as though that *were* the case. Connecting the two narratives is the odyssey of Herbert Stencil, world traveler, whose quest for the knowledge of V.'s history leads him into contact with Profane and his friends. Even Stencil, who bridges the two narrative structures, does not have, any more than V. or Profane, the centripetal force Ricks sought that would hold the novel together; the true connections we eventually come to see are made in Pynchon's thesis, in the ideological framework of the novel.

Nevertheless, the search for V. constitutes Herbert Stencil's identity, and the chapters which tell of the elusive lady are (with the single exception of the epilogue) narrated through his mediation. Stencil's search, in a sense, represents a third major narrative line. Stencil was born in 1901, "in time to be the century's child," Pynchon informs us, thus granting Stencil some sort of allegorical significance (1963, p. 52). His father is a British Foreign Office agent named Sidney Stencil; his mother is unknown. Until 1945 Stencil leads a torpid existence, spending as much time asleep as possible, and devoting his waking hours to cadging favors from the network of good will his father had set up in the "old boy" circuit. In 1945, however, he comes across a passage in his father's diaries dated Florence, 1899: "There is more behind and inside V. than any of us had suspected. Not who, but what: what is she? God grant that I may never be called upon to write the answer, either here or in any official report" (1963, p. 53). Somehow, this awakens Herbert Stencil from his sloth: although he had seen the passage before, it suddenly has meaning enough to force him into initiative, "a single great movement from inertness to—if not vitality, then at least activity" (1963, p. 55). (Why 1945? Was it some unstated aspect of Stencil's experience of World War II? The atomic bomb, perhaps? Pynchon allows us to guess at will, but never satisfies our curiosity.) Some of the motivation behind Stencil's search is implied in his conversation with the Margravine di Chiave Lowenstein; she asks Stencil why he must suddenly leave her:

MARG: A woman.
STEN: Another woman.
MARG: Is it she you are pursuing? Seeking?
STEN: You'll ask next if he believes her to be his mother. The question is ridiculous. (1963, pp. 53–54).

V. may or may not actually be Stencil's mother, but in her he seeks, in some sense, the mother he has never had. It is at any rate an excuse, and an excuse is all that Stencil needs, for the search rapidly becomes an end in itself. The activity of the search compares so favorably with the half-consciousness of his former life that he dares not stop, dares not even find V., in fact, for success would dictate the end of the quest as much as admitting failure would. His strategy is to "approach and avoid," to keep the thing going as long as possible; it bears—as we shall later see—considerable resemblance to Pynchon's strategy as well. In any case, we are allowed from the first to see V. as something that must be sought but must not be found. Like Stencil, we participate in putting together V.'s story as we would help out in some enormous jigsaw puzzle, as the various scraps of information are slowly uncovered for us. We can best see what V. adds up to by presenting the fragments we are shown, not in the order in which we are given them, but in the chronologically progressive order that reveals the pattern the pieces eventually form.

The puzzle in the past

We first meet V. in chapter three ("In which Stencil, a quick-change artist, does eight impersonations") as Victoria Wren, the beautiful eighteen-year-old daughter of a British diplomat, traveling with her father and sister in Egypt during the Fashoda crisis of 1898. There amid the tense backdrop of international intrigue and imminent war, she becomes involved with one Goodfellow, a colleague (perhaps) of Sidney Stencil's in the English Foreign Office. Even here, as an innocent girl, the destructive nature of her personality is implicitly evident; in her conversation with Porpentine (a fretful secret agent working for Sidney) someone's death is foreshadowed:

> "You love Goodfellow," he said.
> "Yes." Nearly a whisper. . . .
> "What would you have me do, then?"
> Twisting ringlets round her fingers: "Nothing. Only understand."
> "How can you—" exasperated—"men can get killed, don't you see, for 'understanding' someone. The way you want it. Is your whole family daft? Will they be content with nothing less than the heart, lights and liver?" (1963, p. 93).

Porpentine is right: a very short time later, he is himself killed by Goodfellow's antagonist agent, Bongo-Shaftesbury.

Goodfellow is only the first of her conquests, Porpentine the first of her victims. After Fashoda she proclaims herself a citizen of the world, divorces herself from family ties, and takes a series of lovers. By the time she appears again, in chapter seven ("She hangs on the western wall"), she has had four, none of whom has meant anything to her. Her only souvenir from Fashoda—aside from her lost virginity—is a peculiar ornament emblematic of her nature: a five-toothed ivory comb "whose shape was that of five crucified . . . soldiers of the British Army . . . hand-carved by . . . an artisan among the Mahdists" (1963, p. 167). A momento, in other words, of the tortures inflicted upon the English prisoners unfortunate enough to survive the Mahdi's victory over General Gordon at Khartoum. Attempting to develop in herself the Machiavellian quality of virtù, she arrives in Florence in April 1899. She takes up with the aging polar explorer, Hugh Godolphin, discoverer of Vheissu (a country, Godolphin explains, without a soul—an image of the Void), and his young aesthetic son, Evan. The three of them, more by accident than design, become involved in a complicated, though fatuous, diplomatic plot which culminates—as the jokes become less and less funny—in an armed confrontation between an expatriate mob and the Italian carabinieri in front of the Venezuelan consulate:

Victoria . . . turned away to gaze, placid, at the rioting. Shots began to ring out. Blood began to stain the pavements, screams to punctuate the singing of the Figli di Machiavelli. She saw a rioter in a shirt of motley, sprawled over the limb of a tree, being bayoneted again and again by two soldiers . . . her face betrayed no emotion. It was as if she saw herself embodying a feminine principle, acting as complement to this bursting, explosive male energy. Inviolate and calm, she watched the spasms of wounded bodies, the fair of violent death, framed and staged, it seemed, for her alone in that tiny square. From her hair the heads of the five crucified also looked on, no more expressive than she (1963, p. 209).

This "feminine principle, acting as complement to this bursting, explosive male energy," is the Inanimate itself, the essence of V. The Victoria who, one year before, was a bruisable postadolescent, has now become cold and emotionless, one step toward the realization of that essence.

At Victoria's next chronological appearance, in chapter fourteen ("V. in love"), nobody knows her name: she is simply V. It is in the Paris of 1913, with the foreboding of the world war about to break loose, but V. this time has nothing to do with politics: she is in love with a ballerina, Melanie L'Heuremaudit ("cursed hour"). This perversity is what we have come to expect of V. by this time, but if we imagine their Lesbian love as Melanie's colleagues did, as involving "machines of exquisite torture, bizarre costuming, grotesque movements of muscle under flesh," we are in for a surprise. V.'s love for Melanie takes the form of the contemplation of a fetish, "a well-composed still-life of love at one of its many extremes: V. on the pouf, watching Melanie on the bed; Melanie watching herself in the mirror; the mirror-image perhaps contemplating V. from time to time. No movement but a minimum of friction" (1963, pp. 408–9). For V. love takes on its most inanimate form: using one's beloved as an object, without contact. And Pynchon reminds us here of the link between V.'s form of love and that persistent theme of decadent romanticism, the *liebestod,* in which the lovers, "dead at last, . . . would be one with the inanimate universe and with each other" (1963, p. 410).

We are not allowed, at this point, to see V.'s uncontrollable perversion merely as the creepy travesty of emotion that it is in itself. V. is a symbol for and a symptom of something much wider in its scope, and Pynchon's description of the course of her existence to this crisis point seems to speak not only of her but of the twentieth century as a whole:

> If she were Victoria Wren, even Stencil couldn't remain all unstirred by the ironic failure her life was moving towards, too rapidly by that prewar August ever to be reversed. The Florentine spring, the young entrepreneuse with all spring's hope in her virtù, with her girl's faith that Fortune . . . could be brought under control; that Victoria was being gradually replaced by V.; something entirely different, for which the young century had as yet no name. We all get involved in the politics of slow dying, but poor Victoria had become intimate also with the Things in the Back Room (1963, p. 410).

Is Pynchon really speaking of the twentieth century, with its enormous store of hope in its virtù? of the struggle to subdue and control nature that would lead to the fearful discovery of atomic energy, with its threat to all life? Is it specifically this that Pynchon has in mind when he wonders whether V. knew that her fetishism was part of some "conspiracy leveled against the animate world," or even some "'sudden establishment here of a colony of the Kingdom of Death"? (1963, p. 411). If the author knows, he never tells: he is willing to let us imagine any form of apocalypse we please, so long as we understand V.'s love as some form of step towards Armageddon.

V. next turns up in Malta during the period preceding the June disturbances ("Epilogue: 1919"), this time under a *nom de guerre*, as Veronica Manganese; here she becomes involved in politics once more, now as an agitatrix stirring up discontent among those whom the Great War has dispossessed, in the company of "various renegade Italians, among them D'Annunzio the poet-militant, and one Mussolini, an active and troublesome anti-socialist" (1963, p. 473). Working against her, trying to control the International Situation, is Sidney Stencil, who is by no means a complete stranger to her: during the Vheissu crisis, when mobs fought trained soldiers in a Florentine square, she had "seduced him on a leather couch in the . . . consulate twenty years ago."[4] Stencil recognizes his long-lost paramour, even though she has changed: one of her eyes is gone, replaced with a clock-iris, and she has had a star sapphire sewn into her navel. Even the Mahdist comb has become a part of her. Here her fascination with the inanimate and her fetishism have combined, as she incorporates dead objects into herself in an attempt to make herself into an object. She is, apparently, succeeding in her ambition, for her "live eye" is as "dead as the other" (1963, p. 487).

Again she is found during death—violent death. In the preceding episode, in Paris, her beloved Melanie was accidentally impaled on a spear during her ballet while the audience—a mob of aesthetic partisans—fought among themselves. Now, in Malta, her agitation culminates in a full-scale riot, with crowds attacking the haunts of the politically unpopular parties. And three days after the June 7 riots, Sidney Stencil is mysteriously swallowed up by a waterspout in the Mediterranean, and with him the ethos of honor and fair play in international relations that he had embodied.

V.'s next chronological appearance comes much earlier in the book, in chapter nine ("Mondaugen's story"), when in the German Southwest Africa of 1922 she turns up during a native uprising under the name of Vera Meroving ("where-am-I-roving"). She is recognizable here by the initial V of her name and by the clock-iris she wears as a false eye. Hugh Godolphin—whom we met in Florence—is here too, still paralyzed by the vision of Vheissu, the Void that fascinates the lady V., and Fräulein Meroving alternates between nostalgic conversations with Godolphin and her enjoyment of the spectacle of violent death taking place all about her. Her companion this time is one Lieutenant Weissmann—a professional Aryan even in name—who has connections with Adolf Hitler (who in 1922 would have been about to begin the writing of *Mein Kampf*); Weissmann offers Mondaugen, our narrator, a position in the Hitler government that is to be. Echoes of Hitler and foreshadowings of Nazism are frequent in this chapter: the party of Europeans is beseiged by the Bondelswaartz natives in a minor rebellion that recalls the far greater uprising of 1904, when General Lothar von Trotha, during one year's "cleaning-up" operations, managed to exterminate sixty thousand natives of the "inferior" race. The narrator anachronistically points out that "this is only 1 per cent of six million, but still pretty good" (1963, p. 245). The reference to the number of Jews exterminated during Hitler's "purification

campaign" is anything but accidental: V. is associated with all
the horrors that the twentieth century is to produce.[5]

The conversations between old Godolphin and Vera Meroving
bring out this sense of coming disasters:

> She leaned forward. . . . "Don't you see? This seige.
> It's Vheissu. It's finally happened. . . ."
> Godolphin laughed at her. "There's been a war, Fräulein,
> Vheissu was a luxury, an indulgence. We can no longer
> afford the likes of Vheissu."
> "But the need," she protested, "its void. What can fill
> that?"
> He cocked his head and grinned at her. "What is
> already filling it. The real thing. Unfortunately" (1963,
> p. 248).

The private image of the Void vouchsafed to Godolphin, he tells
her, can no longer be his alone, or even confined to his own
circle: it is taking over the world. " 'God knows how much of it
the world will see, or what lengths it will be taken to. It's a pity;
and I'm only glad I don't have to live in it too much longer' "
(1963, p. 248).

V.'s final appearance, in chapter eleven ("Confessions of
Fausto Maijstral"), comes during the blitz bombing of Malta in
1942, where she appears, nameless, as the Bad Priest, whom
Fausto puts into "a radius along with leather-winged Lucifer,
Hitler, Mussolini." As a priest, V. has the privilege of counseling
others: true to form, she advises the girls "to become nuns, avoid
the sensual extremes—pleasures of intercourse, pain of child-
birth. The boys he told to find strength in—and be like—the rock
of their island." The object of male existence—so went the
sermon—"was to be like a crystal: beautiful and soulless (1963,
pp. 339–40). V. has thus not only become an object herself—one
no longer even identifiable as female, able to masquerade as a
continent male—she preaches to others the virtue of becoming
inanimate, refusing to reproduce. To Fausto's wife, Elena, she
counsels abortion, which, however liberal an issue its advocates
today consider it, symbolizes for Pynchon the utter rejection of
the essence of human life for man.

The Bad Priest is not strictly identified as V. until the Day of
the Thirteen Raids, when, during a bombing attack, she is crushed
by a fallen beam. Helpless, dying, she lies on the pavement as the
children to whom she had preached strip and dismantle her: they

take off her hat and wig to reveal the bare scalp beneath, remove false teeth, the clock-iris, the star sapphire in her navel, a slipper attached to an artificial foot. A little girl gets the Mahdist comb (she turns out to be Paola Maijstral, Fausto's daughter, who is one of Benny Profane's friends in the narrative present). Fausto himself, observing, wonders where the disassembly will end: "Surely her arms and breasts could be detached; the skin of her legs peeled away to reveal some intricate understructure of silver openwork. Perhaps the trunk itself contained other wonders: intestines of particolored silk, gay balloon-lungs, a rococo heart." And so V. dies, crying inanimately, with a sound "so unlike human or even animal sound that [her death-cries] might have been only the wind blowing past any dead reed" (1963, pp. 343–44). In death V. has fulfilled herself by becoming, in the most ultimate sense, an object.

V.'s progress is along a simple straight line: as one critic put it, "throughout this history she has become . . . more reified, political, deracinated, defeminized, 'anti-life,' fetishistic, abstract, nameless" (Feldman, 1963, p. 258). As V. incorporates more and more of the inanimate world into herself, the events with which she is associated—basically, the political movements of the twentieth century—grow in the scope of their cruelty to culminate in the multiple horrors of World War II. From the absurd misunderstandings between two colonial powers who threatened war at Fashoda, through the fatuous diplomatic maneuverings that preceded World War I, we have come to the manufacture of death on a massive scale: the extermination of six million Jews foreshadowed in Mondaugen's story, and the wholesale bombing of civilian populations practiced by the Luftwaffe over Malta and other Allied outposts (and of course by the Allies as well, though Pynchon never explicitly alludes to it, over Germany and Japan in 1945).

The rhetorical problem here, though, is that our vision of V.'s straight-line progress is distinctly after the fact. The chapters set in 1913 and 1919 are placed *after* the disclosure of V.'s death, so that the chronological history is something we must piece together. Pynchon's motive for manipulating temporal sequence here can, of course, simply be put down to his tendency to arch cuteness—one suspects that he withholds information for its own sake—but I believe that it may point to Pynchon's intentions for closure, a problem we shall take up a little later in the chapter.

In any case, it would seem that the death of V.—or rather Herbert Stencil's knowledge of V.'s death—would bring an end to his quest for her. In fact it does no such thing: Stencil keeps on digging out fragments of the V. jigsaw until finally he is driven to Malta to investigate at first hand the scene of her apotheosis. Here he is frightened by the nearness of the quest's end no less than by the "ominous logic" into which "events seem to be ordered" (1963, p. 449). Panicked by the fear of death, the end of his identity as he-who-searches-for-V., he leaves for Stockholm where one of V.'s fetishes may (or may not) turn up in the possession of one Mme Viola. Deserting his friends, he goes off on a quest that we now know will be without end.

John W. Hunt sees Stencil's quest as a "vision" about which Pynchon skillfully weaves his anti-vision in an effort to suppress the former. According to Hunt,

> The V.-story takes on a general meaning beyond [Stencil's] personal destiny. All the while, the narrator is pursuing his strategy of anti-vision by keeping sheer boundless multiplicity of both event and meaning before the reader: V. is Victoria, Vera, Veronica, but also Valletta on the island of Malta, as well as Vesuvius and Venezuela; and the mysterious letter seems also to stand for the "V" of perspective lines made by lights on a receding street, the "V" of spread thighs or of migratory birds; it is the V-Note, where the Whole Sick Crew listens to jazz, as well as Veronica the sewer rat, the Venus of Botticelli, the Virgin Mother, and the *mons Veneris*. . . . By functioning as historian-reporter, finding the letter V. everywhere, the narrator competes with Stencil to defeat the meanings he is trying to build . . . forcing V. to mean everything and thus nothing (in Scott, 1968, pp. 103–4).

Hunt is certainly correct in that, as an all-purpose symbol, V. is virtually omnipresent.[6] At the same time, however, it would be a mistake to assume, as Hunt apparently does, that these are all red herrings which Pynchon scatters across the trail of Stencil's quest. Stencil's V. is rather the principal symbol for a "locus," a syndrome, aspects of which appear in weird harmony (or one had better say counterpoint) in the little V's one finds throughout the novel.

Chapter seven ("She hangs on the western wall"), for example, contains three of these mini-symbols. One of them is Venezuela, which a mysterious character called only The Gaucho dreams of liberating with fire and the sword. But he happens to be in Florence, not South America, and so can only drum up a demonstration against the Venezuelan consulate, one that turns swiftly into a full-scale riot in whose carnage—as we have seen before—the lady V. basks. The second V. is Botticelli's painting *The Birth of Venus*, which has a fetishistic fascination for Signor Rafael Mantissa: he plans to steal the masterpiece and convey it out of riot-torn Florence in the hollowed-out trunk of a Judas tree. The plan seems to be working: the police are drawn by The Gaucho's demonstration away from the Uffizi Gallery where the painting hangs (on the western wall—hence the chapter title), and Mantissa is about to take possession of his beloved when, all of a sudden, the vision fades;

He could not move; as if he were any gentle libertine before a lady he had writhed for years to possess, and now that the dream was about to be consummated he had been struck suddenly impotent. . . .
What sort of mistress, then, would Venus be? What outlying worlds would he conquer in their headlong, three-in-the-morning excursions away from the cities of sleep? What of her God, her voice, her dreams? She was already a goddess. She had no voice he could ever hear. And she herself (perhaps even in her native demesne?) was only. . . .
A gaudy dream, a dream of annihilation. . . . Yet she was no less Rafael Mantissa's entire love. (1963, pp. 209–10).

The third V. has already been mentioned: Godolphin's Vheissu, a vision of the Void. Godolphin confides to Mantissa that " 'it was not till the Southern Expedition last year that I saw what was beneath [Vheissu's] skin.' "

"What did you see?" asked Signor Mantissa, leaning forward.
"Nothing," Godolphin whispered. "It was Nothing I saw. . . . If Eden was the creation of God, God only knows what evil created Vheissu. The skin which had wrinkled through my nightmares was all there had ever been. Vheissu itself, a gaudy dream. Of what the Antarctic in this world is closest to: a dream of annihilation" (1963, pp. 204, 206).

V. as violence, as an inanimate, fetishistic love, as a dream of annihilation: parts of a single whole: the lady V. And the pattern is continued in Pynchon's other V's, which are not at all a suppression of the vision of Stencil's V. but a further adumbration of the symbol's content.

Puzzle in the present

We have thus far restricted our discussion to the "historical" chapters of Pynchon's novel which, as we stated before, may be thought of as representing the inception and progress of the disease that is killing Western civilization. Let us now turn to the "contemporary" chapters, in which the sickness of present-day society is analyzed.

The opening chapters present a world which is recognizably our own, and yet is only a parody of it, a world of grotesques in which sailors drink beer from foam-rubber taps shaped like enormous breasts (a travesty, but of what? Sex, or beer-swilling? Or an American Dream that encompasses both?), where girls caress and fondle their sports cars, where the only job one can get involves shooting the alligators that have made their homes in the New York City sewer system.

Inhabiting this world is Benny Profane, who, as a schlemihl, is a sworn enemy of the Inanimate—and its constant victim:

> Cut himself shaving, had trouble extracting the blade and gashed a finger. He took a shower to get rid of the blood. The handle wouldn't turn. . . . He put on his skivvy shirt backwards, took ten minutes getting his fly zipped and another fifteen repairing a shoelace which had broken as he was tying it. . . . It wasn't that he was tired or even notably uncoordinated. Only something that, being a schlemihl, he'd known for years: inanimate objects and he could not live in peace (1963, p. 37).

As a walking protest against the Inanimate, Profane should be a true hero within the novel, and in a sense he is. But at the same time he too is in a sense inanimate himself: a human yo-yo, he spends his time mechanically traveling up and down the east coast of the United States or, in New York, back and forth on the Times Square—Grand Central shuttle. Furthermore, he is unable to form, through his fear of being responsible for others, the kind of interdependent human relationships which make living and loving meaningful. He does his level best, in his own way, but it it is not good enough. It is hard, in fact, to blame him much for his lack of success, for the v-ness of V., the Inanimate, has by

1956 got into everyone's guts, shackling the human spirit, so that true meaning in human relationships has become practically impossible.

Other comparatively sympathetic characters besides Profane are treated in the same ambivalent way. Rachel Owlglass (her last name is the English translation of "Eulenspiegel," though the relevance of the allusion escapes me), who seems genuinely to care about Profane, about her roommates Esther and Paola, about her friend Roony Winsome, is initially presented making love to her MG:

> "You beautiful stud . . . I love to touch you. . . . Do you know what I feel when we're out on the road? alone, just us?" She was running the sponge caressingly over its front bumper. "Your funny responses, darling, that I know so well. The way your brakes pull a little to the left . . ." (1963, p. 28.)

And on and on, until the eavesdropping Profane begins to gag.

Profane and Rachel, however, can manage to seem virtually heroic against the backdrop of their associates, known collectively as the Whole Sick Crew. Symbol of that group—Pynchon describes him at significant length—is Fergus Myxolydian, whose principal activity—his hobby, if you will—is sleeping. His life (financed by a foundation grant) is spent alternately sleeping and watching television. To do this with the least possible trouble to himself, Fergus has contrived an ingenious switch that will turn the set on when he reaches a sufficient level of awareness and switch it off when he drops below it. And the rest of the group is equally ingenious, equally dead:

> Raoul wrote for television, keeping carefully in mind, and complaining bitterly about, all the sponsor-fetishes of that industry. Slab painted in sporadic bursts, referring to himself as a Catatonic Expressionist and his work as "the ultimate in non-communication." Melvin played the guitar and sang liberal folk songs. The pattern would have been familiar— bohemian, creative, arty—except that it was even further removed from reality, Romanticism in its furthest decadence; being only an exhausted impersonation of poverty, rebellion and artistic "soul." . . . Perhaps the only reason they survived, Stencil reasoned, was that they were not alone (1963, pp. 56–57).

The characters are representative, obviously by design, of the three major branches of the arts: literature, painting, and music. But they are debased into a kind of formal play, because the "soul" is lacking. Their art, their parties, and their lovemaking are all mechanical, a robotic imitation of life. The tone in which Pynchon relates their machinations is "comic," in inverted commas because there is really nothing very funny about it: much of *V.*, in fact, is narrated as though Pynchon were telling an endless series of bad jokes. There is a desperation about the "contemporary" narrative that saps the potential humor out of the grotesque characters and events.

It is possible to go on being "sick," quietly accepting one's progress towards the full reification of the Inanimate, so long as one does not perceive that one is doing so. The most desperate member of the Whole Sick Crew, therefore, is Roony Winsome, who understands the decadence of American life for what it is: as a Southerner, with historical roots, he perhaps can best comprehend the alterations V. has made on his society. Having done so, however, he can see no way out but suicide: " '. . . Anybody who continues to live in a sub-culture so demonstrably sick has no right to call himself well. The only well thing to do is what I am going to do now, namely, jump out this window' " (1963, p. 361). But suicide is a mere surrender to the Inanimate; even the most depraved of his comrades in decadence can point out the preciousness of life—without it, you're dead—so that it is just as well that Roony is rescued from his suicide attempt and carted off to Bellevue to join the other dropouts from an insane world.

Implicit in this vision of a world whose most talented members have surrendered to the Inanimate, is the possibility of escape through the formation of meaningful interpersonal relationships: the kind of love that is real, not fetishistic or otherwise perverse. But equally implicit is the difficulty, perhaps the impossibility, given the extent to which V. has corrupted men in their very souls, of forming such a relationship. Two pairs of lovers try within *V.*, and demonstrate the limitations on success.

The couple that comes closest is McClintic Sphere, a really creative alto saxophonist, and Ruby the whore, who is Paola Maijstral in blackface disguise. At first McClintic sees people in terms of a universal dialectic of on/off, flip/flop, crazy/cool, in which the former state is one of insane, meaningless excitement, the latter of inanimateness, torpor, quiescence:

"Ruby, what happened after the war? That war, the world flipped. But come '45, and they flopped. Here in Harlem they flopped. Everything got cool—no love, no hate, no worries, no excitement. Every once in a while, though, somebody flips back. Back to where he can love. . . ."
     "Maybe that's it," the girl said, after a while. "Maybe you have to be crazy to love somebody."
     "But you take a whole bunch of people flip at the same time and you've got a war. Now war is not loving, is it?" (1963, p. 293).

There is clearly not much comfort in the flip/flop dichotomy. Later, however, through Paola's real affection, McClintic sees some kind of path through the horns of the dilemma: "there came to McClintic something it was time he got around to seeing: that the only way clear of the cool/crazy flipflop was obviously slow, frustrating and hard work. Love with your mouth shut, help without breaking your ass or publicizing it: keep cool, but care. . . . It didn't come as a revelation, only something he'd as soon not've admitted." The problem, of course, is that loving is indeed hard work, given the way the world is: " 'there's no magic words,' " he concedes to Paola; " 'not even I love you is magic enough' " (1963, pp. 365–66). And the answer, in any case, comes too late: Paola will be leaving soon, with Stencil and Profane, to return to Malta.

And "keep cool, but care" is mighty slim pickings as affirmations of life go. Love may exist, but it cannot be expressed in terms of human joy. It is rather a private thing, clutched fiercely to oneself, a way to thwart the inanimate sickness in one's vitals, and it may be lost in the very act of its expression. But in the world Pynchon has drawn, it stands out as a tight-lipped revolt against the doom that has infected the Western world.

If McClintic and Paola manage to make contact with each other, however briefly, Profane and Rachel merely come close; like live wires that don't quite touch, they set off sparks that illuminate the problem Pynchon sees in present-day human relationships. One of the most poignant scenes shows Rachel trying to enlist Profane's help in stopping her roommate Esther from getting an abortion:

     "I don't know if it's murder or not," she said. "Nor care. How close is close? I'm against it because of what it does to the abortionee. Ask the girl who's had one. . . . Because

Esther is weak, Esther is a victim. She will come out of the
ether hating men, believing they're all liars and still knowing she'll take what she can get whether he's careful or not.
. . . I love Esther like you love the dispossessed, the way-
ward. What else can I feel? . . . . It is myself, what I could
slide back into . . . part of me that I can see in her. Just as
it is Profane the Depression Kid, that lump that wasn't
aborted, that became an awareness on the floor of one old
Hooverville shack in '32, it's him you see in every no-name
drifter, mooch, square's tenant, him you love" (1963, pp.
357–58).

But the appeal falls flat: Profane is rather mystified than moved
by Rachel's declaration of love for a fellow human being; he
thinks she is "acting weird"—selflessness being distinctly
"weird" in the world of V.—and has impulses to run away. And
perhaps Profane's reaction is not utterly contemptible: he may
be repelled by something more sinister than Rachel's saccharine
sentimentality, by the implicit narcissism in her love. So that when
Rachel's rhetoric shifts, as it soon does, from protestations of
affection for Esther to an offer of herself to Profane, he suddenly
sees her as an inanimate object following the impulse of automatic
glands:

Thus the maverick daughter of Stuyvesant Owlglass
perched like any pinup beauty. Ready at the slightest pressure surge in the blood lines, endocrine imbalance, quicken-
ing of nerves at the lovebreeding zones to pivot into some
covenant with Profane the schlemihl. Her breasts seemed to
expand toward him, but he stood fast; unwilling to retreat
from pleasure, unwilling to convict himself of love for
bums, himself, her, unwilling to see her proved inanimate
as the rest (1963, pp. 358–59).

But the impulses are there in Profane, too: knowing he can give
her nothing, he takes what she has to offer. He warns her that all
a schlemihl can do is take, secure in that he knows she has no ears
for this admonition. And so they drift on for awhile, her demanding affection smothering him (the biblical Rachel was the mother
of Benjamin), while his inability to love chills and hurts her. In
the terms of McClintic's dialectic, Rachel fails to keep cool and
Profane doesn't care. Neither has really found the formula, and
if we feel somewhat more sympathetic to Rachel's demands for
contact, we are forced to remember her equally passionate affair

with her MG: passion can be as mechanical as aloofness, at times more so. Thus their "love affair," the only one analyzed in any depth, becomes a form of prostitution (even Rachel recognizes this), a travesty of the possibilities inherent in human life.

Can things get worse? The view Pynchon presents of contemporary love and contemporary art—those two peculiarly humane aspects of man's life—is chilling enough, but he also includes a brief nightmare vision of the future. This is propounded in the scene of Profane at work for Anthroresearch Associates, a defense contractor in the business of making dummies for testing purposes. One model is SHROUD (Synthetic Human, Radiation OUtput Determined), used for testing the effects of atomic radiation on civilian populations; the other is SHOCK (Synthetic Human Object, Casualty Kinematics), which is placed in automobiles on which weights are dropped to test the effect of various kinds of motor accidents. To the men of Anthroresearch, man has become an object, something which exists to absorb X-rays, gamma rays, and neutrons on the one hand, or death-dealing physical blows on the other. SHROUD, however, has a better theory, which it enunciates in a weird conversation with nightwatchman Profane:

> On the way back to the guardroom [Profane] stopped in front of SHROUD.
> "What's it like," he said.
> Better than you have it.
> "Wha."
> Wha yourself. Me and SHOCK are what you and everybody will be someday. (The skull seemed to be grinning at Profane.)
> "There are other ways besides fallout and road accidents."
> But those are the most likely. If somebody else doesn't do it to you, you'll do it to yourselves.
> "You don't even have a soul. How can you talk?"
> Since when did you have one? . . .
> "What do you mean, we'll be like you and SHOCK someday? You mean dead?"
> Am I dead? If I am then that's what I mean.
> "If you aren't then what are you?"
> Nearly what you are. None of you have very far to go.
> "I don't understand."
> So I see. But you're not alone. That's a comfort isn't it?
> (1963, pp. 286–87).

A tantalizing glimpse of Pynchon's prophecy: man seen as a soulless mannikin, immortal because it never was alive, built out of indestructable plastics and metals. The vision stays with Profane, who even improves upon it, imagining "an all-electronic woman. . . . Any problems with her, you could look it up in the maintenance manual. Module concept: fingers' weight, heart's temperature, mouth's size out of tolerance? Remove and replace, was all" (1963, p. 385). The future in store for mankind is thus what the lady V. dreamed of but never lived to achieve: the ultimate triumph of the Inanimate.

The puzzle completed

V. is not a simple novel, because Pynchon refuses to draw parallels and connections for us: he provides the evidence, but the work of ordering and evaluating it we must do for ourselves. The lack of narrative juncture, for the most part, between the "historical" and the "contemporary" chapters at the novel's outset forces us, as we have already suggested, to find coherence in terms of the only important link between them: Pynchon's thesis. Similarly, the convergence of the two kinds of chapters later in the novel in one unified vision of apocalypse provides, as we shall see, much of the impetus toward a sense of ending.

We have already mentioned the confusing order—or rather disorder—in which the "historical" chapters are placed. On the other hand, we might see these chapters as providing a kind of literary counterpoint to the events in the "contemporary" chapters and thus justify the puzzle Pynchon sets for us in thematic terms. "The confessions of Fausto Maijstral" present more than simply the death of V.: they chronicle the effects of the Second World War upon a sensitive and poetic individual, his spiritual journey from active rebelliousness to virtual catatonia under dint of siege and constant air raids. The main focus of the alteration is the change Fausto's affliction causes in his young wife, Elena, and her struggle to go on loving him even as he becomes estranged from her and alienated from himself. It cannot, I think, be mere accident that this chapter immediately follows the establishment of that doomed, incomplete "love affair" between Rachel and Profane, nor that his vision—provoked by Rachel's automatic drives—of the "all-electronic woman" precedes the chapter on V. in love, within which we see something very similar:

[V.] at age seventy-six: skin radiant with the bloom of
some new plastic; both eyes glass but now containing
photoelectric cells, connected by silver electrodes to optic
nerves of purest copper wire and leading to a brain
exquisitely wrought as a diode matrix could ever be.
Solenoid relays would be her ganglia, servo-actuators
move her flawless nylon limbs, hydraulic fluid be sent
by a platinum heart-pump through butyrate veins and
arteries. Perhaps . . . even a complex system of pressure
transducers located in a marvelous vagina of polyethylene;
the various arms of their Wheatstone bridges all leading to
a single silver cable which fed pleasure-voltages direct to
the correct register of the digital machine in her skull
(1963, pp. 411–12).

This kind of interplay becomes progressively more important as
the novel draws to a close. At the outset, the connections between
the "contemporary" and "historical" chapters are established
formally, through Stencil's search for V. at the same time that he
hangs about at the parties of the Whole Sick Crew; and thematically, through the vision of the decadence of humanity into
the Inanimate expressed in both parts. As the novel progresses,
however, the connections between the two types of chapter become more concrete and explicit; references, characters, even
phrases cross over the divide.[7] Throughout the last hundred
pages or so, both "historical" and "contemporary" chapters con-
spire to produce a vision of apocalypse resulting from the trends
we have already seen growing up; Pynchon is, however, less than
explicit about when such an Armageddon would take place, or
of what the doom would consist. Without defining it any more
closely than he has to, the author is content to suggest through
his characters that the end, whatever it might be, is not very far
off. After closing out the minor narrative lines which had given
textural continuity to the whole, Pynchon takes three of his most
significant characters to the ends of their respective ropes, at
once completing the exposition of his thesis and providing a
semicadential closure for his novel.

Stencil's trip to Malta, on which he takes Paola and Profane,
provides the impetus for most of these elements of closure, including the tying off of the various minor narrative strands.
Paola's return to her native country requires her to break off with
McClintic, and, on Malta, she accidentally meets and is reunited

with the sailor husband she had deserted in the very first chapter.[8] Similarly, Profane says farewell to the women who loved and depended so foolishly on him: first Josefina Mendoza, the Puerto Rican girl he had met in his alligator-hunting days, for whose troubles Profane (in an uncharacteristically unschlemihl-like manner) admits responsibility before she leaves to return to San Juan; then Rachel, from whom Profane takes leave at a tête-à-tête wherein the effervescence of the champagne reminds him of clicking radiation counters; finally Paola, who leaves Profane on Malta while she returns to Norfolk, Virginia, to await her husband's return. The other participants return to the *status quo ante*: Pig Bodine, who had deserted his ship in Norfolk, is apprehended by the Shore Patrol during a last party with the Crew, while Roony Winsome, back from Bellevue, is carefully tended by Rachel before he returns to his nymphomaniacal wife, Mafia: the ripple made by Stencil, Profane, and V. passes as they do, and life returns to its customary inanimate patterns. These closure devices control our expectations, in that we are not allowed to foresee a return for the travelers from Malta to New York: their boats are burnt behind them. All this increases the sense of foreboding that Pynchon has carefully been building up.

Stencil himself feels the foreboding, knows somehow that the end of the quest that has kept him active lies on Malta, so that he is both drawn to and repelled from that island.

"Stencil doesn't want to go to Malta. He is quite simply afraid. . . . Stencil's father mentioned [V.] in his journals: this was near the turn of the century. Stencil became curious in 1945. Was it boredom, was it that old Sidney had never said anything of use to his son; or was it something buried in the son that needed a mystery, any sense of pursuit to keep alive a borderline metabolism? Perhaps he feeds on mystery.

"But he stayed off Malta. . . . Young Stencil has been in all her cities. . . . All her cities but Valletta. His father died in Valletta. He tried to tell himself meeting V. and dying were separate and unconnected for Sidney.

"Not so. Because: all along the first thread, from a young, crude Mata Hari act in Egypt . . . while Fashoda tossed sparks in search of a fuse; until 1913 when she knew she'd done all she could and so took time out for love—all the while, something monstrous had been building. Not the War, nor the socialist tide which brought us Soviet Russia. These were symptoms, that's all. . . . Not even as if she were

any cause, any agent. She was only there. But being there
was enough, even as a symptom" (1963, pp. 385–86).

Does Herbert Stencil—speaking of himself in the third person—
expect to find V. on Malta? Will he discover how Sidney died?
Stencil doesn't know, doesn't even know—for reasons we have
already pointed out—whether he *wants* to succeed, for he is
equally afraid of finding V. and of not finding her. All he knows
is that the time is ripe for him to go to Malta. Paris for love,
Malta for war—Stencil quotes his father—and the brewing crisis
in the Middle East over Suez is propitious for Stencil's movement
into the Mediterranean.

Once on Malta, Stencil goes into his customary routine, inter-
viewing those who have known V. Fausto Maijstral, with whom
the travellers are staying, confirms what he had written in his
memoirs, that he saw V. die:

> Maijstral shrugged. "Why have you come? She is dead."
> "He must know."
> "I could never find that cellar again. If I could: it must
> be rebuilt now. Your confirmation would lie deep."
> "Too deep already," Stencil whispered (1963, p. 445).

Stencil tacks about, looks for the children who had been present
at V.'s disassembly, but with little luck, apparently. (Stencil gives
no clue that he knows—as we readers already do—that Paola
had been one of them.) As the search seems to become more and
more futile, Stencil reverts to his pre-1945 condition; he sleeps
endlessly, as though in sleep he could escape the terrible knowledge he seeks. At length Stencil feels as though he were being
haunted by V.'s spirit (if, indeed, she can be said to possess a
spirit):

> "She cannot be dead," Stencil said.
> "One feels her in the city," he cried.
> "In the city."
> "In the light. It has to do with the light."
> "If the soul," Maijstral ventured, "is light" (1963, p. 447).

Stencil finally, in desperation, looks up old Father Avalanche, to
see if he has any information about V. on Malta in 1919. Avalanche, his memory already fading, refers him to a Father Fairing,
his predecessor on Malta, " 'though the poor old man, wherever
he is, must be dead by now' " (1963, p. 449). The name Fairing,

little as it conveys to Stencil, is not unfamiliar to us: we have heard it before in the alligator-hunting chapters. Fairing's Parish is the name the sewer-shikaris have given to a section of main on the upper East Side of Manhattan where Father Fairing, anticipating that the rats were about to take over the depression-torn country, decided to convert the vermin to Catholicism; it was in Fairing's Parish that Profane had cornered and killed a pinto alligator in a chamber lit by a phosphorescence whose frightening radiance reminds us of Godolphin's description of Vheissu.

As Stencil learns of Fairing's connection with V., and as the elements of the coincidence are confirmed by Maijstral and Profane, from their respective vantage points, his fear begins to mount to panic proportions. " 'Events seem to be ordered into an ominous logic,' " Stencil repeats endlessly. Meanwhile Profane comes down with an inexplicable fever, even as Stencil and Maijstral begin to feel the haunting presence of V., and the conclusion comes to Stencil that V. must be in demonic possession of Profane's body. He rushes to Maijstral (who, priestlike, had heard V.'s last confession) to get him to perform an exorcism:

> "She possesses him," Stencil whispered. "V."
>
> "You are as sick."
>
> "Please."
>
> ". . . No," Maijstral said, "you wouldn't get what you wanted. What—if it were your world—would be necessary. One would have to exorcise the city, the island, every ship's crew on the Mediterranean. The continents, the world. Or the western part" (1963, pp. 450–51).

Stencil has come to the end of his rope, for he has found what he was after. There is indeed an ominous logic to events; it is true, as he guesses, that " 'Stencil has never encountered history at all, but something far more appalling' " (1963, p. 450). What he has discovered is the "conspiracy leveled against the animate world," the "sudden establishment here of the Kingdom of Death," the "Things in the Back Room" of which V. was a symptom, but a more pervasive, more deadly symptom than even Stencil had imagined. It was something he had not wanted to know—that V. was not dead, but growing like a cancer in everything around him —and he abjures the knowledge: " 'Stencil went out of his way to bring Profane here. He should have been more careful; he wasn't. Is it really his own extermination he's after?' " (1963, p.

451). This is the last of Stencil's unanswered questions about his
own motivations, the last spoken word of his in the novel. A few
days later, Stencil is gone, leaving only a note that he is off after
the "frayed end of another clue," continuing the search rather
than face the truth he had unwittingly found out.

Profane too, in his own way, comes to the end of his string.
Like Stencil, Profane is on an endless pursuit along "a single abstracted Street" down which he wanders, where "overhead,
turning everybody's face green and ugly, shone mercury vapor
lamps, receding in an asymmetric V" (1963, p. 10). It is on Malta
that Profane, again like Stencil, comes to understand how the
pursuit of his own version of V. has shorn his life of the meaning
that would have made it worth while:

> It made him shudder: as if all his homes were temporary
> and even they, inanimate, still as wandering as he: for
> motion is relative, and hadn't he, now, really stood there
> still on the sea like a schlemihl Redeemer while that enormous
> malingering city and its one livable inner space and one
> unconnable (therefore hi-valu) girl had all slid away from
> him over a great horizon's curve comprising, from this
> vantage, all at once, at least one century's worth of wavelets?
> (1963, p. 453).

He can always go back to the endless Street, which "was nowhere,
but some of us do go nowhere and can con ourselves into believing it to be somewhere: it is a kind of talent," one which Profane
possesses in the highest degree (1963, p. 453). Following Stencil's search for V., privy to the secrets he had uncovered, as well
as to SHROUD's diagnosis and prediction, Profane has simply
not absorbed any of it. He can go on "through the abruptly absolute night, momentum alone carrying" him "toward the edge of
Malta, and the Mediterranean beyond," together with a silly girl
who picked him up as Rachel had previously done, fearless because of his invincible ignorance. Brenda, the pickup, can ask
him about his "fabulous experiences": " 'Haven't you learned?'
Profane didn't have to think long. 'No,' he said, 'offhand I'd say
I haven't learned a goddamn thing' " (1963, pp. 454–55). This
may be the "anti-vision" of which Hunt writes: the ability, conscious or otherwise, to ignore the plain truth—so long as it is
horrible enough.

Both Profane and Stencil, each in his own way, come to the end
of the road; not seeing, or not accepting, the vision that lies in

their path, they go on, doing as they have done before, letting pattern and routine dictate their motions. What would happen, though, if someone were to see, understand, and accept the truth that V. represents? The answer is in the epilogue, the protagonist Sidney Stencil. We have met Sidney before in the Florence of the Vheissu crisis, where he was dubbed Soft-shoe Sidney by his colleagues in the Foreign Office because of his near-obsession with teamwork in diplomacy. Sidney is not normal, especially by comparison with the collection of freaks that populate *V.*; his commitment to "liberal" or "humane" values—to cooperation with others, to dedicated understanding of the jigsaw puzzles in human and political relations that diplomacy creates, to honor and just dealing—these make him nearly unique, the more so because he manages to be humane and liberal without being pompous about it. It is possible for Sidney because he was born early enough to "come in on the tail end" of "a time where which side a man was on didn't matter: only the state of opposition itself, the tests of virtue, the cricket game" (1963, p. 458). But the time is gone now: the year is 1919 and more than World War I is over: Sidney's career and its ethos are also things of the past.

It is tempting to think that there is some connection here, that it was the Great War itself that spelled the end of Sidney's particular brand of virtù. But Sidney himself knows, although he refuses to disquiet his superiors by telling them so, that the war was no "Nameless Horror," no "sudden prodigy sprung on a world unaware. . . . There was no innovation, no special breach of nature, or suspension of familiar principles" (1963, p. 459). At its root, the Great War was no different than any other major war in the latter half of the nineteenth century. Things have changed, but the war was an effect, not a cause. And the changes have made Sidney Stencil a back number awaiting his end:

> "As a youth I believed in social progress because I saw chances for personal progress of my own. Today, at age sixty, having gone as far as I'm about to go, I see nothing but a dead end for myself, and if you're right, for my society as well. But then: suppose Sidney Stencil has remained constant after all—suppose instead sometime between 1859 and 1919, the world contracted a disease which no one ever took the trouble to diagnose because the symptoms were too subtle—blending in with the events

of history, no different one by one but altogether—fatal"
(1963, pp. 460–61).

What this disease is, we already know: it is the Inanimate. The
year 1859 rings a couple of interesting bells: the publication of
Darwin's *Origin of Species* and of Marx's *Critique of Political
Economy*—two men whose philosophies were to alter funda-
mentally our conception of ourselves and of the political world;
two works which espouse a determinist, historicist conception of
man which is at its roots mechanistic. Did Pynchon have any of
this in mind when he had Stencil speak of a disease that might
have begun as early as 1859? The text does not answer these
questions: the origin of the disease of which V. herself and all
her avatars are symptoms is never precisely pinned down.

If the etiology of the disease is unknown, the prognosis is clear
enough: morbidity proceeding towards death. And Sidney Stencil,
staring his own end clearly in the face, is vouchsafed a vision of
the future as he muses over the parallels between politics and
religion:

> The matter of a Paraclete's coming, the comforter, the
> dove; the tongues of flame, the gift of tongues: Pentecost.
> Third Person of the Trinity. None of it was implausible to
> Stencil. The Father had come and gone. In political terms,
> the Father was the Prince; the single leader, the dynamic
> figure whose virtù used to be the determinant of history.
> This had degenerated to the Son, genius of the liberal
> love-feast which had produced 1848 and lately the over-
> throw of the Czars. What next? What Apocalypse? (1963,
> p. 472).

The Epilogue foreshadows the rise of Mussolini and the fascisti,
just as other chapters have limned the rise of Hitler, the Second
World War, the Suez crisis. The world has survived these, just as
Stencil had the First World War. Sidney's end comes rather out
of a cloudless sky, when while sailing from Malta to Sicily "a
waterspout appeared and lasted for fifteen minutes. Long enough
to lift the xebec fifty feet, whirling and creaking . . . naked to the
cloudless weather, and slam it down again into a piece of the
Mediterranean" (1963, p. 492). Does Pynchon expect our apocalypse to arrive as Sidney's private one did, out of a clear day,
with waterspouts created by mushroom-shaped clouds, along

with other deadly phenomena? SHROUD's prophecy of its like-lihood, and Profane's weird association of bubbly champagne with the sound of radiation counters lends such a speculation plausibility. But perhaps it hardly matters how it comes, or even if; the takeover of the Inanimate, that "ominous logic" which destroys the humane potential in man, is apocalypse enough.

Flies in the ointment

The vagueness and conditionality of our statements about Pynchon's ending are not simply a matter of our being unwilling to fix upon a single interpretation; they point to real ambiguity on Pynchon's part. Our hypothesis posits an ending in which the two main characters of the "contemporary" chapters have come face to face with that "something more appalling than history" of which Pynchon's thesis speaks; they then willfully (in the case of Stencil) or through intellectual flabbiness (in the case of Profane) decide to ignore it. This is followed by a similar revela-tion to Sidney Stencil, who understands and accepts all its im-plications, including the doom for himself personally and for the ethos which he represents. It would be pleasant to claim that all this is made very clear, but that is not the case. Chapter sixteen ("Valletta") is not entirely, perhaps not even mainly concerned with Stencil and Profane: it opens with a twenty-page scene of naval horseplay, reminiscent of similar scenes in chapter one, but in a somewhat lower key, in which the Suez crisis and Paola's return are mentioned, but are decidedly kept in the background. Similarly, the Epilogue opens with Sidney Stencil's philosophical musings cited above—material relevant for the posited denoue-ment—but goes on to chronicle at great length from an unusual omniscient point of view the events leading up to the disturbances of June 7, 1919. None of it is wholly irrelevant to Pynchon's thesis, but at the same time it does not display the necessary attention to the task of pulling together the loose paratactic struc-ture of *V.* Thus the sense of ending is weakened by the bulk of tangential material—as well as by the purposely semicadential quality of the last scenes involving Profane and Herbert Stencil. One can well understand Pynchon wanting to end his "contem-porary" narrative on a semicadence: if our notion of his thesis is correct, he would wish to imply, through the half-closure of his ending, that the decadence of the twentieth century caused by the v-ness of V. would continue and progress. He would leave final closure to the Epilogue and Sidney Stencil, whose humanity and honor—and by implication that of the Western world—have in fact come to an end. But why such an ending need be weakened further, I am unable to understand. One may be tempted to offer explanations, from mere speculations (made plausible by the rest of the novel) that Pynchon simply likes to write about horseplay and diplomatic intrigues, to elaborate re-drawings of Pynchon's thesis (which would palliate the rest of the novel); what cannot be explained away, on any hypothesis, is that the two final chapters (except for the parts which we have already tied to Pynchon's thesis) are the least effective part of the novel. Even on a first reading, the scenes of Pappy Hod and Fat Clyde carousing in Valletta and of the elaborate Mizzist conspiracies in 1919 seem tangential; they are part of the occasional longueurs of which most reviewers spoke. As such they represent rather a betrayal than a fulfillment of the open form of *V.*, the triumph of self-indulgence over artistic synthesis.

It might be a stronger temptation to try to make sense of the discordant aspects in Pynchon's conclusion if purposeless ambiguity were a less firmly entrenched habit of his. But as we read *V.*, we are continually striking on and following up allusions that lead only into further enigmas, not to solutions. As in Profane's case, ignorance is bliss, for the more we know the more likely we are to become thoroughly confused. Example one: Kurt Mondaugen, attempting to decode the make-and-break atmospheric disturbances he is investigating in German Southwest Africa in 1922, deciphers his own name plus DIEWELTISTALLESWAS-DERFALLIST (the world is all that is the case), Ludwig Wittgenstein's first thesis in his *Tractatus Logico-Philosophicus*, published in 1922. Now one can see the relevance of such a statement to this apologue, and one can bet that someone, somewhere, is at work on a Wittgensteinian interpretation of *V.*, based either on the *Tractatus*, on the *Philosophical Investigations* that contradict it, or on the *Blue and Brown Books*, which agree with neither. But what is the relevance of this particular coincidence coming at this particular point in the novel? Example two: in the alligator-hunting chapter, reference is made to one "V. A. ('Brushhook') Spugo who claimed . . . to have slain 47 rats with a brushhook under the summer streets of Brownsville on 13 August 1922!" (1963, p. 113). Could this be a veiled reference—for Pynchon delights in *veiled* references—to the "Brownsville Affray," in which a company of black soldiers was accused of armed riot on the summer streets of Brownsville, *Texas,* also on the thirteenth of August, but in 1906? Pynchon certainly knows a good deal about lesser known historical events, but if he meant the knowledgeable to catch on here, the reference leads precisely nowhere, even if one could be sure it was being made. Example three: Pynchon's novel deals with Malta at length, with V's of various sorts at greater length, and there is a single reference to Stencil being "all quite mysterious and Dashiell Hammettlike" (1963, p. 127). Are we being treated to an allusion to *The Maltese Falcon,* Hammett's greatest mystery novel, which opens: "Samuel Spade's jaw was long and bony, his chin a jutting v under the more flexible v of his mouth. His nostrils curved back to make another, smaller, v. . . . The v *motif* was picked up again by thickish brows rising outward from twin creases above a hooked nose" (1965, p. 295). A parallel could be drawn, of course, between the two novels, which share not only an intricate mystery that leads to nothing, but a bitter malaise about America. Perhaps Pynchon was intrigued with the ending of *The Maltese Falcon,* too, in which Sam Spade rejects the attractions of love for the dubious pleasures of playing by the mechanical rules of the private-eye game. But then Hammett's V's, belonging only to Spade's satanic face, have little to do with Pynchon's; the parallel is inexact at its most crucial point and at any rate tells us more about *The Maltese Falcon* than about *V.*

What is common, in fact, to all these examples is that they point outward, not inward, that they explain nothing internal to *V.* Novelists often use allusion as a method of commenting briefly and pointedly on the fiction they have created. With Pynchon, however, allusion is a game for the cognoscenti to play, a game which adds nothing either to the pleasure or the meaning of the novel, and which adds greatly to the opacity of a work which, as even its fans agree, is hard enough to read without artificial enigmas. As a technique, its use rests on the old fallacy of imitative form, which dictates that if you wish to express a vision of chaos, your novel must itself be chaotic; the fallacy of this line of reasoning, of course, is that if your novel is sufficiently chaotic it will express nothing at all. The problem in *V.* is that once one has investigated enough allusions that turn out to be red herrings, one may hesitate to respond to others which may in fact prove productive. A number of scenes, parts of scenes, and throwaway lines indicated to me that Pynchon had meant us to consider the possibility of atomic holocaust as one probable form which the apocalyptic triumph of the Inanimate might take, and I presented these hints in the course of my analysis of the novel. But despite my feelings that Pynchon actually had this in mind, I was reluctant to describe this aspect of *V.* as anything more than a speculation, simply because it is not developed in much greater detail than a number of other chains of references that turned out to be mere distractions. If the notion is correct, then Pynchon has artfully succeeded in concealing something rather important; if not, then he has merely succeeded in confusing one careful reader, and probably a good segment of his public as well.

(Of course it is possible to take another view of Pynchon's use of allusion: that it is deliberately quirky and confusing, designed precisely to run the reader on assorted sleeveless errands, and that this, in turn, should alert the perceptive and self-conscious reader that he is treating the novel as a crossword puzzle and thus participating in the decadence of art. But Pynchon's ad hominem thrust at the reader admits of an obvious riposte: since it is the author who has painstakingly laid down the false trails, is he not far more decadent, more possessed by the inanimate critical game of symbol-hunting than the reader could ever be? But this response does not entirely vitiate the original argument, so that it may well be that Pynchon's allusiveness is in fact meant to entrap the reader—and may very well succeed in embarrassing him.)

Allusion is not the only trick that has gotten out of hand in *V.* Pynchon also tries to trick us with ambiguously unreliable narration. Let us take chapter nine ("Mondaugen's story"), which is introduced in the following way:

> . . . in one of the secluded side rooms of the Rusty Spoon,
> Mondaugen yarned, over an abominable imitation of
> Munich beer, about youthful days in Southwest Africa.
> Stencil listened attentively. The tale proper and the questioning after took no more than thirty minutes. Yet the next Wednesday afternoon at Eigenvalue's office, when Stencil retold it, the yarn had undergone considerable change: had become, as Eigenvalue puts it, Stencilized (1963, p. 229).

Indeed it had: chapter nine runs over fifty pages and could scarcely have been read, much less read aloud, in half an hour. Clearly the reliability of the story has been undermined for us.

But to what purpose? Mondaugen (or is it Stencil?) makes few value judgments, and those few are unexceptionable. There is little for him to be unreliable about; what Stencil is interested in is the bare facts of the narrative, and to make a narrator unreliable about such matters is thoroughly pointless.[9] The tale is told more or less dramatically, and we have nothing against which to test the facts related except the encyclopedia—which confirms them. Thus to the extent that we take the warning on page 229 we are led astray, a fine reward for the close reader. A similar trick is played in chapter three ("in which Stencil, a quick-change artist, does eight impersonations"), wherein Stencil relates information about Victoria Wren at Fashoda which neither he nor his father was in a position to collect. The chapter, even without this caveat (made explicit at p. 63, but implicit throughout), would be hard enough to follow, for the point of view shifts rapidly among seven fictional Cairo residents and one disembodied voice— waiters, bellboys, train conductors, spongers—all of whom speak mainly of their own troubles, but manage nevertheless to overhear snatches of conversation revealing a diplomatic intrigue which forms the center of the chapter but is never quite made clear. As a tour de force the chapter is impressive,[10] but it is not, I think, made more so by our knowledge that each of the centers of consciousness is actually Herbert Stencil, in disguise, making up the whole thing as he goes along. Especially since the information we get in chapter three about the lady V. is substantially confirmed in the more "reliably" narrated chapter fourteen ("V. in love") and the omnisciently narrated Epilogue.

What partially saves Pynchon and his novel from the obscurity into which his obsession with technique might have driven him is the law of *Prägnanz*, that rule of Gestalt psychology that predicts the tendency of any mental form or structure towards meaningfulness, completeness, and relative simplicity. As we read the novel, the false clues, red herrings, and learned trifles which would lead us astray tend to be forgotten as the pattern of Pynchon's thesis shapes the rest into a meaningful picture. Annoyed as we may be at the distractions the author has placed in our path, we cannot fail to be impressed by his achievement.

But the law of *Prägnanz* can only partially rescue *V.*, for while that novel's most obvious defect is obscurity, there is a flaw which cuts deeper and which cannot be so easily explained away. Irving Feldman, in his review of *V.* for *Commentary*, puts a finger on the novel's major defect:

As in some anti-novel or anti-play, Pynchon's characters seem always on the verge of demanding their author to grant them their freedom. But given their screwball beginnings in the novel and the air, breathless and hypomanic [sic], of pastiche continuously surrounding them, nothing could be more meaningless than the problem of Rachel finding fruitful love, Esther having an abortion, Benny Profane reaching the end of the Street. Maybe Pynchon himself is secretly on the characters' side, since he frequently introduces a sane and sympathetic note into his weird scenes. As it stands, however, the characters do not struggle with one another but against their premises. The real source of the Inanimate in V. is the author (Feldman, 1963, pp. 259–60).

Now it would be easy to dismiss Feldman's criticisms as inappropriate to the genre to which V. belongs. After all, Candide is not diminished by the "screwball beginnings" given the characters, nor does the undeniable "air . . . of pastiche" that surrounds them detract from the excellence of that novel. Feldman, we might claim, is judging the novel from the standpoint of realism, a standard which need not apply to an extended fable, a rhetorical fiction, like V. And we might further argue that the fact that Feldman finds the characters' problems meaningless only points to Pynchon's success in portraying the universality of the Inanimate's grip on the soul of twentieth-century man; if we found the characters fully sympathetic and their struggles thoroughly moving, it would diminish our sense of the pervasiveness of civilization's malaise. Wholly sympathetic characters with whom the reader might feel great empathy must be sacrificed to the demands of consistency.

But whatever abstract validity these lines of reasoning might seem to possess, they are specious: Feldman is basically in the right, even though he stops well short of explaining why he is right. To begin with, to defend V. by comparing it with Candide is not to the point. There is a difference of kind between the controlling theses of Voltaire's and Pynchon's fables, and techniques which serve the former well may prove deadly for the latter. Voltaire's thesis is one with which he may expect his audience to be already in sympathy; he may thus indulge himself to the hilt in ironies at his characters' expense, carrying the reader along with him easily. Again, given his thesis, his pastiche characters' foibles are by no means repellent, and Voltaire can easily work up sympathy for them any time he needs to. But Pynchon's thesis, a complex proposition regarding the cause, course, present state, and prognosis of a putative disease afflicting Western civilization, could by no stretch of the imagination be regarded as a received opinion; it is a thesis of which we must be persuaded emotionally —intellectual assent is not enough.

And it is here that Pynchon falls short. The consciousnesses through which we view Pynchon's world—mainly Profane's and Stencil's—are undercut from the start; it may be through Profane and Stencil that we learn of the world sickness, but it rapidly becomes clear that they are not the solution—they are part of the problem. And the narrator, identified closely as he is with the consciousness of Profane or Stencil, offers little in the way of corrective (unlike the narrator of *Candide*). Most of the other main characters are no better. I would hazard that Pynchon would like us to sympathize with "the problem of Rachel finding fruitful love," and not find it "meaningless," and yet one could hardly say he has given us much help. At the moments when Rachel most wants to "connect" with Profane we can hardly forget the vivid picture of her cuddling up to her MG, and in case we had forgotten, Pynchon has Profane remember it for us; similarly, Esther's desire to get an abortion can hardly seem as tragic to us as it does to Rachel, for we have seen too much of the mechanical and inanimate in Esther's sex life to care particularly about the fetus it produced. The few characters who seem to offer an alternative—Paola, McClintic, Sidney Stencil—show up too seldom, too late in the novel, and with too little intensity to give us any insight into how all this inanimateness looks from the outside; the rest, who show us the Inanimate from the inside, are pathetic at best and repulsive at worst—so that none of them is capable of giving us the emotional understanding of Pynchon's thesis that is a necessary prelude to intellectual acceptance. As a result, Pynchon's argument is complete, fully traceable, and entirely consistent, but at the same time the novel as a whole does not present its thesis as an experience carrying emotional conviction. His metaphors remain cold conceits; the novel is itself inanimate.

But if it was necessary for Camus, in showing us an absurd universe, to restrict us to the consciousness of his absurd hero, may it not have been equally necessary for Pynchon to use the schlemihl Profane and the mechanical Stencil to bring us the vision of an inanimate universe? The temptation to agree with this ominous logic is strong, but the answer is better given by the event. In his second novel, *The Crying of Lot 49*, Pynchon tells a similar story (complete with conspiracies reminiscent of the diplomatic intrigues in *V.*) with a similar moral, but this time the central consciousness, Oedipa Maas, is one that is able fully to involve us in her problem, and to that extent the novel is more successful.[11] More successful, too, is Nathanael West's *Miss Lonelyhearts*, which portrays a loathsome world replete with absurdly unnecessary suffering through the eyes of the only character (other than the individual sufferers) who cares.

Yet another more successful modern fable is *Catch-22*, which was published two years before *V.* Like Pynchon's novel, *Catch-22* is informed by a thesis which must be experienced emotionally before it could carry intellectual conviction; like *V.* again, Heller's novel is incredibly inventive, filled with a rich supply of weird characters and events which would be unacceptably improbable except in terms of the author's world-view. *Catch-22* contains, in other words, all the elements *V.* does—including the intentionally distorted time-scheme—but unlike Pynchon, who was unable in the last analysis to shape *V.* as a convincing apologue, Heller managed to create a novel which, immensely funny at times, profoundly moving at others, subordinates these deftly evoked emotional responses to our understanding of his doctrines. In the next chapter we shall have a look at Heller's fully realized rhetorical novel.

6 · The Achievement of Shape in the Twentieth-Century Fable Joseph Heller's Catch-22

My title for this chapter implies—states outright, rather—that *Catch-22* not only has a definable shape but that its form represents an achievement towards which contemporary rhetorical fiction had been groping. Whatever might be thought of such a view today, it would have seemed outrageous to most of Heller's early reviewers, who were repelled by the novel's seeming disorganization. The reviewer for the *New York Times* called Heller the Jackson Pollack of fiction, "a brilliant painter who decides to throw all the ideas in his sketchbooks onto one canvas, relying on their charm and shock to compensate for the lack of design. . . . The book is an emotional hodge-podge; no mood is sustained long enough to register for more than a chapter" (Stern, 1961, p. 50). The *New Yorker* found Heller's techniques symptomatic of a childish mind, one who "wallows in his own laughter and finally drowns in it. What remains is a debris of sour jokes, stage anger, dirty words, synthetic looniness, and the sort of antic behavior . . . children fall into when they know they are losing our attention" (Balliett, 1961, p. 247). Despite its treatment by the critics, *Catch-22* acquired many staunch supporters, particularly in the colleges, where the novel became the object of cult study.[1] By 1967 its popularity, especially in academic circles, was so great that Jan Solomon could write: "Arrived, admired and analyzed, *Catch-22* is now something of an institution; there are no more comments on its formlessness. The novel has been accepted as some sort of gifted example of what in literature must be thought to approximate the drip-and-smear school of modern painting" (1967, p. 47). The tenor of Solomon's article, like that of the spate of criticism on *Catch-22* that has come out in the last five years, is that the novel is not in fact formless, that its madness is under tight control (most of the time, that is), and that the principles of its shape yield to analysis. All this is quite correct. The problem with many of the analyses of this work (a few of which we shall be discussing in some detail later on) is that they concern themselves with Heller's techniques in isolation from the ends for which he developed and used them. As a result we have tended to see *Catch-22* as a queer, surrealistic sort of represented action, queer in that Heller seems to pay little attention to temporal sequence and naturalistic probability, perhaps doubly queer in that Heller will frequently hold whatever narrative lines we can follow in abeyance without having considerations of suspense in mind. These oddnesses in Heller's novel become more readily understandable when *Catch-22* is seen in relation to the tradition of the rhetorical novel.

How not to tell the story

The main story line of *Catch-22*, stripped of its connection with the other structural and textural elements of the novel, is surprisingly simple. The hero, Yossarian, is a bombardier in the Army Air Corps during World War II who competently but unenthusiastically flies his assigned bombing raids until the gruesome death in his plane of a young radio-gunner named Snowden makes him desperate to stay on the ground. The main conflict with Yossarian's desires is generated by his group commander, Colonel Cathcart, who, in order to bring himself to the attention of his superiors and become General Cathcart, refuses to allow the fliers who have served the required tour of duty to go home and instead raises the number of missions the men in *his* group must serve to incredible figures. Finally, Yossarian simply refuses to go up in his plane again, and Cathcart, unwilling to dramatize in a court-martial how he had exceeded his orders and driven his men to rebellion, offers to send Yossarian home if only he will undertake public relations work for Cathcart and the Army when he gets back to the States. Yossarian does not want to be court-martialed, but neither does he want to sell out and praise publicly the organization he loathes with all his being; in the novel's last chapter he learns that his former roommate Orr, thought to have been shot down and killed, had been able to paddle his life raft from the Mediterranean all the way to Sweden. Yossarian takes this cue and deserts, hoping to join Orr away from bombing

missions and Cathcarts, in that Scandinavian oasis where life is
sweet and the women willing.

It would not have been difficult to tell such a story directly, if
that had been Heller's intention, but Heller is so far from wanting
to tell it that he keeps this narrative line from coming into focus
until the last pages of the novel. Instead, the scene is taken over
with a host of characters and a skein of subordinate story lines,
while the temporal sequence is so jumbled—far more so than V.'s
—that only elaborate notes and an excellent memory can piece it
back into order.

The first chapter typifies Heller's method of obscuring the main
narrative line of his novel. During this chapter we learn that our
hero's name is Yossarian and that he is a captain in the Air Corps,
but as exposition for the main narrative line as described above
that doesn't come to much. In fact the term "narrative" itself, im-
plying a chain of events connected by cause and effect, seems to
be thoroughly irrelevant here. What we have is not a narrative in
that sense at all but a sequence of apparently unconnected comic
turns—involving the Texan, Yossarian's ambiguous liver ailment,
a fire in the hospital, the soldier in white, Yossarian's adventures
in mail censorship, a visit from the chaplain, a discussion of the
dying colonel attended by the huge string of specialists (including
a cetologist drafted into the Medical Corps by mistake who tries
to discuss *Moby Dick* with his patient)—comic turns allied to
one another only by the consistency of their absurd tone. The
temporal sequence is either jumbled within the chapter or left
deliberately vague; not even point of view is consistent: some of
the "bits" are narrated using Yossarian as a third-person reflector,
but others seem to take place outside his ken. The unity of tone
is, in a sense, all the reader gets in the way of structure during
the early chapters of the novel; we know who the hero is, and we
are witness to a good many happenings—all equally significant or
insignificant, depending on one's point of view—but there is
nothing that could reasonably be called a plot. Early on we know
what is troubling Yossarian (they're trying to kill him), but we
are not allowed to develop any sense of what we want for him,
much less anything in the way of discrete expectations regarding
his fate. Though Heller will later (in his own good time) develop
a main narrative line which would seem to lend itself to treatment
as a serious action, we are allowed no inkling of this for quite a
while. We are instead forced to structure the novel paratactically:

the coherence of the events is a matter of thematic repetition. The sequence of "bits," related to one another in nothing save their absurdity, forces us to find the structuring principle in rhetorical statement rather than (as in represented actions) in plot, to generalize a thesis about the absurdity of the world. In the chapters following the first one, the world expands from a military hospital to a wide-angle view of the war, but the sequence of bits continues unaltered, so that Heller gradually convinces us of the absurdity of the war. By a process of induction, of successive approximations, we little by little come to understand Heller's thesis. And it is only after the rhetorical structure of the novel is firmly established, after we have begun to react to each incident as an exemplum and are in no danger of grafting the alien notion of plot onto *Catch-22*, that Heller can bring up the important elements of the main narrative line.

Heller's moral vision

Throughout the first chapter of *Catch-22*, Yossarian wears motley, censoring letters in various arbitrary ways, malingering in the hospital with a fictitious liver complaint, playing practical jokes on the Texan and the chaplain. We are even encouraged to think him thoroughly mad, for in his dialogue with the chaplain he shows the crackpot's conviction that only he is sane while the rest of the world is out of its mind. And, as we soon find out, he may very well be right. For the world outside the hospital is at war, which inverts sane values; in war, as the narrator points out, "men went mad and were rewarded with medals. All over the world, boys on every side of the bomb line were laying down their lives for what they had been told was their country, and no one seemed to mind, least of all the boys" (1961, p. 16). To a man committed to his own survival, such a world is indeed absurd, even insane, while he himself will appear insane to those who believe in the war. Yossarian's idealistic friend Clevinger, who is forever getting people into chop-logic arguments, considers him crazy:

> "I'm not joking," Clevinger persisted.
> "They're trying to kill me," Yossarian told him calmly.
> "No one's trying to kill you," Clevinger cried.
> "Then why are they shooting at me?" Yossarian asked.
> "They're shooting at *everyone*," Clevinger answered.
> "They're trying to kill everyone."

"And what difference does that make?" (Heller, 1961, p. 16).

Even Dr. Stubbs—the only reasonably humane physician we meet—considers Yossarian insane, though with a difference:

"That crazy bastard."
"He's not so crazy," Dunbar said. "He swears he's not going to fly to Bologna."
"That's just what I mean," Dr. Stubbs answered. "That crazy bastard may be the only sane one left" (1961, p. 109).

Heller undoubtedly runs some risk in presenting his hero as a malingerer, a goof-off, and a philosophical coward, especially since the war against which we see him operating is not an immoral mess like the recent one in Indochina, nor a series of futile and bloody campaigns like Korea, but rather the Last Great War for Humanity, World War II. Heller succeeds by manipulating our sense of perspective: we are never allowed to view the war as a contest of ideologies, as democracy versus fascism, or the free world versus the master race, nor are we allowed to view it even in conventionally nationalistic terms. The author makes it quite clear that the men in Colonel Cathcart's group who fall in battle are sacrificed to nothing higher than Cathcart's ambition.

Even Cathcart, Yossarian's main antagonist, is never seen as a thoroughly worthy villain. Like many of the higher officers, Cathcart is simply a ridiculous stooge, "daring in the administrative stratagems he employed to bring himself to the attention of his superiors and craven in his concern that his schemes might all backfire" (1961, p. 185). Complacent that at thirty-six he is already a full colonel, and dejected that at thirty-six he is still merely a colonel, he is a slave to the army's hierarchical chain of command. It is the system as a whole, rather than his character, that has thus made him what he is, so that we are forced to blame it rather than him. And yet he is capable of sending men up in planes to be shot and killed who were long overdue for rotation back to the States and safety.

Thus the alternatives which face a man in Yossarian's position are few. One can be a knave like Colonel Cathcart or his sarcastic subordinate, Lieutenant-Colonel Korn, at once a pillar and a victim of the army's death-mills, dehumanized—robbed of one's soul—by the motives and responsibilities of command. Or one can be a fool, like Clevinger or Nately, going up on sortie after sortie until finally, inevitably, one simply does not come back; one is dehumanized this way, too, for "the spirit gone, man is garbage" (1961, p. 438). Between the upper and the nether mill-stones, there is no way to avoid becoming soulless garbage except by getting out; Yossarian's eventual desertion thus becomes the only meaningful and sane form of heroism Heller's world allows.

We cannot, of course, understand all this at the beginning of the novel. Nor are we meant to. Heller first shows us the world of the war as absurd and insane, ridiculous in its queer perversions of normal logic and values. It is only after we have begun to take for granted this apparently comic universe that Heller starts to deepen the mood. Gradually we are shown death, first the deaths of men we have never seen, later the deaths of men we have become acquainted with—Yossarian's friends—and in grimmer and gorier detail. Slowly but inexorably Heller reveals the skull beneath the grinning face of the war, so that what we finally come out with—the thesis that governs Heller's fable—is that beneath the absurdity and insanity of war lies the grim reality of death and dehumanization.

"I see everything twice!"

The method of "successive approximations" by which we come to understand first the absurdity of the universe, then the insanity of war, and finally the horror beneath the surface depends on a technique peculiar to *Catch-22*. Instead of going from incident to new incident, with each successive event darker in tone than the last (the essential technique in, say, Mordecai Richler's *Cocksure*), incidents and situations are repeated, frequently with few factual changes, but with detail added to bring out the grotesque horror that underlies their absurd comedy. The characters and events remain what they were, but more is revealed about them. According to James M. Mellard, the first time through we *see*; later, as the experience is repeated, we *understand*: "Because it raises questions that must be answered, . . . Heller's essentially lyrical method forces the recurring images to accumulate meanings until their full significance, their essence, is finally perceived" (1968, p. 31). It is not, as James L. McDonald thinks (in an article strikingly similar to Mellard's in other respects), simply a matter of Heller manipulating "the characters, events, and situations into elaborate parallels which," through their bumping about together in our minds, help to "illustrate the novel's central themes" (1968, p. 177). There is order and pattern to the way in which Heller manages his repetitive structure.

One simple and relatively unimportant example of this pattern is the "soldier in white," who appears three times in the course of the novel. The first time is in the initial chapter, where he appears, swathed in bandages, with an intravenous input and a catheter output whose bottles are periodically switched. Nurse Cramer takes his temperature, finds that he is dead, and Yossarian and Dunbar accuse the bigoted Texan, jokingly, of having murdered him on account of his race. The second time he shows up is during a repetition of the very same hospital scene with which the novel began. (One can tell that it is the same only by noting that the number of missions Yossarian has to fly—forty-five—is unchanged. The number of missions Cathcart has set for the group is virtually the only "calendar" we are allowed in the book.) This time, though, Dunbar and Yossarian are moved almost to rage by the soldier in white's presence and by the orderly, efficient, and thoroughly nonsensical care he receives. Dunbar frantically asks the Texan whether he perceives any kind of life behind the bandages, while Yossarian gets angry at Nurse Cramer for her grotesque solicitude:

> "How the hell do you know he's even in there?" he asked her.
> "Don't you dare talk to me that way!" she replied indignantly.
> "Well, how do you? You don't even know it it's really him."
> "Who?"
> "Whoever's supposed to be in all those bandages. You might really be weeping for somebody else. How do you know he's even alive?"
>
> "Maybe there's no one inside," Dunbar suggested helpfully. "Maybe they just sent the bandages here for a joke."
> She stepped away from Dunbar in alarm. "You're crazy," she cried, glancing around imploringly. "You're both crazy."
>
> "I wonder what he did to deserve it," the warrant officer with malaria and a mosquito bite on his ass lamented after

Nurse Cramer had read her thermometer and discovered that the soldier in white was dead.

"He went to war," the fighter pilot with the golden mustache surmised.

"We all went to war," Dunbar countered.

"That's what I mean . . ." (1961, pp. 168–69).

Here the soldier in white is connected up with the war and his lack of human identity in such a way as to associate the war with dehumanization. The scene is still comic, though in a much grimmer way than before, for there are ominous overtones to the last colloquy, foreshadowing the harvest of corpses that is still to come.

The last time the soldier in white appears (much later—Cathcart now wants seventy missions) there is nearly a riot in the hospital. Dunbar begins screaming eerily, "He's back! He's back!" until the fever-crazed inmates begin to think that some disaster has struck the hospital. Dunbar starts to believe—as before he had jokingly said—that there *is* no one inside the bandages, that the doctors sent the phony patient into the ward in order to mock the airmen's situation. As the panic spreads, the soldier in white begins to take on the tenor of a conspiracy of the doctors against the patients[2] similar to that of the top brass against the ordinary crewmen and officers like Yossarian and his friends:

"They've stolen him away!" Dunbar shouted . . . . "They just took him away and left those bandages there."

"Why should they do that?"

"Why do they do anything?"

"Did anyone see him?" Dunbar demanded with sneering fervor.

"You saw him, didn't you?" Yossarian said to Nurse Duckett. "Tell Dunbar there's someone inside."

"Lieutenant Schmulker is inside," Nurse Duckett said. "He's burned all over."

"Did she see him?"

"You saw him, didn't you?"

"The doctor who bandaged him saw him."

"Go get him, will you? Which doctor was it?"

Nurse Duckett reacted to the question with a startled gasp.

"The doctor isn't even here!" she exclaimed. "The patient
was brought to us that way from a field hospital."
"You see?" cried Nurse Cramer. "There's no one inside!"
(1961, pp. 358–59).

And it is immediately after this incident that Dunbar, like the
soldier in white, is "disappeared," lost to sight, never found.
Another relatively minor character who is developed in this
way is Aarfy—Captain Aardvark—who seems to be merely an
extremely conventional ex-fraternity boy who has never quite
grown up. His jovial confusion—" 'I don't think we're at the target yet. Are we?' "—tends to place him in our good books: he is
not manic, like Clevinger, so perhaps he is, like Dunbar, one of
the finest, least dedicated men we know. But during the investigation of Yossarian's conduct at the bombing of the bridge at
Ferrara, where as lead bombardier he took the entire squadron
past the target twice, getting the bridge the second time but killing Kraft and his crew, a sour note is added to Aarfy's thought-
less incompetence: the reason Yossarian was unable to get the
bridge the first time around, he says, is that " 'I didn't have
enough time. My navigator wasn't sure he had the right city' "
(1961, p. 137).

Almost immediately afterwards, Aarfy's thoughtlessness contributes to a nightmarish scene. In the second mission over
Bologna, Yossarian's squadron runs into a ferocious barrage of
antiaircraft fire. Having dropped his bombs on the ammunition
dump, Yossarian looks up to find Aarfy in the bombardier's nose
bubble, blocking his escape route in case the plane is hit by antiaircraft fire. So Yossarian is stuck with trying to do two things at
once: get Aarfy out of the nose back to his station in the body of
the plane, and guide McWatt out of range of the flak. Frantically
Yossarian screams orders to McWatt, while at the same time he
shouts at Aarfy and pummels him with his fists: all the while
Yossarian is bellowing at Aarfy his only response is " 'I can't hear
you, you'll have to speak louder.' " And Yossarian's fists have as
little effect as his words; Aarfy is immovable:

> Punching Aarfy was like sinking his fists into a limp
> sack of inflated rubber. There was no resistance, no
> response at all from the soft, insensitive mass, and after a
> while Yossarian's spirit died and his arms dropped help-
> lessly with exhaustion. He was overcome with a humiliating

feeling of impotence and was ready to weep in self-pity (1961, p. 148).

This scene is replayed once more, later in the novel, when after Yossarian has dropped his bombs on Parma, Aarfy misnavigates the plane over the strongly defended seaport of Leghorn. Another barrage of flak comes up at them and Yossarian is wounded by one of the shots:

"I lost my balls! Aarfy, I lost my balls!" Aarfy didn't hear, and Yossarian bent forward and tugged at his arm. "Aarfy, help me," he pleaded, almost weeping. "I'm hit! I'm hit!"
Aarfy turned slowly with a bland, quizzical grin. "What?" "I'm hit, Aarfy! Help me!"
Aarfy grinned again and shrugged amiably. "I can't hear you," he said.
"Can't you see me?" Yossarian cried incredulously, and he pointed to the deepening pool of blood he felt splashing down all around him and spreading out underneath. "I'm wounded! Help me, for God's sake! Aarfy, help me!"
"I still can't hear you," Aarfy complained tolerantly. . . . "What did you say?" (1961, p. 284).

Aarfy is not actually deaf, but he might as well be. What he has become by this point in the novel is actually much worse: a soulless *golem* insensitive to the most immediate human considerations, only outwardly human and sociable, his fraternity-boy grin fixed to his face like a mask.

The other side of Aarfy is cued by his hilariously bourgeois attitudes toward sex; he is a consummate killjoy. One of the girls Yossarian's squadron picks up in Rome is a slattern in an orange satin blouse whose prized possession is a ring whose bezel is a pornographic cameo. Aarfy gets the girl, but refuses " 'to take advantage of a sweet kid like that.' " At which Yossarian is properly livid:

"Who said anything about taking advantage of her?" Yossarian railed at him in amazement. "All she wanted to do was get in bed with someone. That's the only thing she kept talking about all night long."
"That's because she was a little mixed up," Aarfy explained. "But I gave her a little talking to and really put

some sense into her. . . . I know what kind of girls to prod
and what kind of girls not to prod, and I never prod any
nice girls. This one was a sweet kid. You could see her
family had money. Why, I even got her to throw that ring
of hers away right out the car window" (1961, pp. 155–56).

There is low comedy in this, as in Aarfy's repeated asseverations
that never in his life has he paid for sex. But after the scene recounted above we find a streak of cruelty—of which Aarfy, of
course, is totally unconscious—within his fraternity-produced
system of values. When Nately hires his own whore and her two
girl friends, Aarfy declines to help him by taking one of the girl
friends off Nately's hands (" 'Nobody has to pay for it for good
old Aarfy. I can get all I want any time I want it.' "), but he has
another suggestion:

> "Why don't we keep the three of them here until after the
> curfew and then threaten to push them out into the street
> to be arrested unless they give us all their money. We can
> even threaten to push them out the window. . . . Gee whiz,"
> he defended himself querulously. "Back in school we were
> always doing things like that. I remember one day we
> tricked these two dumb highschool girls from town into
> the fraternity house and made them put out for all the fel-
> lows who wanted them by threatening to call up their parents
> and say they were putting out for us. We kept them trapped
> in bed there for more than ten hours. We even smacked
> their faces a little when they started to complain. Then we
> took away their nickels and dimes and chewing gum and
> threw them out. Boy, we used to have fun in that fraternity
> house" (1961, pp. 235–36).

The two sides of Aarfy's nature—the bourgeois fraternity
boy given to cruel but childish acts of mischief, and the insensate,
inconscient golem—merge in his final appearance at the climax
of Yossarian's nightmare odyssey through the dark Roman
streets. Searching for sanity where it is not to be found, Yossarian
rushes back to the officers' quarters looking for Michaela, the
homely farm girl who serves as maid in the apartment building:

> She had sallow skin and myopic eyes, and none of the men
> had ever slept with her because none of the men had ever
> wanted to, none but Aarfy, who had raped her once that
> same evening and had then held her prisoner in a clothes

closet for almost two hours with his hand over her mouth until the civilian curfew sirens sounded and it was unlawful for her to be outside.

Then he threw her out the window. Her dead body was still lying on the pavement (1961, p. 408).

Yossarian is horrified at what Aarfy has done, but Aarfy himself shows no remorse. He had to kill her, after all: you couldn't let her go around saying bad things about airmen, could you? And when Yossarian points to her dead body on the street, Aarfy explains that " 'she has no right to be there. . . . It's after curfew' " (1961, p. 409). Yossarian is overjoyed when he hears police sirens coming closer: perhaps there is justice in the world after all, perhaps the irresponsible eventually have to face up to the evils they cause. The sirens close in, and the military police run up the stairs, but it is Yossarian, not Aarfy, that they arrest—for being in Rome without a pass.

Aarfy is Heller's most literal representation of the kind of dehumanization that the war works on men *while they are still alive*. In the course of the novel, he is revealed as a soulless monster, acting out his cruel fantasies and retreating into the irresponsibilities of his frat-boy smile, knowing that amid the enormities of the war, while thousands of soldiers and civilians are being killed every day, his own tiny murder is but a peccadillo of no importance at all. It is certainly, in the eyes of the men of war, a far more venial crime than Yossarian's, for the latter is a breach of army discipline, a sin against the system, while murder is, after all, the army's business.

It is important to note that the change in Aarfy from the beginning of *Catch-22* to its end does not involve any alteration of his character. We are not left, in other words, with the comforting belief that before he went to war Aarfy was a good man and that he became a rapist and a murderer under the pressure of combat. On the contrary, his character is not so much altered as progressively revealed; the only change, if one can call it that, is that his increased opportunities for noxious mischief lend greater plausibility to that revelation.

A more important character, whose function and development are similar to Aarfy's, is Milo Minderbinder, pilot and war-profiteer. Like Aarfy, he is introduced casually, with a brief reference to the fact that the mess hall runs smoothly in his absence; we take Milo, from the description of Yossarian's gourmet dinner,

to be simply one whiz of a mess officer. We soon find out that
Milo is also an entrepreneur of the old school, evidenced when
he trades McWatt's yellow bedsheet for a package of pitted dates
and somehow winds up with both the dates and the bedsheet;
Milo's explanation is in a great American tradition:

> "He stole the whole bedsheet and I got it back with the
> package of pitted dates you invested. That's why the quarter
> of the bedsheet is yours. You made a handsome return on
> your investment, particularly since you've gotten back every
> pitted date you gave me. . . . The remaining quarter of the
> bedsheet I've set aside for myself as a reward for my enter-
> prise, work, and initiative. It's not for myself, you under-
> stand, but for the syndicate. That's something you might
> do with half the bedsheet. You can leave it in the syndicate
> and watch it grow" (1961, p. 65).

And it does grow—the syndicate, not the half-bedsheet. Milo sets
up an international trading cartel: each bomber group in all the
armies (except the Russians—Milo won't trade with Communists)
lends him a single plane to deliver groceries in, and Milo uses the
huge fleet to cruise about the Mediterranean snapping up bar-
gains, buying low and selling high, and making an enormous
profit for himself.

Without seeming to. Yossarian is puzzled by the fact that Milo
buys eggs in Malta for seven cents apiece and sells them to the
mess halls in Pianosa for only five cents. Yossarian—and we
readers—have been wondering about that since page 66, but it is
not explained for another one hundred sixty pages how he manages to do it—or why. At last Yossarian asks him why:

> "I do it to make a profit."
> "But how can you make a profit? You lose two cents an
> egg."
> "But I make a profit of three and a quarter cents an egg by
> selling them for four and a quarter cents an egg to the people
> in Malta I buy them from for seven cents an egg. Of course,
> I don't make the profit. The syndicate makes the profit.
> And everybody has a share."
> ". . . Why don't you sell the eggs directly to you and
> eliminate the people you buy them from?"
> "Because I'm the people I buy them from," Milo ex-
> plained. "I make a profit of three and a quarter cents apiece
> when I sell them to me and a profit of two and three quarter
> cents apiece when I buy them back from me. That's a total

profit of six cents an egg. I lose only two cents an egg when I sell them to the mess halls at five cents apiece, and that's how I can make a profit buying eggs for seven cents apiece and selling them for five cents apiece. I pay only one cent apiece at the hen when I buy them in Sicily" (1961, pp. 226–27).

And everybody has a share. Milo's hilarious business antics reach some sort of apogee when he buys the entire Egyptian cotton crop just for the experience of cornering a market, and too late finds out that there is no market at all for cotton, much less for a year's crop.

It is around this point that the darker side of Milo's business ventures starts to come out. In order to raise some cash for his syndicate operations, he goes into the war business himself, contracting with the Americans to bomb a highway bridge at Orvieto and with the Germans to defend the self-same bridge, all at cost plus six percent, with a merit bonus of a thousand dollars for every plane shot down: since both armies are already present to do the fighting, "in the end Milo realized a fantastic profit from both halves of his project for doing nothing more than signing his name twice" (1961, p. 250). The arrangement was wonderful for everyone—everyone, that is, except a flyer named Mudd, who had no sooner arrived at Yossarian's squadron than he was packed aboard a plane, sent over Orvieto, and shot down with the rest of the crew. Milo denies all responsibility for his death, over Yossarian's furious protests; after all, Milo claims, " 'if I can persuade the Germans to pay me a thousand dollars for every plane they shoot down, why shouldn't I take it?' " (1961, p. 251). Yossarian pleads with Milo: there is a war on; Milo is dealing with the enemy; people are dying all around them. But for Milo the Germans are *not* the enemy—the Germans are members in good standing of Milo's cartel; the real enemy, for Milo, is the people who don't pay their bills to the syndicate on time. And in the insane logic of *Catch-22*, Milo's position is irrefutable.

In an effort to recoup his losses on the Egyptian cotton corner, Milo tries a variation on his Orvieto arrangement:

One night, after a sumptuous evening meal, all Milo's fighters and bombers took off, joined in formation directly overhead and began dropping bombs on the group. He had landed another contract with the Germans, this time to bomb his own outfit. . . . Wounded soon lay screaming everywhere.

A cluster of fragmentation bombs exploded in the yard
of the officer's club and punched jagged holes in the side of
the building and in the bellies and backs of a row of lieu-
tenants and captains standing at the bar. They doubled over
in agony and dropped. . . .
. . . "Milo, this is Alvin Brown. I've finished dropping my
bombs. What should I do now?"
"Strafe," said Milo.
"*Strafe?*" Alvin Brown was shocked.
"We have no choice," Milo informed him resignedly.
"It's in the contract" (1961, pp. 252–53).

And both the outcry in the press and the congressional investigation are defused when it is learned what a tremendous profit the
entire venture had brought in. And everybody has a share. So
Milo goes on and on, more prestigious than ever, buying Egyptian cotton and trying to sell it to the mess halls, covered with
chocolate, as a confection.

A revealing conversation takes place shortly thereafter, as
Milo observes of the tree he has climbed to be with Yossarian,
who is watching Snowden's funeral from a branch, " 'This is a
pretty good tree.' 'It's the tree of life,' Yossarian answered, . . .
'and of the knowledge of good and evil, too.' Milo squinted
closely at the bark and branches. 'No, it isn't,' he replied. 'It's a
chestnut tree. I ought to know. I sell chestnuts' " (1961, p. 257).
This is emblematic of Milo's outlook on life: the knowledge of
good and evil might as well not exist. Milo, like Aarfy, is one
of the irresponsibles whose values produce the needless cruelty of
war. Neither is a villain in the usual sense of the word; neither
actively wills the suffering and death he causes. They are simply
moral imbeciles, unconscious of any ethical dimension to their
actions. Furthermore, both of them, despite their military dress,
represent in exaggerated form civilian attitudes typical of busi-
nessmen and young middle-class climbers,[3] and as such they
extend the absurdity and horror of *Catch-22* well beyond the war
which is its ostensible subject.

We are thus allowed to view Heller's thesis in potentially
broader terms than the novel as a whole develops. Milo's cartel is
not simply American: M & M Enterprises includes all of Europe
as well. And we are explicitly told that the end of the war will not
mean the end for Milo. M & M Enterprises, with Milo at its head,
will go on, absorbing or merging with its competitors (like ex-

Pfc. Wintergreen's rival operation), and staffed with former officers, including the abominable Cathcart, whose executive talents
insure their welcome. The world of Catch-22, in other words, will
be brought back home, so that returning to the States will in
reality be no escape. These peripheral matters become crucial
when Heller is arranging his denouement.

Milo's last appearance, like Aarfy's, comes in the "Eternal
City" chapter, in which all the varieties of human misery are
served up to us at once. Yossarian is looking for Nately's whore's
kid sister, the little girl who represents for him the injured innocent of the world. Yossarian goes to Milo, who has power everywhere, and promises to become a good team-player again, to
stop rocking the boat by embarrassing Colonel Cathcart with his
refusal to fly more missions—if only Milo will use his clout to
help him find the girl. They drive to the police station, where
Milo reveals Yossarian's problem. The police chief would like
to help, he says, but that night he has no manpower: " 'Tonight
all my men are busy trying to break up the traffic in illegal tobacco.' " All at once Milo forgets about Yossarian and the kid
sister while the profit motive wells up in him. As he thinks about
the money he can make smuggling tobacco, he turns into a
fevered automaton, dehumanized himself just as his arrange-
ments with the Germans had dehumanized Mudd and the other
fallen airmen:

> "Illegal tobacco," Milo explained to him with a look of
> epileptic lust, struggling doggedly to get by. "Let me go.
> I've got to smuggle illegal tobacco."
> "Stay here and help me find her," pleaded Yossarian.
> "You can smuggle illegal tobacco tomorrow."
> But Milo was deaf and kept pushing forward, nonviolently
> but irresistibly, sweating, his eyes, as though he were in the
> grip of a blind fixation, burning feverishly, and his twitching
> mouth slavering. He moaned calmly as though in remote,
> instinctive distress and kept repeating, "Illegal tobacco,
> illegal tobacco" (1961, pp. 401–2).

The fascinating thing about both Milo and Aarfy is that, horrifying as they are, they are treated comically throughout Catch-22.
Perhaps this is possible because they are mechanical versions of
men—and the mechanical taking over the human is, according to
Bergson, the root source of all humor. But at the same time they
represent the spiritual death at the heart of Heller's absurd uni-

verse. Heller's economy is such, indeed, that his characters are not a compound of funny and of horrible traits; rather the same characteristic—their dehumanization, their spiritual death—make Aarfy and Milo both comic and horrifying at once.[4]

The soldier in white, Aarfy, Milo: three symbolic characters whose development contributes not only to the texture of *Catch-22* but to its structure as well. Indeed, the opposition is a false one, because in this particular novel structure and texture are one. The structure is a peculiar one, with an element of strict order and an element of apparent randomness. The novel consists of a skein of interweaving threads each developing a single character, symbol, or recurrent action. Within each thread a strict order among the episodes is observed, an order of more and more explicit revelation of the horror inherent in the comic. In symbolic terms, x_1 must precede x_2, x_2 must precede x_3, and so on; and the same would be true of the sequence y_1, y_2, y_3 . . . y_n, and all the other sequences. But the interweaving of the threads is not determined by any such mechanical law: if y_1 immediately follows x_1 early in the novel, there is no guarantee that y_2 will immediately follow x_2: other episodes may be interposed between them, or they may even come in opposite order; furthermore, each thread may have a different number of total episodes, may begin much earlier or much later than other threads. This apparent randomness accounts for the fact that each episode comes upon us as a surprise—there is no predicting when Aarfy, Milo, Hungry Joe will pop up in our field of vision. It is also responsible in large part for the reviewers' accusations that *Catch-22* was the fictional equivalent of an action painting. But the randomness is only apparent: while there is no *mechanical* order observed among the various threads, the skein maintains a remarkable consistency of tone for all its myriad inconsistencies: the degree of darkening of tone alters smoothly, accelerating as we reach the climax in "The Eternal City" and "Snowden." It may well be possible to switch the order of adjacent chapters with little noticeable effect; as the distance between the switched chapters is increased, however, the effect becomes progressively more destructive to the novel's power.

The two most important components of the skein have not been discussed in detail as yet; their especial importance is in the high degree of integration with the main narrative line. Unlike the three discussed earlier, neither is a character: one is a symbol, the other a recurrent action.

Only one catch

The title of Heller's novel is *Catch-22*, and that little phrase, like the characters we have already discussed, is developed through incremental repetitions until its full meaning is understood. The first reference, in Heller's usual practice, tells us little. As Yossarian is censoring letters in the hospital, the narrator reminds us—almost as though it were something that *we* had forgotten —that "Catch-22 required that each censored letter bear the censoring officer's name" (1961, p. 8). Except for the fact of the title and epigraph, we should hardly notice the reference to Catch-22: perhaps it is some clause in the army's regulations. We first begin to understand the elusive power of Catch-22 at the second reference, when Yossarian comes to Doc Daneeka asking to be grounded for medical reasons: he is crazy, he says, and therefore exempt from combat duty. But Doc Daneeka isn't having any— you can't, after all, let crazy people decide whether they're crazy or not—so Yossarian tries a different tack, concentrating on his equally mad tentmate Orr:

> "Is Orr crazy?"
> "He sure is," Doc Daneeka said.
> "Can you ground him?"
> "I sure can. But first he has to ask me. That's part of the rule."
> "Then why doesn't he ask you to?"
> "Because he's crazy," Doc Daneeka said.. "He has to be crazy to keep flying combat missions after all the close calls he's had. Sure, I can ground Orr. But first he has to ask me to."
> "That's all he has to do to be grounded?"
> "That's all. Let him ask me."
> "And then you can ground him?" Yossarian asked.
> "No. Then I can't ground him."
> "You mean there's a catch?"
> "Sure there's a catch," Doc Daneeka replied. "Catch-22. Anyone who wants to get out of combat duty isn't really crazy" (1961, p. 45).

Some catch, that Catch-22. Orr would have to be crazy to fly another bombing mission, and since he is crazy he doesn't have to. But if he refuses, he is showing concern for his own survival, characteristic of a rational mentality; therefore he is sane, and has to fly. Catch-22 is one of those perverse paradoxes of two-valued logic that delighted Lewis Carroll;[5] it becomes, at this point, symbolic of the absurdity of wartime regulations and of the general insanity of the war Heller's characters are fighting.

We lose sight of Catch-22 for a while, but when Heller picks it up once more a touch of cruelty has been added to its absurdity. The next reference is during Captain Black's Glorious Loyalty Oath Crusade, a project anachronistically reminiscent of the McCarthy era. Black has convinced Milo not to let the men eat until they sign an oath pledging their loyalty to the United States government, all the men except Major Major Major Major, whom Black will not allow to sign loyalty oaths—or eat—because he considers him a Communist:

> "What makes you so sure Major Major is a Communist?"
> "You never heard him denying it until we began accusing him, did you? And you don't see him signing any of our loyalty oaths."
> "You aren't letting him sign any."
> "Of course not," Captain Black explained. "That would defeat the whole purpose of our crusade" (1961, p. 113).

And Captain Black's logic in starving Major Major is above reproach: as he himself says, " 'It's just like Catch-22. Don't you get it? You're not against Catch-22, are you?' " Catch-22 is thus extended to cover the insane persecutions—the witch hunts—by which good men are ruined.

But we do not find out the whole truth about Catch-22 until the "Eternal City" chapter, when Yossarian, looking for Nately's whore's kid sister at the bordello where she and Nately's whore lived, finds the place empty except for an old cleaning woman, who tells Yossarian that the girls have all been chased into the street:

> "Chased away by who? Who did it?"
> "The mean tall soldiers with the hard white hats and clubs. And by our *carabinieri*. They came with their clubs and chased them away. They would not even let them take their coats. The poor things. They just chased them away into the cold. . . ."
> "There must have been a reason," Yossarian persisted,

pounding his fist into his hand. "They couldn't just barge
in here and chase everyone out."
    "No reason," wailed the old woman. "No reason."
    "What right did they have?"
    "Catch-22."
    "*What*?" Yossarian froze in his tracks with fear and alarm
and felt his whole body begin to tingle. "*What* did you say?"
    "Catch-22," the old woman repeated, rocking her head
up and down. "Catch-22 says they have a right to do anything we can't stop them from doing. . . . All they kept
saying was 'Catch-22, Catch-22.' What does it mean,
Catch-22? What is Catch-22?"
    "Didn't they show it to you?" Yossarian demanded,
stamping about in anger and distress. "Didn't you even
make them read it?"
    "They don't have to show us Catch-22," the old woman
answered. "The law says they don't have to."
    "What law says they don't have to?"
    "Catch-22" (1961, p. 398).

Catch-22 is thus no longer merely a symbol for the absurdity of
war. While it is no less insane in its workings than before,
Catch-22 has come to include the horror of naked power un-
chained, the evils that man inflicts on his fellow man in the name
of irresponsible authority. And as its essence is inexorably revealed we come to understand the thesis of Heller's novel, that
the insanity, the absurdity, the perverse logic of war is only a
surface phenomenon, and that beneath that surface lies the
horror of death and dehumanization.

But this is not the last reference to Catch-22. It is mentioned
just once more, as the "catch" behind Colonel Cathcart's offer to
send Yossarian home. Catch-22 dictates Yossarian's part of the
bargain: in exchange for release from combat duty and rotation
back to the States, Lieutenant-Colonel Korn tells Yossarian that
he has to " 'like us. Join us. Be our pal. . . . Become one of the
boys' " (1961, p. 416). There, in Cathcart's sunlit office, away
from the horrors of the dark Roman streets, it would seem easy to
forget about what has just happened, to join forces with the
servants and victims of Catch-22, which kills spiritually what it
does not deprive of physical life. And Yossarian is indeed
tempted: Heller cites Yossarian's close shave when he is offered
the opportunity to sell out as an indication of his vital humanity
(1962, p. 23). But he eventually decides not to accept the spiritual

death which the deal involves: Yossarian's desertion to Sweden is a decision to put himself, if possible, beyond the reach of Catch-22.

Snowden's death

In chapter 40 ("Catch-22"), Yossarian has tentatively accepted Cathcart's deal; at the very opening of chapter 42 ("Yossarian"), he tells Major Danby, the confused ex-college professor, that he has decided to reject it. No process of reasoning has intervened, nor has Yossarian met anyone with new ideas or new information. But Yossarian has learned something that changes his view of the deal: he—and we readers—have come to understand Snowden's secret.

Snowden is introduced early in the novel, in the question Yossarian asks everyone "that had no answer: 'Where are the Snowdens of yesteryear?' " The flip parody of François Villon hides more intensity than it seems to, for Yossarian "was ready to pursue" the corporal to whom the question is put "through all the words in the world to wring the knowledge from him if he could." But Yossarian's desperation goes almost wholly unexplained; all we can learn now is that "Snowden had been killed over Avignon when Dobbs went crazy in mid-air and seized the controls from Huple" (1961, pp. 34–35).

As the novel progresses, Snowden's death is referred to again and again, always portentously, as though its freight of meaning were too great to be discharged at once. Almost immediately after the first reference, Yossarian brings into his memory Dobbs "weeping pathetically for help," calling for first aid for the bombardier; when Yossarian radios back that he himself is all right, Dobbs keeps begging, " 'then help him, help him. . . .' And Snowden lay dying in back" (1961, p. 50). Somewhat later, when Yossarian is in the hospital, we find out something new, that Snowden had a secret which he had "spilled" to Yossarian before he had frozen to death in the back of his plane. And almost immediately thereafter Yossarian gives his version of Snowden's secret: "That was the secret Snowden had spilled to him on the mission to Avignon—they were out to get him; and Snowden had spilled it all over the back of the plane" (1961, pp. 170–71). But Yossarian has always known that everybody is out to get him: this is *not* Snowden's secret (although, in a way, it is part of it), and Snowden's death keeps intruding like an unanswered question as the book continues. We continue to find out new details: that Yossarian refuses to wear his uniform after the Avignon mission, and receives his Distinguished Flying Cross standing naked in the ranks; that it was Dobbs's incompetent flying that had caused Snowden's death; that even the cagy and coy Doc Daneeka showed "glum and profound and introverted grief . . . when Yossarian climbed down the few steps of his plane naked, in a state of utter shock, with Snowden smeared abundantly all over his bare heels and toes, knees, arms and fingers (1961, p. 255). The references to Snowden—there are more than a dozen of them—become short scenes, connecting up the details more and more coherently and still referring enigmatically to Snowden's "eternal, immutable secret" (1961, p. 339). But it is not until chapter 41 ("Snowden") that the significance of his death is fully understood.

By chapter 41 we have seen death in many forms, heard how Mudd, Kraft, Colonel Nevers and Major Duluth—all people we never meet—have been shot out of the sky; we have heard that Clevinger flew into a little white cloud, never to fly out again; we have seen Kid Sampson cut in half grotesquely by McWatt's propeller, and McWatt himself suicidally fly into a mountain; we know that Hungry Joe was found suffocated with a cat on his face and that Chief White Halfoat died of pneumonia—deaths they themselves had predicted; we have heard how Orr was lost (as we still think) and how Dunbar was "disappeared" by order of the high command; that Dobbs collided with Nately in the air and that both crews were killed. Dozens of deaths have been reported—and yet the phenomenon is still a mystery, unknown to us emotionally at least. This is thoroughly intentional on Heller's part: though he lets the weight of the numbers of the dead oppress us, he interposes his ironic point of view between us and the final vision of mortality, describing Kid Sampson's death as comic Grand Guignol, and reporting the death of Nately—the idealistic kid for whom we have been made to feel fond affection —as simply as he possibly could: "And Nately, in the other plane, was killed too" (1961, p. 369). Heller thus saves until the climactic spot in his novel the revelation of the horror of death and dehumanization, and here Yossarian's recurrent nightmare is played out in full dress.

The scene begins in the by now familiar manner: the screaming dive, the sound of antiaircraft shells exploding near the plane,

and Dobbs begging for help, which Yossarian crawls back into
the body of the plane to administer. He finds Snowden with an
enormous wound in his thigh, panics at first, then settles down
to stop the flow of blood, administer antibiotics (there is no
morphine—just aspirin and a note from Milo, whose cartel has
taken over the opiates), and bandage the wound. He sits back
at last with a sigh of relief, knowing that Snowden will survive,
when all at once he notices "a strangely colored stain seeping
through the coveralls just above the armhole of Snowden's flak
suit":

> Yossarian felt his heart stop, then pound so violently he
> found it difficult to breathe. Snowden was wounded inside
> his flak suit. Yossarian ripped open the snaps of Snowden's
> flak suit and heard himself scream wildly as Snowden's
> insides slithered down to the floor in a soggy pile and just
> kept dripping out. A chunk of flak more than three inches
> big had shot into his other side just underneath the arm and
> blasted all the way through, drawing whole mottled quarts
> of Snowden along with it through the gigantic hole in his
> ribs it made as it blasted out. Yossarian screamed a second
> time and squeezed both hands over his eyes. His teeth were
> chattering in horror. He forced himself to look again. Here
> was God's plenty, all right, he thought bitterly as he stared
> —liver, lungs, kidneys, ribs, stomach and bits of the stewed
> tomatoes Snowden had eaten that day for lunch. Yossarian
> hated stewed tomatoes and turned away dizzily and began
> to vomit, clutching his burning throat. The tail gunner
> woke up while Yossarian was vomiting, saw him, and
> fainted again. Yossarian was limp with exhaustion, pain,
> and despair when he finished. He turned back weakly to
> Snowden, whose breath had grown softer and more rapid,
> and whose face had grown paler. He wondered how in the
> world to begin to save him (1961, p. 429).

This is the reality behind the absurd business of war, and now
we know it. And yet Heller does not let out all his stops in this
scene: he continues, even here, to distract us with "bits" from
earlier sections of the novel, like the note from Milo put in place
of the morphine, "What's good for M & M Enterprises is good
for the country."[6] Phrases like "whole mottled quarts of Snowden" and "Yossarian hated stewed tomatoes" are inserted to fore-
stall the potential sense of climax. For the true climax of the
scene is to come not with the revelation of Snowden's death-

wound but with the "spilling" of his secret promised since early
in the novel. And it is with this—not the gore—that the frisson
of recognition comes, for it is here that our emotional reactions
are subordinated to, converted into the knowledge that Heller
wishes to convey:

> Yossarian was cold . . . and shivering uncontrollably. He
> felt goose pimples clacking all over him as he gazed down
> despondently at the grim secret Snowden had spilled all
> over the messy floor. It was easy to read the message in
> his entrails. Man was matter, that was Snowden's secret.
> Drop him out a window and he'll fall. Set fire to him and
> he'll burn. Bury him and he'll rot, like other kinds of
> garbage. The spirit gone, man is garbage. That was Snow-
> den's secret. Ripeness was all (1961, pp. 429–30).

The spirit gone, man is garbage. And whatever eliminates that
spirit—physical death, moral death—turns man into garbage.
Fear of the former had kept Yossarian from going up in his
plane, made him refuse to fly more missions. And it is fear of the
latter—spiritual death through moral surrender—that forces
Yossarian to reject Cathcart's deal. For it does not matter whether
one is shot to death or dehumanized through becoming a servant
of Catch-22: garbage is garbage.

Sweden and sanity

The conclusion of *Catch-22* is basically a debate, in dialogue
form, on the merits of Yossarian's decision not to accept the
colonels' deal. Yossarian is not unwilling to be sent home, but it
must be on his terms, not theirs: as he himself demands, "Let
them send me home because I flew more than fifty missions"—by
this time Yossarian has actually flown seventy—"and not because
I was stabbed by that girl, or because I've turned into such a
stubborn son of a bitch" (1961, p. 432). But that is past praying
for: if Yossarian rejects the deal and still refuses to fly more
missions, Cathcart will court-martial him on trumped-up charges,
suborning witnesses (including Aarfy) to testify against him
under the justification that getting rid of Yossarian would be
"for the good of the country." Worse still, the servants of Catch-
22 have closed their ranks, and Yossarian will no longer be able
to play off Milo against Cathcart, or ex-Pfc. Wintergreen—Milo's
competition—against the other two: Cathcart has been made a

vice-president of M & M Enterprises, which has recently merged with Wintergreen's operation. But Yossarian keeps the knowledge of Snowden's secret before his eyes:

> "Danby, must I really let them send me home?" Yossarian inquired of him seriously.
> Major Danby shrugged. "It's a way to save yourself."
> "It's a way to lose myself, Danby. You ought to know that."
> "You could have lots of things you want."
> "I don't want lots of things I want" (1961, pp. 436–37).

It is at this point that the chaplain rushes in bringing news—received God knows how—that Orr, shot down months ago over the Adriatic and never heard from since, had washed ashore in Sweden. Washed ashore, nothing, says Yossarian: Orr planned it that way; he had rehearsed for his escape to Sweden and sanity by getting shot down on every mission he flew. The news of Orr's success restores Yossarian's faith in the possibility of human survival, and he decides to escape to Sweden himself, bringing with him the innocent and defenseless girl he had unsuccessfully sought in the Eternal City—if he can find her. He takes his leave of his friends and sets out for a good place, out of reach of the long arm of Catch-22:

> "Goodbye, Yossarian," the chaplain called. "And good luck. I'll stay here and persevere, and we'll meet again when the fighting stops."
> "So long, Chaplain. Thanks, Danby."
> "How do you feel, Yossarian?"
> "Fine. No, I'm very frightened."
> "That's good," said Major Danby. "It proves you're still alive" (1961, p. 442).

The ending of *Catch-22* has been subjected to a good deal of scrutiny, and several critics—a solid majority of those who discuss it at all—find it wanting in either the philosophical or the aesthetic dimension. Occasionally this is done without much regard to internal consistency: one critic, having claimed that "the ending of *Catch-22* is an attempt to focus upon the major topic of the book itself, the question of survival," later states that "Heller's ending adds a new dimension to the novel. However it is sharply inconsistent with the bulk of material presented before the last five pages" (Pinsker, 1964–65, pp. 160, 161–62).

One does not know whether Pinsker's objection is to the novelty of the material or to the fact that it still focuses "upon the major topic of the book itself"—whether the ending is too inconsistent or too consistent. Actually I suspect that Pinsker is more troubled by the probability of the ending than with Heller's credentials as a thinker with a unified point of view, for he goes on, "The *deus ex machina* character of Orr's miraculous journey is unacceptable to modern sensibilities which demand a greater sense of 'reality' " (1964–65, p. 162). It is hard to accept this, however, as legitimate criticism, for Heller's mode of probability, which corresponds to Aristotle's category of the "possible improbable," has been fully consistent throughout the novel: to reject the ending on the grounds that we readers "demand a greater sense of 'reality'," is to reject also the soldier in white, Milo's business deals, the biographies of Chief White Halfoat and Major Major Major Major, Nately's whore's murderous peregrinations—the entire novel, in fact, to a greater or lesser extent.

A more pertinent objection is offered by Vance Ramsey, who notes what he calls a "discursive quality" about the last four chapters of the novel:

> This loss of the dramatic quality at the end of the novel points to an even deeper problem, the change in Yossarian. The first part of his story, his reaction to death and his need to disengage himself from all that threatens him, is made poignantly convincing; the last stage of his development, the decision that there is something greater than survival, is not so convincing. Yossarian's morality in saying "no" to the forces which threaten to take him over is supposed to become a morality of social involvement; he is to go to Sweden to try to do something about all of the horrors he has seen in his last night in Rome (in Whitbread, 1966, p. 117).

And Ramsey's objection is echoed in a later biographical and critical article by Richard Lehan and Jerry Patch, who declare that the author finished the novel under pressure of a deadline set by his publishers: "Heller, faced with the task of drawing together his sprawling materials, finally did so, but with an abrupt shift of gears." Lehan and Patch quote with approval Sherman Wincelberg's criticism of the denouement (*New Leader*, May 14, 1962) as putting Yossarian into "one of those soul-searching conflicts between conscience and self-interest which used to be so popular on live TV. . . . In contrast to the rest of the book's splendid contempt for such niceties, I find it a little on the square side" (Lehan and Patch, 1967, p. 243).

Had Heller initially created Yossarian as an egoist devoid of all conscience, concerned with his own survival to the exclusion of all outside claims, and then had him fly off to Sweden after profound self-examination to do social service, these criticisms would be justified. As it is, they are based on a profound misreading of Yossarian's character and Heller's intentions for him. Yossarian is indeed concerned about his own survival and with the forces that threaten it, but at the same time he is concerned for the survival of his friends, acquaintances, and mere colleagues. It is because of this that he interrogates Milo unmercifully, trying to get him to admit responsibility for the death of Mudd over Orvieto; because of this that he is willing to pursue "through all the words in the world" the answer to his riddle, "where are the Snowdens of yesteryear?"; because of this that he mourns in his own unconventional way when Orr is lost over the Adriatic; because of this that he takes his life in his hands to break the news of Nately's death to the latter's girl friend. And on the other side, there is no indication of any incredible altruism in Yossarian's escape to Sweden—barring his intention to take Nately's whore's kid sister with him. Perhaps Ramsey has been misled by Yossarian's talk of his "responsibilities": " 'I'm not running *away* from my responsibilities. I'm running *to* them,' " Yossarian declares at one point. But the context makes it clear that Yossarian's "responsibilities" add up to survival—saving his own life and soul: immediately after the above quotation, Yossarian explains: " 'There's nothing negative about running away to save my life. You know who the escapists are, don't you, Danby? Not me and Orr' " (1961, p. 440). There is indeed a change in Yossarian at the end of the novel, but it is not an inexplicable shift in character and motivation; it is rather that he knows at the end, through his understanding of Snowden's secret, that it would be as fatal for him to accept Cathcart's deal as to fly more missions, that neither is an acceptable alternative. Ramsey even seems to understand this, for he suggests that "it is possible to intellectualize [Heller's] result: if Yossarian were to accept the deal offered to him in order to survive, he might still lose his self to the system" (Whitbread, 1966, p. 117). But since Ramsey also considers the Milo Minderbinder story and other portrayals of dehumanization of the living as "excrescences" irrelevant to the main theme of the novel—ignoring half of Heller's thesis by doing so—he does not consider such a reading of *Catch-22*'s denouement "artistically convincing" (Whitbread, 1966, pp. 116–17).

It is not clear just what sort of ending would have satisfied Heller's captious critics—they themselves do not presume to suggest alternatives that would have been an improvement. It is clear that there are only a few possibilities: Heller could have killed Yossarian off,[7] or he could have had Yossarian mindlessly accept the colonels' deal, or he could have done neither, but at the same time given us the feeling somehow that, no matter what Yossarian did, he would never, never get outside the reach of Catch-22. Any of these would have provided a sense of closure by settling our curiosity about Yossarian's fate, but only the last would have provided a denouement equal in force to the one Heller actually chose; only the last would come as close as Heller's ending to providing a sense of completeness. But it would have been an impossible ending given Heller's character and views: Daniel Rosoff, for thirty-seven years an intimate friend of Heller's, informed Lehan and Patch that "Heller could not have written a different ending, could not have concluded his novel on a note of hopelessness" because of his staunch liberal commitments to human and civil rights (Lehan and Patch, 1967, p. 243).

The only thing which I personally find hard to accept about Heller's conclusion is the notion that any country—Sweden, Switzerland, or Shangri-La—could really be beyond the reach of Catch-22: if Milo's planes trade in Denmark `for pastry, could they not get to Stockholm? One can easily see that Heller was caught in a bind here, for to the extent that Sweden is vividly portrayed as an island of sanity, the force of the universal horror of Catch-22 is palliated, and to the extent that it remains a mystery, unexperienced by us—we learn only that the girls are sweet and the people advanced—its credibility as a refuge is undermined. Heller gets around this problem by ending his novel with Yossarian just starting on his way, leaving open the question of what he finds when he gets there—or even whether he makes it. Heller has even stated off the record, in fact, that Yossarian does not make it to Sweden,[8] while in the novel itself Yossarian explicitly defines the value of his desertion as lying in the attempt rather than the fulfillment:

"... I've got to get to Sweden."

"You'll never make it. It's impossible. It's almost a geographical impossibility to get there from here."

"Hell, Danby, I know that. But I'll at least be trying"
(1961, p. 441).

Yossarian's valuing existence for its own sake, his irrational
commitment to the attempt to get to Sweden—even though he
knows he will never make it—and his absolute revolt against
the absurd values of the army which exalt death: all these call
up the image of Camus's rebel. The intellectual connection between Heller and Camus has not, in fact, escaped one of Heller's
critics. John W. Hunt, whose "Comic Escape and Anti-Vision"
we examined in the last chapter, draws a number of significant
parallels between French existentialism and the guiding vision of
several contemporary novelists. Of Heller, Hunt writes that, although that author has "no quarrel with Camus," he shows little
interest in the metaphysical nature of absurdity" (in Scott, 1968,
pp. 90–91). This is perhaps an overstatement: certainly the creation of Dunbar, the Camus hero par excellence, betrays a concern
on Heller's part for the more "metaphysical" aspects of existentialism; at times Dunbar's dialogue might be a comic pastiche of
The Myth of Sisyphus:

> "Do you know how long a year takes when it's going
> away?" Dunbar repeated to Clevinger. "This long." He
> snapped his fingers. "A second ago you were stepping
> into college with your lungs full of fresh air. Today
> you're an old man."
>
> "Old?" asked Clevinger with surprise. "What are you
> talking about?"
>
> "Old."
>
> "I'm not old."
>
> "You're inches away from death every time you go out on
> a mission. How much older can you be at your age? . . ."
>
> "Well, maybe it is true," Clevinger conceded unwillingly
> in a subdued tone. "Maybe a long life does have to be filled
> with many unpleasant conditions if it's to seem long. But
> in that event, who wants one?"
>
> "I do," Dunbar told him.
>
> "Why?" Clevinger asked.
>
> "What else is there?" (1961, pp. 38–39).

But at the same time Hunt is right in that Heller sees—or at
least portrays—the existential revolt in terms of action rather

than thought: Meursault's revolt could consist of the realization of his happiness and freedom, but Yossarian cannot succeed if he remains passive. And since Yossarian cannot fly more missions or accept Cathcart's deal—both alternatives being forms of suicide, the surrender to the absurd—the only meaningful revolt he can accomplish on Pianosa is to run away. He need not get anywhere, but he will "at least be trying," and the revolt is what is important, not the final results.

It is not only in Yossarian's activity (so unlike Meursault's passive acceptance of the world about him) that he differs from Camus's rebel; Doctor Rieux, the narrator of Camus's *The Plague*, is as "active" a hero as one could wish, and yet the quality of his revolt is different in kind from Yossarian's and points to a basic incompatability between Camus's thought and Heller's. In a word, there is for Camus no Sweden: the absurdity of the universe inheres in its nature and in that of man. For Heller, on the other hand, it is man's attitudes and institutions—both susceptible of alteration—which are absurd; thus utopia, no matter how far out of reach, is a meaningful ideal for which man may strive. There is, therefore, a sense in which the absurd is for Heller less a metaphysical commitment than a literary technique. Once used by Camus in exposition of his philosophical ideas, the representation of the divorce between purpose and human need, or acts and ends, or man and fellow man, was available to be used by libertarian progressives like Heller for wholly different ends. The conclusions of the two novels, *The Plague* and *Catch-22*, underline the differences between the ideologies of the two authors: Camus uses his denouement, especially Cottard's murderous explosion and the revelation of the death of Mme Rieux, to establish in the most convincing way that the incident of the plague in Oran is but a symbol of the human condition everywhere, that there is no escape. Heller, on the other hand, uses the very desperation of Yossarian's desertion to underline the difference, immense but bridgeable, between the dehumanizing warfare Yossarian is leaving and the more "advanced" and rewarding life he hopes to find.

7 · _Conclusions_

If the reader of this study is left with the impression that many more questions have been raised than have been answered, one can only reply that such a result is not uncommon. Literary questions, especially theoretical ones, are apt to raise a host of disquieting problems which only further work can lay to rest. We began with a relatively simple question: what are the principles which dictate closure and completeness in didactic fiction? In the case of purely imitative fictions—what Sheldon Sacks calls "represented actions"—one can state a principle which, at first glance, may seem both simple and satisfying: actions involve characters in unstable situations, and the removal of the instability and the consequent formation of a new, stable situation provide us with the sense of ending. (Here completeness and closure, while theoretically separable principles, are provided by identical means.) If we ask, however, how we know which conflicts amongst the novel's characters constitute true instabilities and which do not, or if we ask what sort of resolution is achieved by removing an instability, an abyss opens before us. Take so relatively straightforward an action as _Tom Jones_. Why must Fielding provide a happy marriage for Tom and Sophia as a necessary component of the ending of his novel, while he may leave in limbo the fate of those two foils for our hero and heroine, the daughter and son-in-law of Broadbrim the Quaker, who briefly appear in the seventh book of that history? And why does Fielding assure us at great length (through Mrs. Miller, Allworthy, and Tom himself) that Tom's inveterate womanizing will cease after his marriage to Sophia, while no such assurance need be given, apparently, with regard to Tom's other faults of conduct —his somewhat choleric temper, for example, or his notorious imprudence in financial matters? And on what grounds *can* we be assured that Tom *has* changed in respect to his habitual infidelities? I do not mean to suggest that these questions have no answers, only that they are thoroughly begged by the formula suggested above for the endings of actions. And the parallel formula for apologues—that an apologue is complete when it has exhaustively or most thoroughly embodied in a fiction the truth about the external world that is its guiding principle—is even more egregiously question-begging. In the chapter on *Rasselas* and *Candide* we saw how the devices of completeness and closure differ because of the different relationships between moral truth and fictional example that were established by Johnson and Voltaire. On the other hand, we saw also how the differences, slight but significant, between the "morals" of the fables made their contribution to the differences in their resolutions. Once again, this is by no means to say that we cannot intelligibly discuss the ways in which rhetorical fictions exhibit the two principles of completeness and closure. It is just that neither "form" nor "content" alone provides a simple explanation: rhetorical fictions are too complex, too varied, and have developed too rapidly as a genre to be adequately described by blanket generalizations. The problem of ending is one which each author we have dealt with has had to face individually, in terms of the materials and techniques at his disposal. In working out the problem, each managed to create a radically new work, one which constituted a step in the development of the form. To study them at all one must examine them, as we have done, individually and in detail.

And yet we can say that modern apologues, like *The Stranger* and *Catch-22*, differ in the manner in which they achieve this sense of completeness from eighteenth-century fables like *Rasselas* and *Candide*. All four, of course, end when they have "exhaustively or most thoroughly embodied" the theses which are their raisons d'être; the difference lies in the particular kind of exhaustiveness pursued. In both *Rasselas* and *Candide* an attempt is made to universalize the thesis by representing as broad a range as possible of situations which demonstrate its truth. We have already shown how *Rasselas* divides experience into categories, examining each one's capacity for producing and sustaining human happiness, so that our sense of the completeness of the prince's quest depends on our agreeing to the implicit but illusory claim that all the possible situations, occupations, philosophies, and schemes for promoting happiness had been tried and found wanting. Similarly, we showed how *Candide* contains a virtual catalogue of the sources of human misery current at the date of writing, and that the absurdity of believing in the perfection of the universe is thoroughly demonstrated in proportion to the exhaustiveness of the catalogue.

With *The Stranger* and *Catch-22*, however, completeness is less a question of the universality of the thesis's application than it is of the intensity with which we experience its truth. It is a matter of the depth of our response, rather than the breadth of our vision. *Catch-22* leads up to a double climax in the chapters entitled "The Eternal City" and "Snowden." The former demonstrates through a sequence of expressionistic images (the chapter is constructed with the pictorial quality of a film by Pabst or Murnau) the horror of a soulless, inhuman world; the latter conveys in a single powerful scene the ultimate dehumanization of death. Now these chapters do not simply suggest the universality of war's dehumanization; this has already been done for us in two-score earlier chapters which lead up to and prepare us for this double climax. "The Eternal City" and "Snowden" are rather the most intense, violent, direct, dramatic revelation of Heller's thesis. Up to this point, Heller had only hinted at his ideas, had presented them coyly and half-jokingly: here all the stops are let out. Like most rhetorical climaxes, Heller's needs all the preparation it gets—surely we would not have been so affected by such scenes without the careful foreshadowing provided by the first four hundred pages of the novel. But the scenes which complete *Catch-22* do so not by merely summarizing what has gone before, or by extending the application of the thesis, or by completing an unfinished logical argument: they work by increasing to an almost unbearable degree the emotional force of Heller's ideas.

In *The Stranger*, again, the last scenes, which complete Camus's vision of an absurd universe, do so not by establishing the breadth or scope of this absurdity (the conclusion would be utterly ineffective did we not feel already that there can be no escape from the absurd), but by showing in the most powerful way how man in revolt reacts to the most extreme of earthly situations. In a prose style which lyrically intensifies the spirit of the moment, the climax of *The Stranger* reveals the freedom and happiness inherent in what one would think to be the bleakest possible circumstance. Our understanding of how Meursault can say, during the last hours before he is beheaded, that he had always been happy and was happy still, our apprehension of the grim joy with which Meursault expresses his desire to be greeted before the guillotine with cries of hatred—these are the objects at which the last few pages of *The Stranger* aim, for here it is most powerfully demonstrated that life is the more worth living because it is without meaning. It is true, of course, that the denouement of *The Stranger* also universalizes the thesis. To accept the idea that one may with reason be happy in the moments preceding an inevitable and ignominious death is to accept Camus's principle as true, a fortiori, in less extreme circumstances. But it is the emotional force of the revelation, the intensity with which we are made to experience its truth, which is maximized, not just its inflexible logic.

Indeed, the limited aesthetic value of mere "inflexible logic" is demonstrated by the failure of *V*. The kinds of formal patterning which produced completeness in *Rasselas* and *Candide* are in evidence in *V*.; here, however, it is not enough. Pynchon's thesis—like Heller's and Camus's—demands emotional conviction as a precondition for intellectual assent; our involvement is wanting, and as a result Pynchon's novel remains an intricate and fascinating failure. The relationship we have attempted to define between the new kinds of theses used by contemporary novelists as the structural principles of rhetorical fictions and the new modes of achieving the sense of completeness which these necessitate is the most important result of the preceding essay.

At the same time, the argument up to this point makes it possible to erect hypotheses along two different lines which may throw light on aspects of the novel not systematically considered here. The first line has to do with the application of the distinction between principles of completeness and principles of closure to works other than fully realized fables; the second has to do with the formal history, in the strict sense, of the rhetorical novel.

Completeness and closure

Anyone who has ever written himself into a corner appreciates, at least intuitively, the distinction between completeness and closure. Typically, you find yourself in a rhetorical "corner" when you exploit the known devices for achieving a sense of climax too early in the work, so that you find you have brought your piece to an end before saying everything you meant to. The essay, speech, or whatever form of discourse is closed before it has been completed, and it is often the work of hours before you can figure out how to reinsert the points you forgot to make earlier. What makes it possible to write one's self into a corner is simply the fact that the devices for closing off an essay—notably repetitive summary—can be used at any time; the sense of the essay's completeness, on the other hand, depends instead on the use of the many arguments or other means of persuasion which are appropriate to the essay's purpose.

Similarly in the novel: we can dissociate the devices used for achieving good closure from the means of attaining completeness, in the case of fables at least.[1] In our discussion of *Rasselas*, for example, there was no great difficulty in ascertaining just how Johnson makes us feel that anything following the forty-ninth chapter would be at best a sequel to his novel. In any quest novel, the abandonment of the quest is as obvious a closure device as repetitive summary would be for an essay. The problem, rather, was to discover just why this obvious closure device should be invoked after the forty-eighth, rather than, say, after the twenty-fourth chapter; in other words, what makes us feel that the quest for a choice of life, potentially infinite in its duration, was rightly abandoned at a certain point? *Candide* presents a similar case: again, some of the ingredients of good closure are readily predictable—Candide's marriage with Cunégonde and an end to their wanderings—but since these events do not take place as a result of a necessary or probable sequence of events, it is clear that, except for questions of completeness, closure might well have been invoked at almost any point in the narrative. If we feel that *Candide* has not been arbitrarily ended where it stops, it is because we have been made to feel that because Candide's reeducation in the school of the world's miseries is complete, he at last can understand and accept the wisdom of the old farmer and the dervish, and find moderate pleasure and contentment in cultivating his garden.

In fables, as we have found, the aesthetic pleasure of endings is at least as much due to achieved completeness as to good closure devices. We found in *Rasselas*, and again in *The Stranger* and *Catch-22*, that it was possible to sacrifice the most effective closure to the greatest sense of completeness in such a way that the works are the better for it. We might well ask, however, whether works exist which have taken the opposite tack, which have sacrificed completeness to closure. Such a novel might well appear to have been finished too quickly by the author who had inadvertently written himself into a corner. In the theater, there is a classic example of a play whose ending seems strangely inadequate to the lines of plot which had been developed: Shakespeare's *Cymbeline*. In the novel, the case which most obviously springs to mind is Oliver Goldsmith's flawed masterpiece, *The Vicar of Wakefield.*

The conclusion of *The Vicar of Wakefield* has come under a good deal of criticism ever since Walter Raleigh's attack in the late nineteenth century: "the plot," said Raleigh, "is loosely constructed, and hastily huddled up at the close." Goldsmith, in his efforts to "multiply misfortunes on the head of the ill-starred Vicar . . . found he had raised more troubles than he could lay." The conclusion, which illustrates the restoration of the Vicar and his family to the good graces of fortune, is, according to Raleigh, "conducted in the same summary and ineffective fashion as in the tag to the Book of Job" (1894, p. 207). This criticism is echoed by Edgar Pelham, who wonders whether the novel "triumphs by reason of its faults," particularly since "almost everything seems to be wrong and yet turns out in the result to be astoundingly right" (1933, p. 77). The most crafty analysis of the defective ending of Goldsmith's novel, however, is by Ernest A. Baker:

> So in the end, [Goldsmith] manages to have it both ways. Imprudence, though it always meant well, has come to grief. And now the good genius, in the shape of Prudence personified, comes to the rescue. But the reversal of fortune, if strictly interpreted, reverses the moral, for it is not repentence and amendment that is the agency of [the Primroses'] salvation, but mere coincidence. Thus Goldsmith shuffles off his comic pose, and out of pure tenderness for the children of his brain gives everybody a prize. Even the villainous seducer [Mr. Thornhill], a meaner scamp than Jonathan Wild himself, is left in a fair way of redeeming his character and being reunited to the fair Olivia after all (1934, vol. 5, p. 83).

The ending, according to Baker, is not merely tacked on roughly; it also fails to be consistent with the ethical norms of Goldsmith's novel, and, as Baker points out somewhat later, with the earlier characterization of the Vicar as well.

The other major flaw in Goldsmith's novel, to which numerous critics have called attention, is that the work does not seem all of a piece: the first half is rather different from the second. Raleigh, though he is not explicit about what he means, may have been alluding to this when he called *The Vicar of Wakefield* "loosely constructed." Writing more directly on this point, Ralph Wardle, in his biography of Goldsmith, mentions that while "Fanny Burney believed that the second half of [*The Vicar of Wakefield*] was superior to the first," and while the moralistically inclined Victorian reader might well have agreed with her, "a modern reader is more apt to prefer the first half of the book and to delight in its slow pace, its gentle humor, and especially the complex characterization of the Vicar" (1967, pp. 170–71). Curtis Dahl also feels it necessary to deal with criticism of the novel's "lack of coherence and . . . inclusion of seemingly extraneous passages" in an overly ingenious essay which attempts to show that the theme of disguise is the glue which holds the discordant elements of the novel together (1958, p. 90). The thematic pattern of reality vs. appearance can indeed be found in *The Vicar of Wakefield* (as it can in practically every novel written, from *Don Quixote* to *Valley of the Dolls*), which need not prevent us from seeing, with Ernest A. Baker, that "Goldsmith started in one direction, lost his way before he had gone far, and presently found himself going without being able to stop, in a direction entirely opposite" (1934, vol. 5, p. 81).

Only Baker, and maybe Raleigh, seem to be cognizant of both faults, but neither of them grasps the inextricable connection betwixt them: it is not simply that *The Vicar of Wakefield* contains an unconvincing ending and is *also* composed of two parts not easily reconcilable; rather the denouement of Goldsmith's novel is defective precisely *because* the two halves of *The Vicar of Wakefield* are written to diverse ends.

The first half of Goldsmith's novel is that of a morally serious comedy of a kind with which readers of Fielding are familiar. The hero, Parson Primrose, is a man who, like Tom Jones, is made sympathetic to us because of his naturally good and generous nature, and who, like Abraham Adams, inspires our respect for his wisdom, religious conviction, and learning. Like Adams, however, his knowledge of the world is defective, and, like Jones, he is imprudent and indiscreet. The most piquant difference between Fielding's comedies and the first half of *The Vicar* lies in Goldsmith's magnificent use of Primrose himself as the first-person narrator. The comedy is thus enabled to proceed in two directions at once: on the one hand, the Vicar can be used to comment on the vanity and folly of his even more imprudent and indiscreet family (in this context, Primrose serves as an ethical paragon), while on the other hand, the Vicar's own errors of pride or vanity are treated with gentle, but nonetheless richly comic irony. We thus spend half the time laughing with the Vicar at his family's mortifications (the comic consequences of Moses' pride of learning, or his wife's pride of place, or his daughters' pride of person), and the other half laughing at Primrose himself, especially his ludicrous naïveté. Goldsmith broke fresh comic ground here, not so much in drawing a character who could be at once admirable and ridiculous, for Fielding and Cervantes before him had done that, but in managing to do so without the mediation of a narrator. Goldsmith was in a fair way to create the first fully realized example in English of first-person morally serious comedy. As we come to the break between the two halves of the novel (at chapter seventeen or thereabouts), the form Goldsmith intended is clear: more adventures, in which the folly of the Primrose family, abetted by the ignorance and imprudence of the Vicar himself, will more and more jeopardize their already insecure position, until fortune, whom we expect will soon favor the Primroses, reverses herself and places them again in that comfort and security from which they started. And that is almost what happens.

The structure begins to break down at the point where Mr. Thornhill (Primrose's landlord) starts to pose a serious threat to the happiness, safety, virtue, and even the lives of the Primrose family, a threat which is pushed too far for the fragile world of comedy to sustain. As a result, the situations move from the comic to the pathetic and, unlike Fielding, who managed within *Tom Jones* to control our sentiments in such a way as to avoid the maudlin entirely, Goldsmith exploits such situations to wring tears. The comedy is dealt a blow from which it never recovers. Instead, as Primrose goes out into the world to recover his lost daughter, and as more and more calamities are piled on the supine Primrose family, our ironic view of the Vicar alters. No longer the good but limited individual who evoked our sympathetic laughter, he becomes a latter-day Job, the Good Man

Tested by Adversity, and the novel accordingly turns into an apologue testifying to the power of faith to remain steadfast in a world replete with evils. In accord with the altered end of the novel, Goldsmith obliges his hero by subjecting him to almost every disaster short of death that could be visited upon a man in his condition: his elder, flightier daughter is first ruined by a sham marriage, then reported dead; his younger, wiser daughter is carried off, supposedly to the same fate as the elder; he himself is carted off to jail by the machinations of the villain, where he meets his eldest and most promising son lying wounded and under sentence of death. And while in prison, insult is added to his manifold injuries by his fellow-prisoners, who mock at him while he attempts to reform their souls. Through all this, the Vicar is subjected to a further test. He can be released from prison if he will submit himself to the perpetrator of all his family's misfortunes, and consent to ally the villainous Mr. Thornhill with his eldest son's intended, Arabella Wilmot. But in spite of the temptation to relieve his own miseries by complying with an evil action, and in spite of his wife's entreaties (Mrs. Primrose plays a kind of comforter to Primrose's Job), he refuses to betray his faith and his moral convictions. And as the second half of the novel proceeds to its end, the questions, so relevant before, of our desires for the Primrose family and our expectations about their fate, drop out of sight. The alteration of Mr. Thornhill from a comic to a serious threat to the Primroses does not, as one might have expected, change the plot from comedy to melodrama; it rather takes it entirely out of the realm of what we have called represented actions, as our hopes and fears for the Primrose family are subordinated to the moral lesson which the Vicar's behavior under the stress of multiplied calamities inculcates. The sermon which the Vicar preaches from the prison is by no means an irrelevancy, nor even a digression away from the story's general direction, but rather an integral part of the fable which Goldsmith's novel has more or less suddenly turned into.

How can one effectively end a comedy turned apologue? It is reasonably obvious, I think, that there could be no single conclusion which would satisfy the requirements of both forms. To end the fable would require the most convincing possible demonstration of the ability of the true Christian to surmount the obstacles of fortune and human wickedness, which can only take place with the Vicar in the greatest adversity; such an ending, however, would make comedy impossible, for comedy minimally requires that the characters' fates be compatible with their ethical deserts. True, the Book of Job manages to end happily, but it is hardly a conclusion famous for its artistry or probability, nor are the Lord of Host's arguments against the three comforters as convincing as Job's steadfastness had been. To carry the apologue to its proper logical conclusion would, besides, have been opposed to the tenor of Goldsmith's genius, which delighted in the amiable. So, forbearing to complete the fable, our author instead wrote the closure sequence for the comedy. This was, of course, unsatisfactory on several counts. For one thing, as Ernest A. Baker very properly mentions, the final disposition of Mr. Thornhill, whose punishment is limited to being a companion at the home of a relation, where his pride may be mortified by taking his dinner "at the side-table" instead of at the place of honor, and where his sensuous nature may be frustrated by having to humor his kinsman and play the French horn, is far too mild, considering the enormities which he perpetrated or intended. After his behavior in the novel's second half, nothing short of seeing him turned off at Tyburn would seem truly fitting—but reconciliation is the mood proper to comedy. For another, the character of the Vicar in the conclusion, which returns to the gentle and ironic view of the opening, feels strangely off-color: Primrose has stood too long for a concept of the greatest sublimity to return to his charming but silly self. Most important, though, is the fact that the conclusion, while it may close off the novel, cannot complete either section of the fiction with any probability. There are novels, of course, *Tom Jones* among them, which accomplish astonishing reversals of fortune in an extraordinarily brief space —but think how painstakingly Fielding prepared for his comic peripeties! In *The Vicar of Wakefield*'s second half, however, the lines of comic probability have been left slack while the apologue worked itself out, and while Sir William Thornhill (alias Mr. Burchell) may swiftly step in to resolve the Primroses' predicaments, it can only be as the most outrageous sort of deus ex machina. The ending comes less as a surprise than as a shock. Nothing can rob the denouement of its status as an effective device of closure, for indeed, anything we might subsequently read about Goldsmith's characters would have the force of a sequel; neither the comedy nor the apologue, however, is complete: the comedy lacks a middle and the apologue an end.

The preceding analysis of *The Vicar of Wakefield,* whatever its merits in itself, finds its place here as an example of the kinds of formal insights into fictions other than fully realized fables which may be achieved through studies in completeness and closure.[2] Moreover, it should be clear that, while it was the much-criticized defects in the form of Goldsmith's novel which suggested it to me as an object of study, the methods and principles used in this essay could as well be applied to fully realized forms, which raise equally fascinating and unsolved problems for further study and analysis.

One such form is that usually termed the picaresque novel, a fiction consisting of a series of episodes without a subsuming plot structure. What—if anything—is meant by completeness in such novels? And can such forms be artistically closed, even if they cannot in any strict sense be complete? The fact that controversy persists over the conclusion of Defoe's *The Fortunate Mistress,* while nothing of the kind hovers over the denouement of *Moll Flanders,* suggests that further work along these lines might lend some insight into the ways in which such imitative biographies contributed to the development of fully realized fictional forms.

Another is the fictional satire. While many, perhaps most English novels have been accused (rightly or wrongly) of containing thematic elements of satire, there have been very few fictions which use satire as the principle of structure. *Gulliver's Travels* and *Shamela* are the two most important; *Our Gang,* by Philip Roth, is a recent example. It is not hard to see why there are not many which have attained novelistic length and complexity: satire, in any medium, is a difficult mode to sustain, and it is next to impossible to find a fictional framework flexible enough and pregnant enough with objects to ridicule for full-length treatment. Though we have not been wanting studies of *Gulliver's Travels,* it might be interesting to see if one could find out just why the last book attains its peculiar finality (for Swift obviously could not have written a fifth book to follow the adventures in Houyhnhmnland that would function either as a part of the whole or even as an effective sequel). Furthermore, the very notion of wholeness in satires is a particularly vague one: if satire is, as Edward W. Rosenheim suggests in *Swift and the Satirist's Art,* the ridicule of discrete butts in the external universe, then what, aside from the use of the rhetorical mode itself, could unify a series of ridiculing passages? Would the principle be inherent in the fiction through which the satire takes place, or in some unity intrinsic to those real objects?

The third problem is occasioned by works which, regardless of their generic form, lead a dual existence both as separate, fully realized wholes and as parts of a larger scheme. It is so customary to look upon Galsworthy's *The Man of Property* as the first third of *The Forsyte Saga*, that it is easy to forget that fourteen years lay between its publication and that of the second volume of the trilogy, *In Chancery*. The obvious question is of the completeness and closure of the trilogy as a whole and the extent to which that is compatible with the full closure of either of the nonfinal parts.[3] The question has no one simple answer: there are trilogies and trilogies. Some romans-fleuves, like *Remembrance of Things Past*, are so clearly conceived of as a whole that individual volumes make comparatively little sense separated from what precedes or follows them. Others, like the philosophical fantasy of E. R. Eddison (*The Worm Ouroboros, Mistress of Mistresses, A Fish Dinner in Memison*), are thoroughly separable and, indeed, are only tangentially and thematically related. Still others, like *The Forsyte Saga*, fall into the wide space between these two extremes. Furthermore, each volume of a roman-fleuve need not have the same discreteness and integrity as every other: frequently the earlier volumes may have been conceived explicitly as wholes, while the later ones, thought through more firmly in terms of the larger framework, may be less separable from it. (The obvious example here is the twelve-volume biography of Lewis Eliot, by C. P. Snow, under the general title of *Strangers and Brothers*: early novels like *The Light and the Dark* and *The Masters* can be read on their own, but the last two, *The Sleep of Reason* and *Last Things*, are practically incomprehensible unless the reader has read most of the others.) No doubt we are dealing here with a different sort of unity from that which informs works designed to stand alone, but I believe that a good deal of light might be shed on the structure of such romans-fleuves by the analysis of the completeness and closure of the segments which must serve both as parts and as wholes.

A fourth form—the last we shall consider here—is one which has developed very recently, in the late nineteenth and early twentieth centuries: represented actions whose instabilities devolve about changes in character or in state of consciousness rather than in the agents' external circumstances. Such fictions, for which Joyce's *Portrait of the Artist* and Bellow's *Herzog* may stand as specimens, have been taken by the apostles of "open form" as perfect examples of the kinds of literary openness with which the twentieth century, in their view, abounds. At the same time, few readers of these fictions have any doubt that they are in fact over where they end; their completeness and closure simply rest upon somewhat different principles from those governing more conventional represented actions. The reader's expectations and desires, hopes and fears refer rather to a desirable (or undesirable) change in consciousness on the part of the protagonist than to a desirable (or undesirable) alteration in fortune. A study of this sort of represented action would indeed be useful, but it may well be that it would deal only indirectly with how such plots are brought to an end. (This, after all, is tolerably obvious: the anticipated change in character or consciousness either does or does not take place.) The more important question might be how such works manage to focus the plot machinery onto character to such an extent that what is usually thought of as the fate of the protagonists—of Stephen Dedalus and of Moses Herzog in our examples—could be left more or less up in the air without destroying the sense of the novel's completeness.

These four lines for further research stem not so much from the results of our essay on the fable as from the principles and theories which prompted it. The further development of that essay is indeed possible, although along rather different lines. To say what lines, we must make a detour into the theory of literary history.

Narrative histories of form

In his essay "Critical and Historical Principles of Literary History" R. S. Crane discusses the two dominant modes of writing the history of literature: the *grammatical* (what we today would call the philological), and the *dialectical*. The former operates by means of "the literal exegesis and comparison of texts in terms of the material traits of their content and form in a context of the circumstances of their composition"; its tools are "textual and historical criticism, grammar (including prosody), the grammatical parts of logic, and bibliography in the traditional sense." The latter, or dialectical, school is oriented "not to the historical origins of works but to their effects upon readers. Its major concern, therefore, is not to describe the material and conventional traits of dramas, novels, and poems," but rather "their qualities, or 'values,' . . . which any work shares with any other work by partaking in the common causes of all human discourse—language, the mind, society, history, and so on" (1967, vol. 2, p. 48). Both the grammatical and the dialectical school rely in their criticism upon the distinction between "content" and "form," but the former take the terms simply as "the distinguishable elements of any grammatically complete utterance," while the latter customarily set up an opposing and (usually) hierarchical relationship between them (1967, vol. 2, p. 50). One famous example of the dialectical content/form relation is in the poetic criticism of Cleanth Brooks, where the essence of poetry resides in its "form," a complex semantic structure held together through paradox and irony, and where "content" is simply the dry husk of literal meaning contained within prose paraphrase.[4] Examples of the "grammatical" literary history include historical surveys and reference texts like *A Literary History of England*, edited by Albert C. Baugh, et al.; examples of the "dialectical" would include literary histories of a more "philosophical" tenor, such as those of Louis Cazamian or Hippolyte Taine, or of the "New Critics."

Both these schools have made many fruitful contributions to our understanding of literary works, but both, according to Crane, "are necessarily limited in the kinds of propositions they permit the historian to make about literary works" (1967, vol. 2, p. 55). For one thing, neither is concerned with the literary work as a whole determined by the artistic decisions of the author. The "grammatical" critic would see the wholeness of *Hamlet* as its merely grammatical completeness, while the "dialectical" critic would see it as a certain synthesis of the opposed "form" and "content." As a result, neither is able to deal with anything except the characteristics of the play's parts. Furthermore, while the "grammatical" critic is able to deal with what Crane calls the "preconstructional aspect" of literary works (the relation of a work to its sources, either in the poet's biography, his milieu, or the tradition), and while the "dialectical" critic is able to deal with the postconstructional aspect (the effect of such works on readers), neither can deal adequately with the constructional aspect: "the artistic principles and judgments operative in their

composition." Crane suggests as a remedy for this lacuna in critical methods "a third mode of deriving critical predicates for
works—that which rests upon what I may call the concept of
artistic synthesis" (1967, vol. 2, p. 55).

This "concept of artistic synthesis" is nothing more nor less
than the notion, derived from Aristotle and explicit in Crane's
work since the nineteen-forties, that any criticism of an artistic
object must take into account first its purpose in terms of the
effects it is designed to produce, and then the particular causes
of those effects—the linguistic materials of which they are composed, the humanely interesting action, character, and thought
which they reveal, and the techniques by which all this is represented and ordered. To move from the criticism of a given text
to literary history, however, requires one more notion, the idea
of genre—for how can history be written but by the discussion
of the likenesses and differences between objects, and what sense
would it make to compare two objects unless we knew them to
be comparable members of the same category? The other two
schools of literary history also have their genres, but while the
"grammatical" school derives its genres from tradition (the "ode,"
the "chronicle play"), and while the "dialectical" school derives
its own from application of the a priori terms of its particular
dialectic (the "synthetic" and "analytic" of T. S. Eliot, for example), Crane derives his genres empirically through grouping
works according to definable similarities in their organizing
principles. What would a literary history based upon such critical
ideas be like? Crane's definition is as follows:

> The collective enterprise of historians in this mode would . . .
> have as its ultimate purpose the writing of a narrative-causal
> history of the various literary arts in terms of four things:
> (1) the successive shifts in the artistic or formal ends which
> writers at different times and in different places have
> pursued, (2) the successive changes in materials through
> which the different ends were realized, (3) the successive
> discoveries of more effective or at least new devices and
> techniques for the achievement of the different forms in the
> different materials, and (4) the successive actualizations
> of all these changing possibilities in the production of
> artistically valuable or historically significant works in the
> different arts with which the history deals. . . . It is
> appropriate . . . to describe this mode of literary history
> as the narrative history of forms (1967, vol. 2, pp. 81–82).

It is a tall order indeed. But while our preceding essay makes no claim actually to be the sort of literary history Crane describes, it seems to me that we have touched a number of the bases and have indicated directions for the actual completion of a highly selective and limited history of this sort, the narrative history of the rhetorical novel.

Of the four aspects of this new type of literary history, Crane calls the first three "independent variables," any of which might be held as a constant in writing a selective history of this type. Accordingly, one might hold materials as a constant in writing of the way in which, say, the Joan of Arc legend had been used, with varying techniques down through the centuries, to achieve very different formal ends. Or one might hold techniques as a constant if one wished to study, say, how the use of stream-of-consciousness narrative had been adapted to different materials and for differing formal ends. We have instead held constant the formal end to which the fictions in our study have been written, and the subject of our study thus becomes how the particular didactic intent of each novelist was reflected in his choice of materials and techniques, and how new materials and developments in novelistic techniques taking place in other genres made possible developments in the kinds of informing principles which apologues could possess.

The first half of our task, the study of representatives of the apologue in their concrete actualizations "as unique artistic wholes the production of which marked the coming into being of values, great or small, such as the world had not previously known," has, I think, been accomplished with some thoroughness on the small number of novels with which this essay has dealt in detail. This was, in fact, the inevitable result of dealing with the idea of completeness in rhetorical fiction, for completeness is by its very nature a notion which strikes at the essence of each work. To speak of the completeness of *Rasselas* or *Candide* or any fable necessitates talking about the didactic principle which informs the work, about the action and characters which are created and set in motion to serve its exposition, and about the particular relationship between fictional construct and normative statement which each work sets up. Completeness and closure are functions not of individual parts of works but of the works as realized artistic wholes.

The second half—the study of how new materials and techniques made possible developments in the kinds of didactic ends

fables might take as their informing principles—has scarcely
been begun: one could claim that this essay has dropped a few
hints about the kinds of changes which have taken place and
why. We have given grounds for believing that the rhetorical
novel has undergone considerable development over the last two
hundred years of its history, not only in the philosophical material which makes up its subject matter, but also in the technical
means of representation by which authors achieve their didactic
purposes. At a minimal level, recent fables like *Catch-22* and
Lord of the Flies have demonstrated that the rhetorical novel is
no less capable than the represented action of making strong
appeals to the emotions in a way that would have been impossible
in the mid-eighteenth century. This, as we have suggested, is due
to the incorporation into the fable of techniques for representing
states of consciousness which were developed for represented
actions; our deeply empathic response to the heroes of rhetorical
novels is owing to our engrossing view of their private, internal
world. A further, and perhaps more far-reaching development of
this new empathy produced by inside views has been the ability
of contemporary fabulists to propound through their fictions
doctrines which are relatively novel and not generally accepted.
The novelty of *Rasselas* and *Candide* certainly was not their
philosophical stances, which had the status of commonplaces in
their time.[5] It was rather the fictional form, with its human interest, that was new. But the doctrine propounded by *The Stranger*
or earlier in the century by Hermann Hesse's *Siddhartha*—was
far more original than the fictional form. (The comparison of the
plot of *The Stranger* with the plots of relatively banal tales of
crime proved this.) Once more, it is the use of inside views which
makes this possible, for it is by the audience's vicarious
participation in the protagonist's experience that it may be
"convinced" of the truth of propositions which, on a literal
philosophical level, it would resist or even fail to understand.
The absurdity of the universe is hard to grasp as a concept, but
Meursault's perceptions of it are intuitively convincing; similarly
one may in one's daily life consider World War II a glorious effort
on the part of humanity, but it is difficult to resist seeing it as
thoroughly and horribly dehumanizing when one looks at it
through Yossarian's eyes.[6]

When we say that the rhetorical novel "developed," by the
way, we do not mean to suggest that the course of change was a

universal improvement, or even that the change was universal. In the first place, one can say that *The Stranger* represents
a development over *Candide* without saying that the former is the
better novel. Clearly *Candide* is a classic, while time will still
have to test *The Stranger's* durability. The question of relative
quality is moot, and I do not intend to argue it here. The development spoken of is not an improvement per se so much as an
extension of the possibilities inherent in the form, so as to make
the rhetorical novel capable of wider and deeper emotional effects,
more difficult and unusual doctrines. The improvement, if there
can be said to be one, is in potentia, not necessarily in re. And in
the second place, the development did not affect all—or even
most—contemporary rhetorical novels. Though the doctrines
differ as much as one might expect, *Animal Farm* shows slight
technical advance over *Pilgrim's Progress*, *Brave New World* none
over *Rasselas*. While the new forms are being worked out, and
for a long time after, the old are still being written, rewritten,
and read.

What questions remain, then, for a future narrative history of
the rhetorical novel? First, some further research into the origins
of didactic fiction, back to Bunyan or perhaps to Thomas More.
Second, a more complete study of the apologue in the eighteenth
century, especially of Fielding's *Jonathan Wild* and Sterne's
Tristram Shandy. Third, some speculative investigation of the
relative disappearance of formally interesting fables in the nineteenth century. Inartistic specimens of the genre abound, but
there are few developments and very few attempts at fable by
novelists of real talent. Was the interest of the most creative
spirits working in fiction absorbed in the development of the
psychological novel and the novel of society, in the development
of techniques to increase the range and power of the represented
action? (There are a few important examples of the form during
this century: Melville's *The Confidence Man* is one.) Fourth, we
might ask about the reasons for the resurgence of the form in the
twentieth century. Had the psychological novel, in the hands of
James, Conrad and Joyce, come to some kind of dead end, leaving
only the investigation of abnormal states of consciousness (as in
Faulkner, Robbe-Grillet, Céline, and many others) as a fertile
field for experimentation? And might this have been a reason
why novelists turned to a neglected form, the fable, where there
was the possibility of doing something new and original? Or had

some novelists who were repelled by the moral ambiguity of fashionably impersonal narrative (documented so thoroughly by Wayne C. Booth) taken up the apologue as a means of making their philosophical and ethical convictions widely known? These speculative explanations, whatever their apparent merits, deserve further investigation as a test for their truth.

It is obvious, in any case, that the vogue of the rhetorical novel on the contemporary literary scene cries out for explanation. Fable is no longer a strange or unusual item; many of our most respected recent masterpieces, and most of the truly original and provocative ones are apologues.[7] John Barth, probably the most striking American talent of the last decade, has five novels to his credit, all in the rhetorical mode, all arguing (I believe) a single doctrine but in dazzlingly varied fictional forms. John Gardner, whom many believe will be one of the most important writers of the seventies, has begun his oeuvre with three pungent and striking apologues, the most recent of which (*The Sunlight Dialogues*) was a popular as well as a critical success. Donald Barthelme, perhaps the most virtuoso prose stylist of our day, has been adapting the complex, involuted structures of Jorge Luis Borges to American themes; he has a single fiction of novelistic length to his credit (*Snow White*), a fable. The novel voted the most distinguished prose fiction of the period 1945–65, Ralph Ellison's *Invisible Man*, is also in the rhetorical mode. The practitioners of fable by this time are legion; their names are a virtual roll call of the most interesting contemporary writers: Kurt Vonnegut, Bruce Jay Friedman, Richard Brautigan, Jeremy Larner, John Hawkes, Jerzy Kosinski among our native novelists; Alan Paton, Mordecai Richler, Anthony Burgess, and Nigel Dennis in England and its former colonies; and among the continental novelists some of the most powerful influences on our own: Jean-Paul Sartre and André Malraux, Franz Kafka and Hermann Hesse, Evgeny Zamiatin, and Alexander Solzhenitsyn. There is little wonder that Sheldon Sacks sees in the new fable "the most promising single development of contemporary fiction in the Western world." It is in such developments as we have chronicled that he finds "evidence that the Western novel is not dead. Its soul is merely transmigrating, possibly to reappear in the Divine Comedy of our day." (1969, pp. 290–91).

Appendix A
Bellow's Herzog

One of the basic problems Bellow had to solve in writing *Herzog* was common to all represented actions with plots of character: keeping the reader's expectations focused on the psychological change in the protagonist rather than on any circumstantial alterations which may be taking place concurrently. The eponymous hero, Moses Elkanah Herzog, is an intellectual, a historian of ideas whose attempt to come to terms with the failure of his second marriage brings him face to face with the void. Bellow's problem, more specfically, is that he must describe a set of labile relationships Herzog participates in with his colleagues, family, and friends without creating the expectation that they will be resolved: we must be made to understand fully the intricate twists and turns in Herzog's relations with others without seeing them as instabilities of the sort that plots of action customarily devolve around. The true instability, whose alterations and final resolution will provide the shaping form of the novel, must be Herzog's mental state.

Bellow begins by having the question of Herzog's shifting and ambiguous mental state open the novel: "If I am out of my mind, it is all right with me, thought Moses Herzog. Some people thought he was cracked and for a time he himself doubted that he was all there. . . . His friend, his former friend, Valentine, and his wife, his ex-wife Madeleine, had spread the rumor that his sanity had collapsed. Was it true?" That is the initial question, and although we come back to this scene much later in the novel, knowing that Herzog is at this time securely on the road back to recovery and mental stability, at the outset it is a question we cannot answer. The information Bellow gives us is thoroughly ambiguous. "He was taking a turn around the empty house and saw the shadow of his face in a gray, webby window. He looked weirdly tranquil. A radiant line went from mid-forehead over his straight nose and full, silent lips." What are we to make of this? Is Herzog's smile one of pure human joy or of dementia? And why is Herzog writing "to the dead, his own obscure dead, and finally the famous dead"? (pp. 1–2.). The scale seems tipped to the side of madness, and the disconnected fragments that line the opening pages pique of our curiosity: if this be madness yet there is method in't. The opening launches us in the main groove down which the novel runs: Herzog's state of consciousness. The relationships that have affected and produced that state are not baldly set forth in exposition but sketched in gradually, in brief allusions at first. Only when the story of Herzog's spiritual crisis is firmly under way do whole episodes appear in the narrative. We are thus prevented from viewing Herzog's relationships with Madeleine and Valentine Gersbach, with Tenny, and Zelda, and Himmelstein, and Simkin, and Ramona as "instabilities" until we already have a fair notion (intuitive and inchoate, perhaps) of what sort of story we are reading.

It is important, too, that the characters who most threaten Herzog—Madeleine, Gersbach, Himmelstein, Edvig—are portrayed as ridiculous people, and that they pose no problems which Herzog must necessarily solve once he is in shape to deal with them. Those who have done him harm are in no position to do more. Herzog may threaten to damage himself by getting involved with them again—as he indeed does—but the divorce and most of its painful aftermath are over before the mental drama begins: the bastards and bitches who have taken Patient Griselda Herzog for all he is worth have no further claims to press. This would, of course, be no less the case even if Madeleine, Gersbach, & Co. were *not* made to seem ludicrous as antagonists for the infinitely more sensitive, truthful, worthy Moses Herzog. But their ridiculousness serves to define more sharply the fact that our hero's problems are only in his consciousness. We know that Herzog could cope with these schmegagies easily were he only in his right senses. The disparity between the quality of the threat and the actual threat to Herzog's consciousness that is posed is what is largely responsible for the serio-comic tone of the novel. One other factor, not to be neglected on any account, is Herzog's response to his own misery, a pungent wit that thinly masks the self-pity beneath: "On the knees of your soul? May as well be useful—scrub the floor" (p. 4).

So far I have been speaking of *Herzog* as though the hero's problems were imaginary, as though Moses Herzog were an intellectual hypochondriac with a taste for weltschmerz. There is a sense in which this is true, and this perspective on the hero is part of what gives the novel its marvelous ironic tone. At the same time, Herzog's malaise is perfectly real: he suffers, and we readers who find him a sympathetic character are moved by his intellectual predicament, which, in him, amounts to a genuine spiritual threat to his happiness. As Wayne C. Booth says in his review of *Herzog*: "The Void threatens us, after all, as *idea* fully as much as it does in what is ordinarily called 'experience.' Herzog *experiences* threatening ideas as other modern heroes experience more spectacular forms of degradation"[1] (1964, p. 1). And the ideas which threaten Herzog are the social, political, and metaphysical notions common in this century, the ideas of mass men.

> His recent misfortunes might be seen as a collective project, himself participating, to destroy his vanity and his pretensions to a personal life so that he might disintegrate and suffer and hate . . . down in the mire of post-Renaissance, post-humanistic, post-Cartesian dissolution, next door to the Void. Everybody was in the act. "History" gave everyone a free ride. The very Himmelsteins, who had never even read a book of metaphysics, were touting the Void as if it were so much salable real estate. This little demon was impregnated with modern ideas, and one in particular excited his terrible little heart: you must sacrifice your poor, squawking, niggardly individuality—which may be nothing anyway . . . to historical necessity. And to truth. And truth is true only as it brings down more disgrace and dreariness upon human beings, so that if it shows anything except evil it is illusion, and not truth (Bellow, 1964, p. 93).

The ideas of the late nineteenth- and early twentieth-century intellectuals, first perverted so as to deprive them of grandeur, even of human dignity, and then reified as action—by Gersbach, Madeleine, Himmelstein and the rest—these are what cause Herzog's suffering, and it is with these that he joins issue. Bitterly, Herzog takes on the new theology in a letter to his existential psychoanalyst, Edvig:

> Valentine Gersbach . . . brought me books (by Martin Buber). He commanded me to study them. I sat reading *I and Thou, Between God and Man, The Prophetic Faith* in a nervous fever. Then we discussed them.
>   I'm sure you know the views of Buber. It's wrong to turn a man (a subject) into a thing (an object). By means of spiritual dialogue, the I-It relationship becomes an I-Thou relationship. God comes and goes in a man's soul. And men come and go in each other's souls. Sometimes they come and

go in each other's beds, too. You hold the poor fellow's
hand. You look into his eyes. You give him consolation.
All the while, you rearrange his life. . . . You deprive him
of his daughter. And somehow it is all mysteriously trans-
muted into religious depth. And finally your suffering is
greater than his, too, because you are the greater sinner.
And so you've got him, coming and going (p. 64).

Similarly, in his letter to the *New York Times*, Herzog inveighs
against the masters of war who would reconcile post-Nietzschean
man to the prospect of nuclear annihilation by appealing to the
Philosophy of Risk; he chastises a colleague, Egbert Shapiro, for
swallowing "the canned sauerkraut of Spengler's 'Prussian So-
cialism,' the commonplaces of the Wasteland outlook, the cheap
mental stimulants of Alienation, the cant and rant of pipsqueaks
about Inauthenticity and Forlornness" (pp. 74–75). In his letter to
Pulver, he notes how man, newly self-conscious, "is provoked
to take revenge upon himself, a revenge of derision, contempt,
denial of transcendence"; Herzog counters with his belief in "the
inspired condition," in which man, transfigured, is free to know
the truth and love his fellow-man—even "to abide with death
in clarity of consciousness" (pp. 184–85). Herzog's response to
the nay-sayers of his time is a glorious intellectual "Aye!"—and
yet it is, after all, but an intellectual affirmation. He confutes his
enemies in trenchant letters full of furious mental fire and finds
that it is not enough for him. He is himself still tortured. Within
himself, he asks, "can thought wake you from the dream of existence?"—and answers, "Not if it becomes a second realm of
confusion, another more complicated dream, the dream of intellect, the delusion of total *explanations*" (p. 166). In the last
analysis, the letters themselves, seemingly Herzog's defense
against the threat that twentieth-century nihilism poses for him,
are not only symptoms of our hero's malaise but are a disease in
their own right. So long as Herzog must noisily affirm the hidden
joys of life, the hopefulness inherent in human existence, so long
will Herzog be unable to accept that joy and that hope for himself. Silence is a necessary condition for Herzog's contentment.
    Herzog's letters, in other words, represent a necessary stage
in his spiritual convalescence, and when Bellow finally informs
us that "thus began his final week of letters," we know that the
spiritual disease that had begun with Herzog's second divorce is
coming to a full close (p. 318). In the week that preceded Herzog's return to his summer home in the Berkshires, he had come
to terms with his ex-wife Madeleine and her lover, his former
friend Gersbach. In deciding to kill that precious pair as an *acte*

gratuite and then deciding, in almost as arbitrary a fashion, not to kill them, Herzog had purged his hatred of them—and the remains of his love. So that he is not even shaken when he must confront Madeleine in the chill indignity of a Chicago police station: she and Gersbach had become strangers whose opinions and passions mattered nothing to Herzog. But at Ludeyville in the Berkshires, amid the natural beauties of his estate, he has still something with which he must come to terms: his own questioning soul. He must ask the most probing questions in an effort to conquer his spiritual malaise, so that he may finally fall silent. And he must make his adieux.

So some of the letters, this last week, bid farewell to his tormentors, of whom he now takes leave, finally, without rancor. "Dear Madeleine—you are a terrific one, you are! Bless you! What a creature! . . . And you, Gersbach, you're welcome to Madeleine. . . . You will not reach me through her, however. I know you sought me in her flesh. But I am no longer there" (p. 318). And Edvig, the unconscious tool in their betrayal, can be dismissed with a laugh. Letters follow to Herzog's son Marco, to his mistress Ramona, to his old friend Luke Asphalter, affirming with the hesitancy of the convalescent the strength of his feeling for them and acknowledging (as he writes to Ramona) "that we owe a human life to this waking spell of existence, regardless of the void" (1964, p. 314).

The other letters are Herzog's final explanation: his attempt to understand and explain the suffering through which he has already gone, and explain it *without* justifying it. This, I think, is the rationale of Herzog's polemical letter to Mermelstein, in which he rejects the latter thesis that "truth has lost its force with us and horrible pain and evil must teach it to us again . . . before mankind turns serious once more." It is at this point that Herzog, having climbed up to the "inspired condition" he now evinces at Ludeyville by means of the intellectual malaise which brought on his confrontation with the void, now means to kick over the ladder. (Intellectually, this may make no sense, but it works emotionally.) One can conceive, romantically, of pain which is ennobling, which brings us closer to God and his works, but "more commonly suffering breaks people, crushes them, and is simply unilluminating" (pp. 316–17). Herzog rejects here that salving image of himself as "that suffering joker": "I am willing without further exercise in pain to open my heart. . . . I've had all the monstrosity I want. . . . I will never expound suffering for anyone or call for Hell to make us serious and truthful" (pp. 317–18). The last polemic is addressed to the long-dead Nietzsche himself, that apostle of joy and pain whose philosophy was

twisted by his self-styled disciples not only into Nazism (first
and foremost) but also into the countless other denials of the
human spirit that Herzog has defended himself against all his life.
And in his letter Herzog seems to sum up all his former arguments:

> No, really, Herr Nietzsche, I have great admiration for you.
> Sympathy. You want to make us able to live with the void.
> Not to lie ourselves into good-naturedness, trust, ordinary
> middling human considerations, but to question as has never
> been questioned before, relentlessly, with iron determination,
> into evil, through evil, past evil, accepting no abject comfort.
> The most absolute, the most piercing questions. Rejecting
> mankind as it is, that ordinary, practical, thieving, stinking,
> unilluminated, sodden rabble, not only the laboring rabble,
> but even worse the "educated" rabble with its books and
> concerts and lectures, its liberalism and its romantic the-
> atrical "loves" and "passions"—it all deserves to die, it will
> die. Okay. Still, your extremists must survive. No survival,
> no Amor Fati. Your immoralists also eat meat. They ride
> the bus. They are only the most bus-sick travelers. Human-
> kind lives mainly upon perverted ideas. Perverted, your
> ideas are no better than those of the Christianity you con-
> demn. . . . Yours, under the veil of Maya, M.E.H. (319–20).

The polemics, the "baiting of great men," is over now, and Herzog begins to see what we have long understood: that there must
be an end to explanations. To Rozanov, the nineteenth-century
Russian mystic, he confides that "the explained life is unbearable," even though the explanations "have to be made." And to
himself, even while the explanations grind slowly to a halt, he
admits that, luckily for him, he didn't "have the means to get too
far away from" mankind's common life. "I am glad of that. I
mean to share with other human beings as far as possible and
not destroy my remaining years in the same way" (pp. 322–23).

Significantly, the last letter is not a letter at all, but a prayer,
and as Herzog speaks to God, he ceases to explain, to invent reasons, and like Job, with the wholeness of an opened heart,
accepts:

> How my mind has struggled to make coherent sense. I have
> not been too good at it. But have desired to do your
> unknowable will, taking it, and you, without symbols.
> Everything of intensest significance. Especially if divested
> of me.

I look at myself and see chest, thighs, feet—a head. This
strange organization, I know it will die. And inside—
something, something, happiness . . . "Thou movest me."
That leaves no choice. Something produces intensity, a holy
feeling, as orange produces orange, as grass green, as birds
heat. Some hearts put out more love and some less of it,
presumably. Does it signify anything? There are those who
say this product of hearts is knowledge. "Je sens mon coeur
et je connais les hommes." *But now his mind detached itself
also from its French.* I couldn't say that, for sure. My face
too blind, my mind too limited, my instincts too narrow.
But this intensity, doesn't it mean anything? Is it an idiot
joy that makes this animal, this most peculiar animal of all,
exclaim something? And he has it in his breast? But I have
no arguments to make about it. "Thou movest me." "But
what do you want, Herzog?" "But that's just it—not a
solitary thing. I am pretty well satisfied to be, to be just as it
is willed, and for as long as I may remain in occupancy"
(pp. 325–26, 340).

The instability inherent in Herzog's changing mental states comes
to its final resolution here: not only will he "do no more to enact
the peculiarities of life"; he has reached that point of transcendence, that inspired condition within which he can "abide with
death in clarity of consciousness." At one time, he fled from his
friends the Sisslers, sneaking off like a criminal to avoid their
loving protection; at another, he ran from Ramona, afraid that
she might demand something from him that he was unwilling to
share; but now, we can be confident, he can accept the manifold
joy that life offers "with intensest significance": his children, his
brothers, his friends, Ramona. We do not know precisely what
he will do: we do not know, say, whether he will marry Ramona,
whether he will ever pull together his book on romantism and
politics. What we do know—and this is what keeps us from having anything more than a vague curiosity about Herzog's future
—is that he is finally in his right mind. For even Herzog (always
the last to understand himself) knows that:

Perhaps he'd stop writing letters. Yes, that was what was
coming, in fact. The knowledge that he was done
with these letters. Whatever had come over him during
these last months, the spell, really seemed to be passing,
really going. . . . In a few minutes he would call . . . "Damp
[the dust] down, Mrs. Tuttle. There's water in the sink."
But not just yet. At this time he had no messages for anyone.
Nothing. Not a single word (1964, p. 341).

Bellow's method of providing us with the sense of completeness in *Herzog* is thus surprisingly direct and simple, considering the complexity of the element of thought in the novel. Bellow has very early on established the conditions for completeness: (1) Herzog's own arguments against the apostles of apocalypse are intellectually honest and convincing, so that we are made to agree (provisionally, as we do to the intellectual norms established in fictions) that this is not a doomed time, in which we are merely "waiting for the end"; it is a time of crisis but nevertheless one in which human joy is as possible as it is necessary. (2) At the same time and as a result of this, we are made to see Herzog's letters as a defense mechanism, which can compensate for his existential problem but cannot solve it. Insofar as the necessity to write them keeps him from accepting his life itself in all its comic and tragic and romantic manifestations—the letters are a threat to his spiritual stability. (3) The element in his life which Herzog can least accept is his love-hatred for Madeleine and Gersbach, who have not only betrayed him but may also be mistreating his daughter June. By first deciding to kill his ex-wife and ex-friend, by witnessing the very real love these two "actors" have for his daughter, by confronting Madeleine in the police station the next day and observing her "performance" with amused indifference, Herzog is finally able to come to terms with this element in his problem and can dismiss Valentine and Madeleine as having no further claims on his soul. Having set up the problem in this way, Bellow can complete the form by showing us how Herzog's letters work themselves out of his system: the farewell notes, the last polemics, the prayer and (at last) the silence.

Appendix B
A Selective Checklist of Formally Interesting Rhetorical Fiction

FICTION TO 1800
> Thomas More: *Utopia*
> John Bunyan: *The Pilgrim's Progress*
> Henry Fielding: *Jonathan Wild*
> Laurence Sterne: *Tristram Shandy*
> Henry Mackenzie: *The Man of Feeling*
> Samuel Johnson: *Rasselas*
> Francois Marie Arouet de Voltaire: *Candide*
> Denis Diderot: *Rameau's Nephew*
> Jean-Jacques Rousseau: *Emile, or Education.*

THE NINETEENTH CENTURY
> Mary Shelley: *Frankenstein*
> Walter Scott: *Redgauntlet*
> Herman Melville: *The Confidence Man*
> Samuel Butler: *The Way of All Flesh*
> Leo Tolstoy: *Resurrection*

THE TWENTIETH CENTURY
> Samuel Clemens: *The Mysterious Stranger*
> James Branch Cabell: *The Cream of the Jest*
> George Orwell: *Animal Farm*
> Aldous Huxley: *Point Counter Point*
> Nathanael West: *The Day of the Locust*
> Ralph Ellison: *Invisible Man*
> William Gaddis: *The Recognitions*
> Alan Paton: *Cry, the Beloved Country*
> Mordecai Richler: *Cocksure*
> Anthony Burgess: *A Clockwork Orange*
> Doris Lessing: *The Golden Notebook*

Katherine Ann Porter: *Ship of Fools*
Nigel Dennis: *Cards of Identity*
John Barth: *The Sot-Weed Factor*
Donald Barthelme: *Snow White*
Ishmael Reed: *Yellow Back Radio Broke Down*
William Golding: *The Spire*
Thomas Pynchon: *Gravity's Rainbow*
John Gardner: *The Wreckage of Agathon*
Jeremy Larner: *Drive, He Said*
Joseph Heller: *Catch-22*
John Hawkes: *The Lime Twig*
Jerzy Kosinski: *Steps*
E. M. Forster: *A Passage to India*
Richard Brautigan: *Trout Fishing in America*
Kurt Vonnegut: *Slaughterhouse-Five*
Andre Malraux: *Man's Fate*
Jean-Paul Sartre: *Nausea*
Albert Camus: *The Fall*
Hermann Hesse: *Steppenwolf*
Bertolt Brecht: *The Threepenny Novel*
Franz Kafka: *The Castle*
Hermann Broch: *The Death of Virgil*
Evgeny Zamiatin: *We*
Alexander Solzhenitsyn: *One Day in the Life of Ivan Denisovich*

Notes

Notes to Chapter One

1. I cannot say whether Friedman would actually agree with this analysis of *Pamela* or not. Perhaps not. One finds it hard to say because it is not enough for Friedman that the "flux of experience" remain open; the expansion of the "stream of conscience" has to be "convincing," the criteria for which are left mystically up in the air. See Friedman, 1966, pp. 35–36.

2. See Friedman, 1966, p. 180. For his partisanship of the "open-ended" novel, coupled with an intemperate and somewhat off-target attack upon critical traditionalists, especially Wayne C. Booth, see pp. 185–86.

3. For a fuller treatment of the problems brought up by this reading of *Herzog*, see Appendix A.

4. All citations are from Beverly Gross's article, "Narrative Time and the Open-ended Novel," *Criticism* 8 (Fall 1966):362–76. This point of view derives from a more extended (and less defensible) argument in her dissertation, "Open-Ended Forms in the Modern Novel," University of Chicago, 1966.

5. Actually one could define the plot of *To the Lighthouse* as being either of action or character, depending upon whether one saw the alteration in (say) Lily Briscoe's situation at the end of the novel as one of circumstances or consciousness. It is uncomfortable for one who likes to keep his categories straight, but I fancy that the novel could be profitably discussed in either way.

Notes to Chapter Two

1. Letter to Elizabeth Carter in *Posthumous Works*, I, 108ff., quoted in Frederick W. Hilles, "*Rasselas*: An 'Uninstructive Tale,' " in *Johnson, Boswell and Their Circle, Essays Presented to Lawrence Fitzroy Powell* (Oxford: The Clarendon Press, 1965), p. 111.

2. See Burke's "*Coriolanus* and the Delights of Faction," in *Language as Symbolic Action* (Berkeley, University of California Press, 1966).

3. George Sherburn, in "Rasselas Returns—to What?" *Philological Quarterly* 38 (July, 1959):383–84, insists that Johnson's statement in the first chapter, "those on whom the iron gate had once closed were never suffered to return," precludes Rasselas's readmission to the "happy valley." Sherburn ignores the context here, which is that no one was permitted to *leave* the paradise-prison, not that those who had left would not be taken back. Leaving was unprecedented, as the text makes clear, so whatever Abyssinian functionary encountered Rasselas and his friends at the gateway on their return would have to make new law for their unique situation.

4. Later in the chapter we shall discuss a way of arranging the experiences of Rasselas and his companions into a fairly shapely framework. We shall also discuss at that point why, nevertheless, this does not make for closure in the novel, though it is chiefly responsible for the sense of completeness in *Rasselas*.

5. C. R. Tracy, " 'Democritus, Arise!' A Study in Johnson's Humor," *Yale Review* 39 (December 1949):305–10, overemphasizes the element of satire in *Rasselas*, possibly under the misconception that all works of literature should have the same virtues, not just the ones proper to their form. Here it is clear that the more satirical Johnson made the passage the *less* effective it would be for his purpose.

6. See such an incident in *Tom Jones*, book 5, chapter 2, where Square is the satiric target. This would surely have been familiar to Johnson at the time of the composition of *Rasselas*.

7. Here and later we shall refer briefly to a sort of geographical exhaustiveness which runs parallel to Voltaire's exhaustive catalogue of natural and man-made evils. In showing the variety of ills occurring in every major country of Europe, Africa (in the Old Woman's story), and America (in Candide's and Cacambo's wanderings), before everyone settles down, bored to death, in Asia Minor, Voltaire makes clear that nowhere is any better than anywhere else—except Eldorado, where one cannot go. The universe is given not only a moral shape, but a physical one as well; we have a strong sense of the extent of this "best of all possible worlds."

Notes to Chapter Three

1. From the anthropologist's point of view, Golding has been rather accurate here: Jack's placing the pig's head on a pike as an offering resembles a ritual done after successful bear hunts by the

Ostiak Indians of Kamchatka Island. See Sir James Frazer's description of this in *The Golden Bough* (1922), pp. 519ff.

2. See Ralph Freeman, "The New Realism: The Fancy of William Golding," *Perspective* 10 (Summer-Autumn 1958):118–28; and John M. Egan, "Golding's View of Man," *America* 108 (January 26, 1963):140–41.

3. See chapter 1, pp. 13–16.

4. In this version, of course, the forest fire would be eliminated.

5. Perhaps this is going too far—nowadays we tend to trace the darker side of human life rather to defective social organization than to the evil nature of the individual. But at the same time, Golding's view has enjoyed wide currency in the past and is part of the dogma of no less towering an intellectual influence than the Catholic church.

Notes to Chapter Four

1. Wayne C. Booth has suggested the possibility of an inconsistency here between Meursault's claim of past and present *happiness* (the word, in the original, is "heureux") and his sense that the four shots at the end of part one were like blows on the door of his *unhappiness* ("malheur"). Booth wonders whether this was an inadvertent inconsistency on Camus's part, or was perhaps meant as a paradox (Booth, personal communication). I am not sure that one need take either view. In accord with Camus's idea that the best living is the most living, Meursault's "unhappiness" is simply his death which, inevitable in any case, he has hastened by shooting the Arab. His assertion, on the other hand, that "I'd been happy and was happy still" is implicit in his act of *revolt against death*, his assertion of freedom and the value of living. But there is more to Booth's objection than my riposte allows for.

2. This is in order to give the audience the sense that Beckett's characters, dead participants in a love triangle, go on speaking their parts forever from the urns onstage in which they are entombed. In *Play*, the repetition is part and parcel of Beckett's intention—the work would be incomplete if it were performed only "once."

3. One could make out a good case that Meursault—unlike ourselves— has actually learned nothing because he knew it all from the beginning: this is implied in his claim, "I'd been right, I was still right, I was always right," which precedes Meursault's exposition of the high privilege of simply being alive (1946, p. 151). The countercase, that Meursault is just now coming to terms with the absurd, would rest on his later statement that "for the

first time, the very first, I laid my heart open to the benign indifference of the universe" (1946, p. 154). This is perhaps a real
paradox but, while one would be happy to resolve it, it is far less
essential for the fulfillment of Camus's intentions for us to find
out whether Meursault has learned something new than for us
to have done so ourselves. The significance of the novel is practically unaffected by which way this question is resolved. But
think what would happen to *Candide* if we were in any doubt as
to whether the hero had learned anything. . . . This illustrates
strikingly the difference in structure between the two kinds of
rhetorical novel.

    4. One had just as well face directly the question of whether
Camus *really* succeeded in the exposition of a highly original
philosophy through his rhetorical fiction. The question is posed
par excellence by the initial reactions to the English-language
publication of *The Stranger*; many reviewers saw little difference
between Camus's philosophical fable and crime fiction of the
Dashiell Hammett/Raymond Chandler school. See especially the
late Edmund Wilson's review in the *New Yorker*, April 13, 1946,
pp. 113–14, and also Richard Plant's review, "Benign Indifference," *Saturday Review of Literature*, May 18, 1946, p. 10, and
Alexander Comfort's unsympathetic remarks in *The Novel and
Our Time* (London: Phoenix House, 1948), p. 41. By a coincidence
that no one will have the least trouble understanding, most British and American criticism of *The Stranger* published between
1946 and 1955 (when the Justin O'Brien translation of *The Myth
of Sisyphus* was published) seems sadly off the mark today. This
pattern of events may make one wish to question my confident
judgment here, a judgment implicit throughout, that Camus's
novel succeeded in presenting its author's ideas, since some of
the most brilliant critics of England and America, with few exceptions, missed those ideas almost completely. (One exception,
perhaps an important one, is Nicola Chiaromonte's "Albert
Camus" in the *New Republic*, April 29, 1946, pp. 630–33.) One
way out—one could think of others—is simply to recognize that
prior to the publication of *The Myth of Sisyphus* the critics
lacked a vocabulary for the discussion of Camus's ideas and an
audience familiar with the premises of existentialism; lacking
these things, they discussed *The Stranger* in terms familiar to
their readers and to themselves, at considerable cost to clarity
and understanding. But all the critics I read, even those most
wildly off base, showed a sense that there was something going
on in the novel that they were probably missing, some ineluctable
depth they felt they were failing to sound. One might claim—and
I *would* claim, in fact—that the critics' understanding of *The*

Stranger was more accurate than their descriptions would indicate. Today, of course, when the Void is touted like so much salable real estate (Saul Bellow's phrase), when absurdity and revolt and the meaninglessness of existence are discussed at cocktail parties, even secondary school students are likely to find *The Stranger* and its ideas accessible.

Notes to Chapter Five

1. Another similarity to *Finnegans Wake*.

2. I mean by this only that there are, theoretically, an infinite number of hypothetical formal ends of which *V.* is the incomplete realization, and none of which it is the complete and perfect realization. As a result, since any hypothesis we might select is more or less inadequate, the selection of one could be regarded as theoretically arbitrary.

3. See above, chapter 1, pp. 17–18.

4. Does this mean that V. is indeed Stencil's mother? It seems impossible, given normal human gestation periods, that the casual fling in April 1899, could have resulted in Herbert's 1901 birth—so we are no wiser than before. (The discrepancy—precisely one year—is intriguing, and makes one think in terms of typographical errors and authorial miscalculations.)

5. One might mention, as well here as anywhere, that Pynchon is fastidiously accurate, so far as I have been able to check him out, in his use of historical detail: what information he gives about Fashoda, or the Malta riots, or von Trotha's activities in 1904 demonstrates fairly thorough research.

6. Hunt has not even exhausted the possibilities: there are also Vheissu, virtù, the Vatican, and, believe it or not, half a dozen more.

7. For example, Mondaugen's enigmatic code-message, consisting of the Wittgensteinian thesis, "the world is all that is the case," is echoed in a song sung by one of the Whole Sick Crew only a few pages later (see Pynchon, 1963, pp. 278, 288).

8. Robert ("Pappy") Hod, Paola's husband, is temporarily stationed in Valletta awaiting developments in the Suez crisis, which forms the background to the Maltese scenes.

9. Exception: when the inability of a narrator to keep straight the surface of events can be taken as evidence of mental instability or psychic deterioration: for examples see such diverse works as Nabokov's *Lolita* and Robbe-Grillet's *Jealousy*.

10. So impressive that it was published separately, as "Under the Rose," in *Noble Savage* 3 (May 1961).

11. *Lot 49* is not, however, the most impressive of Pynchon's novels. Though it is a more fully realized fable than *V.*, the rich

vein of inventiveness that made Pynchon's first novel so brilliant a tour de force wears a bit thin in *Lot 49*. Pynchon published no book-length fiction between 1966, when *Lot 49* came out, and 1973, when he published *Gravity's Rainbow*, which came out too recently to be given mature consideration here. The hiatus probably reflects Pynchon's need to replenish his stock of outré images. At a glance, *Gravity's Rainbow* appears to have combined the power of *Lot 49* with the range and inventiveness of *V.*, although I retain a healthy skepticism with regard to large claims being made for it (in particular Richard Poirier's suggestion [in the March 1973 *Saturday Review of the Arts*] that *Gravity's Rainbow* is the most important novel in English since *Ulysses*). Pynchon's longueurs and cuteness are very much in evidence in his latest effort.

Notes to Chapter Six

1. As a college freshman at the University of Chicago in 1961, I was a member of such a cult.

2. This conspiracy of the doctors against the patients appears again, without benefit of the soldier in white, at pp. 420–21.

3. Perhaps the attitudes are not unduly exaggerated: revelations about present-day entrepreneurs, especially the presidents of certain fast-sinking conglomerates, and news reports about the behavior of "ordinary" GIs at My Lai, together with the embarrassing communications from Laos in March 1971 that the air support units had indeed bombed our own bases (not for money, so far as is known)—all indicate that Milo and Aarfy are very much with us today.

4. According to Vance Ramsey, Aarfy is "the most frightening character of all" because his commitment to Cathcart's values "is so complete as to make him inhuman" (see Whitbread, 1966, p. 113; see also Mellard, 1968, p. 40, for a fascinating, but somewhat too ingenious theory in which Milo's conversation in the chestnut tree is compared with the temptation of Christ by Satan).

5. See Caroline Gordon and Jeanne Richardson, "Flies in Their Eyes? A Note on Joseph Heller's *Catch-22*," *Southern Review*, n.s., 3 (January 1967):96–105; on page 100 is an explicit discussion of the influence of Carroll's logic problems on Heller's paradoxes.

6. Previous use of that "bit," a parody of Charles Wilson's aphorism about General Motors, was at page 302 and els where.

7. He could have killed Yossarian off just as George Mandel, Heller's close friend and—at least in part—the model for Yossarian, did to the protagonist of his own black comedy about

World War II, *The Wax Boom* (see Lehan and Patch, 1967, pp. 242–43).

8. Heller says so, in a passage fraught with irony elsewhere, within his interview with Paul Krassner (see Heller, 1962, p. 26). Whether he succeeded in conveying the dubious success of Yossarian's desertion within the novel—or even whether he meant to—is anybody's guess.

Notes to Chapter Seven

1. In *Rasselas, The Stranger,* and *Catch-22* we noted how relatively weak closure devices were used so that the strongest sense of completeness would result; the possibility of sacrificing completeness to closure (or vice versa) is foreclosed in represented actions because the same event (the removal of the last bar to a new, stable relationship amongst the agents) must produce *both* completeness and closure in all fictions whose organizing principle is plot. This is a major structural difference between fables and represented actions, or between didactic and mimetic modes of organization generally. There is an inherent looseness to paratactic structures which requires the utmost artistry on the part of the novelist to conceal.

2. I hope this brief commentary on *The Vicar of Wakefield* will at least absolve Goldsmith from the charges of ineptness and indolence with respect to the composition of that work: its failings are more the result of overambitiousness, of trying to do too many things at once, than of the sins of which he is usually accused.

3. In the case of *The Forsyte Saga,* the problem is further complicated by the existence of two subsequent trilogies, *A Modern Comedy* and *End of Chapter,* which further advance the histories of the Forsytes and their collateral descendants.

4. See in this connection Brooks's classic volume *The Well-Wrought Urn: Studies in the Structure of Poetry,* together with Crane's reply in *Critics and Criticism.*

5. Commonplaces, even though they were opposed by other, contradictory commonplaces.

6. For a similar point of view on novel doctrines in the contemporary rhetorical novel, see Crane, 1967, vol. 2, p. 143.

7. See Appendix B for a short checklist of formally interesting rhetorical novels.

Note to Appendix A

1. Booth's formulation is, I think, exact. Ideas really *do* threaten Herzog, and he is even conscious of this. After a meditative passage in which Herzog sees the philosophy of the present

generation as a kind of deification of the void ("History is the history of cruelty, not love, as soft men think. . . . the one true god is Death.") we get an inside view of his reaction to these notions: "Herzog heard this as if it were being spoken slowly inside his head. His hand was wet and he released June's arm. Perhaps what had made him faint was not the accident but the premonition of such thoughts. The nausea was only apprehension, excitement, the unbearable intensity of these ideas" (p. 290). When he meets the clever and vicious Madeleine only a few pages later, he has no comparable emotional reaction.

Works Cited

Adams, Robert Martin. *Strains of Discord: Studies in Literary Openness.* Ithaca, N.Y.: Cornell University Press, 1958.

Alkon, Paul. *Samuel Johnson and Moral Discipline.* Evanston, Ill.: Northwestern University Press, 1967.

Allen, Walter. "New Novels." Review of *Lord of the Flies. New Statesman* 48 (September 25, 1954):370.

Austen, Jane. *Persuasion.* Edited by Andrew Wright. Boston: Houghton Mifflin Co., 1965.

Baker, Ernest A. *The History of the English Novel.* 9 vols. London: H. F. and G. Witherby, 1924–38.

Balliett, Whitney. "Mrs. Jolley and Mrs. Flack." *New Yorker,* 37 (December 9, 1961):247.

————."Wha." *New Yorker,* 39 (June 15, 1963):113–17.

Barthelme, Donald. *Snow White.* New York: Atheneum, 1967.

Baugh, Albert C., et al. *A Literary History of England.* New York: Appleton-Century-Crofts, 1948.

Bellow, Saul. *Herzog.* New York: The Viking Press, 1964.

Besterman, Theodore. *Voltaire.* New York: Harcourt, Brace and World, 1969.

Block, Haskell M. "Albert Camus: Toward a Definition of Tragedy." *University of Toronto Quarterly* 19 (July 1950): 354–60.

Booth, Wayne C. *The Rhetoric of Fiction.* Chicago: University of Chicago Press, 1961.

————. "Salvation Justified." *Chicago Literary Review* 2 (October 23, 1964):1.

Bottiglia, William F. *Voltaire's Candide: The Analysis of a Classic.* Vol. 7 of *Studies on Voltaire and the Eighteenth Century,* general editor Theodore Besterman. Geneva: Institut et Musée Voltaire, 1959.

————. *Voltaire*: *A Collection of Critical Essays*. Englewood Cliffs, N.J.: Prentice-Hall, 1968.

Brée, Germaine. *Camus*: *A Collection of Critical Essays*. Englewood Cliffs, N.J.: Prentice-Hall, 1962.

Brooks, Cleanth. *The Well-Wrought Urn*: *Studies in the Structure of Poetry*. New York: Reynal and Hitchcock, 1947.

Bunyan, John. *The Pilgrim's Progress*. London: Dent, 1954.

Burke, Kenneth. *Language as Symbolic Action*: *Essays on Life, Literature, and Method*. Berkeley: University of California Press, 1966.

Camus, Albert. *The Stranger*. Translated by Stuart Gilbert. New York: Random House, 1946.

————. *The Plague*. Translated by Stuart Gilbert. New York: Modern Library, 1948.

————. *The Myth of Sisyphus and Other Essays*. Translated by Justin O'Brien. New York: Random House, 1955.

————. *Récits et théâtre*. Paris: Gallimard, 1958.

————. *Carnets 1935–1942*. Translated by Philip Thody. London: Hamish Hamilton, 1963.

Carruth, Hayden. *After the Stranger*: *Imaginary Dialogues with Camus*. New York: Macmillan, 1955.

Chiaromonte, Nicola. "Albert Camus." *New Republic* 114 (April 29, 1946):630–33.

Comfort, Alexander. *The Novel and Our Time*. London: Phoenix House, 1948.

Cox, C. B. "Lord of the Flies." *Critical Quarterly* 2 (Summer 1960):112–17.

Crane, Ronald Salmon, ed. *Critics and Criticism*: *Ancient and Modern*. Chicago: University of Chicago Press, 1952.

————. *The Idea of the Humanities and Other Essays Critical and Historical*. 2 vols. Chicago: University of Chicago Press, 1967.

Cruickshank, John. "Camus' Technique in *L'Étranger*." *French Studies* 10 (July 1956):241–53.

————. *Albert Camus and the Literature of Revolt*. London: Oxford University Press, 1959.

Dahl, Curtis. "Patterns of Disguise in *The Vicar of Wakefield*." *ELH* 25 (June 1958):90–104.

Daiches, David. *The Novel and the Modern World*. Chicago: University of Chicago Press, 1939.

Dostoyevsky, Fyodor. *Crime and Punishment*. Translated by David Magarshack. Harmon, Middlesex: Penguin Books, 1956.

Dreiser, Theodore. *Sister Carrie*. New York: New American Library, 1961.

Drew, Philip. "Second Reading." *Cambridge Review* 78 (October 27, 1956):79–84.

Egan, John M., O.P. "Golding's View of Man." *America* 108 (January 26, 1963):140–41.

Ellison, Ralph. *Invisible Man.* New York: Random House, 1952.

Feldman, Irving. "Keeping Cool." *Commentary* 36 (September 1963):258–60.

Fielding, Henry. *Jonathan Wild.* London: J. Dent, 1893.

————. *The History of Tom Jones, a Foundling.* New York: Modern Library, 1950.

Frazer, James George. *The Golden Bough.* Abridged edition. New York: Macmillan, 1922.

Freeman, Ralph. "The New Realism: The Fancy of William Golding." *Perspective* 10 (Summer-Autumn 1958):118–28.

Friedman, Alan. *The Turn of the Novel.* New York: Oxford University Press, 1966.

Galsworthy, John. *The Forsyte Saga.* New York: Charles Scribner's Sons, 1934.

Gardner, John. *The Sunlight Dialogues.* New York: Alfred A. Knopf, 1972.

Gide, André. *The Counterfeiters.* Translated by Dorothy Bussy. New York: Modern Library, 1931.

Gindin, James. *Postwar British Fiction: New Accents and Attitudes.* Berkeley: University of California Press, 1962.

Golding, William. *Lord of the Flies.* New York: Capricorn Books, 1959.

Goldsmith, Oliver. *The Vicar of Wakefield.* New York: New American Library, 1961.

Gordon, Caroline, and Richardson, Jeanne. "Flies in Their Eyes: A Note on Joseph Heller's *Catch-22.*" *Southern Review,* n.s., 3 (January 1967):96–105.

Green, Peter. "The World of William Golding." *Transactions and Proceedings of the Royal Society of Literature* 32 (1963): 37–57.

Gross, Beverly. "Narrative Time and the Open-Ended Novel." *Criticism* 8 (Fall 1966):362–76.

Hammett, Dashiell. *The Novels of Dashiell Hammett.* New York: Alfred A. Knopf, 1965.

Hanna, Thomas. *The Thought and Art of Albert Camus.* Chicago: Henry Regnery Co., 1958.

Hassan, Ihab H. *Radical Innocence: Studies in the Contemporary American Novel.* Princeton, N.J.: Princeton University Press, 1961.

Heller, Joseph. *Catch-22.* New York: Simon and Schuster, 1961.

————. "An Impolite Interview with Joseph Heller," *Realist*, no. 39 (November 1962), pp. 18–31.

Hemingway, Ernest. *The Sun Also Rises*. New York: Charles Scribner's Sons, 1926.

Hesse, Hermann. *Steppenwolf*. Translated by Basil Creighton. New York: Frederick Ungar, 1957.

————. *Siddhartha: ein Indische Dichtung*. New York: Macmillan, 1962.

Hilles, Frederick W. "*Rasselas*, An 'Uninstructive Tale.'" In *Johnson, Boswell and Their Circle: Essays Presented to Lawrence Fitzroy Powell*. Oxford: The Clarendon Press, 1965.

Johnson, Samuel. *The History of Rasselas, Prince of Abyssinia*. Edited by Gwin J. Kolb. New York: Appleton-Century-Crofts, 1962.

Johnson, Boswell and Their Circle: Essays Presented to Lawrence Fitzroy Powell. Oxford: The Clarendon Press, 1965.

Joyce, James. *A Portrait of the Artist as a Young Man*. New York: Modern Library, 1928.

————. *Finnegans Wake*. New York: Viking Compass Book, 1959.

Kearns, Francis E. "Salinger and Golding: Conflicts on the Campus." *America* 108 (January 26, 1963), pp. 136–39.

Kermode, Frank. *The Sense of an Ending: Studies in the Theory of Fiction*. New York: Oxford University Press, 1967.

Kolb, Gwin J. "The Structure of *Rasselas*." *PMLA* 66 (September 1951):698–717.

Lehan, Richard, and Patch, Jerry. "*Catch-22*: The Making of a Novel." *Minnesota Review* 7 (Autumn-Winter 1967):238–44.

Liberman, M. M., and Foster, Edward E. *A Modern Lexicon of Literary Terms*. Glenview, Ill.: Scott, Foresman and Co., 1968.

McDonald, James L. "I See Everything Twice: The Structure of Joseph Heller's *Catch-22*." *Kansas City University Review* 34 (Spring 1968):175–80.

Mellard, James M. "*Catch-22*: *Déjà vu* and the Labyrinth of Memory." *Bucknell Review* 16, 2 (May 1968):29–44.

Melville, Herman. *The Confidence-Man: His Masquerade*. Edited by Herschel Parker. New York: W. W. Norton, 1971.

O'Hara, J. D. "Mute Choirboys and Angelic Pigs: The Fable in *Lord of the Flies*." *Texas Studies in Literature and Language* 7 (Winter 1966):411–20.

Orwell, George. *Animal Farm*. New York: Harcourt, Brace, 1946.

Pelham, Edgar. *The Art of the Novel from 1700 to the Present Time*. New York: Macmillan, 1933.

Peter, John. "The Fables of William Golding." *Kenyon Review* 19 (Autumn 1957):577–92.

Pinsker, Sanford. "Heller's *Catch-22*: The Protest of a *Puer Eternis*." *Critique: Studies in Modern Fiction* 7, 2 (Winter 1964–65):150–62.

Plant, Richard. "Benign Indifference." *Saturday Review of Literature* 29 (May 18, 1946):10.

Plimpton, George. "Mata Hari with a Clockwork Eye, Alligators in the Sewer." *New York Times Book Review* (April 21, 1963), p. 5.

Pynchon, Thomas. *V*. New York: Lippincott, 1963.

———. *The Crying of Lot 49*. New York: Lippincott, 1966.

———. *Gravity's Rainbow*. New York: The Viking Press, 1973.

Raleigh, Walter. *The English Novel*. London: John Murray, 1894.

Richardson, Samuel. *Pamela, or Virtue Rewarded*. New York: W. W. Norton, 1958.

Ricks, Christopher. "Voluminous." *New Statesman* 66 (October 11, 1963):492.

Rosenfield, Claire. " 'Men of a Smaller Growth': A Psychological Analysis of William Golding's *Lord of the Flies*." *Literature and Psychology* 11 (Autumn 1961):93–101.

Rosenheim, Edward W. *Swift and the Satirist's Art*. Chicago: University of Chicago Press, 1963.

Sacks, Sheldon. *Fiction and the Shape of Belief*. Berkeley: University of California Press, 1964.

———. "Golden Birds and Dying Generations." *Comparative Literature Studies* 6 (September 1969):274–91.

Scott, Nathan A., Jr., ed. *Adversity and Grace: Studies in Recent American Literature*. Chicago: University of Chicago Press, 1968.

Scott, Walter. *Miscellaneous Prose Works*. 6 vols. Edinburgh: Cadell and Co., 1827.

Sherburn, George. "Rasselas Returns—to What?" *Philological Quarterly* 38 (July 1959):383–84.

Smith, Barbara Herrnstein. *Poetic Closure: A Study of How Poems End*. Chicago: University of Chicago Press, 1968.

Solomon, Jan. "The Structure of Joseph Heller's *Catch-22*." *Critique: Studies in Modern Fiction* 9, 2 (Spring-Summer 1967):46–57.

Stern, Richard G. "Bombers Away." *New York Times Book Review* (October 22, 1961), p. 50.

Thody, Philip. *Albert Camus 1913–1960*. London: Hamish Hamilton, 1961.

Topazio, Virgil W. *Voltaire: A Critical Study of His Major Works*. New York: Random House, 1967.

Torrey, Norman L. *The Spirit of Voltaire*. New York: Columbia University Press, 1938.

Tracy, C. R. " 'Democritus, Arise!' A Study in Johnson's Humor." *Yale Review* 39 (December 1949):305–10.

Viggiani, Carl A. "Camus' *L'Etranger.*" *PMLA* 71 (December 1956):865–87.

Voltaire, Francois Marie Arouet de. *Candide, ou l'Optimisme.* Edited by George R. Havens. New York: Henry Holt, 1934.

———. *Candide, Zadig and Selected Stories.* Edited and translated by Donald Frame. Bloomington: Indiana University Press, 1961.

Wade, Ira O. *Voltaire and Candide: A Study in the Fusion of History, Art, and Philosophy.* Princeton: Princeton University Press, 1959.

Wahba, Magdi L. *Bicentenary Essays on Rasselas.* Supplement to *Cairo Studies in English.* Cairo, 1959.

Walters, Margaret. "Two Fabulists: Golding and Camus." *Melbourne Critical Review* 4 (1961):18–29.

Wardle, Ralph M. *Oliver Goldsmith.* Lawrence: University of Kansas Press, 1967.

Watson, Kenneth. "A Reading of *Lord of the Flies.*" *English* 15 (Spring 1964):2–7.

West, Nathanael. *Miss Lonelyhearts.* New York: New Directions, 1946.

Whitbread, Thomas B., ed. *Seven Contemporary American Authors: Essays on Cozzens, Miller, West, Golding, Heller, Albee, and Powers.* Austin: University of Texas Press, 1967.

Wilson, Edmund. "Albert Camus—Charles Dickens—Lafcadio Hearn." *New Yorker* 22 (April 13, 1946):113–14.

Wimsatt, William. "In Praise of *Rasselas.*" In Maynard Mack and Ian Gregor, *Imagined Worlds: Essays in Honor of John Butt.* New York: Barnes and Noble, 1968.

Woolf, Virginia. *To the Lighthouse.* New York: Harcourt, Brace, 1927.

Young, James Dean. "The Enigma Variations of Thomas Pynchon." *Critique: Studies in Modern Fiction* 10, 1 (Winter 1967–68):69–77.

Index